THAT
VANISHING
SOUND

The Lookout—"All's Well," an oil on canvas by Winslow Homer. *Courtesy Boston Museum of Fine Arts, William Wilkins Warren Fund*

THAT VANISHING SOUND

L. Elsinore Springer

Crown Publishers, Inc. New York

Also by L. Elsinore Springer
The Collector's Book of Bells

Printed in the United States of America

Published simultaneously in Canada by General Publishing Company Limited

Design: Deborah Daly

Library of Congress Cataloging in Publication Data

Springer, L. Elsinore.
That vanishing sound.

Includes index.
1. Bells—United States—History. I. Title.
CC208.S67 1976 681'.81'9509 76-8223
ISBN 0-517-52539-9

CONTENTS

ACKNOWLEDGMENTS

It is a pleasure to acknowledge the assistance of many individuals, publications, institutions, and private industries who have contributed in some way to this book. Though it is impossible to name each, other than in a credit line, thanks are due two librarians in particular: local history librarian Dorothy Mozley, of the Springfield, Massachusetts, City Library, for locating and making usable heretofore unrecorded data; and Tom Holmberg, curator of the Yung-Meyer collection of railroadiana, for long hours spent researching the recently acquired collection without benefit of an index.

Special thanks go also to Congressman Roy A. Taylor, who was instrumental in securing information otherwise not accessible; and to Mrs. Robert Collins, editor of *The Bell Tower*, for her gracious permission to use brief excerpts.

Both *Atlantic Monthly* and the Missouri Historical Society have readily given permission to quote brief passages from their publications: a short verse from the *Atlantic* selection "Buttin' Blood" by Pernet Patterson; and portions of a paragraph from Edwin W. Mills's article describing pioneer bellmaking in the Ozarks, taken from the Missouri Historical Society Bulletin, vol. XVII, No. 4, pt. 1, July, 1961, p. 359.

Mrs. G. Lyle Ringland, Mr. A. E. Mercer, Mr. Thomas J. Collins, and the late Mrs. Maude LaNicca all kindly contributed many pertinent pieces of information relating to bells of their own geographical areas.

So far as illustrations are concerned, the untiring efforts of several persons are gratefully acknowledged, most especially Mike Northrup's creative photography and Dorothy Cole's freehand sketches. Others are credited in the text. Readers should bear in mind that historical pictures from the days when photography was in its infancy leave much to be desired in clarity and sharpness. To bring these up to anything approaching usable standards has required unending patience on the part of many.

Finally, acknowledgments are not complete without a word of gratitude for the editorial wisdom of Mrs. Kathryn Pinney in bringing the book to satisfactory completion in the publisher's office.

Should readers find missing the names of certain famous bells or their makers or their steeples, the omission may be an unavoidable one if no response could be elicited from authorities verifying certain facts. However, in view of the great number who did respond, confirming facts or clarifying troublesome points, such omissions seem less regrettable in the final analysis.

L. E. S.

Asheville, North Carolina
September 18, 1975

PREFACE

Have you listened lately and wondered where in this land of ours, if at all, you might still hear church bells pealing in unison, or a clock chiming over a busy thoroughfare, or perhaps cowbells echoing across a meadow? From colonial days onward, even into the present century, life in America moved to the tinkle and boom, the chime and clank, and occasionally the tolling of bells. To some extent life was even regulated by those sounds.

Zell's U. S. Business Directory for 1898 lists hundreds of firms casting bells. Today fewer than a dozen are still casting them. Like other familiar items, bells have succumbed to fast changes in American taste, to burgeoning technology, to the promotion of new concepts in sound. Our ears are attuned to a shrill noon siren hustling us to the nearest quick-service grill, not to a mellow "nooning" bell beckoning us home for a leisurely dinner; they are accustomed to the harsh blaring horn of a modern diesel train, not to the haunting sound of the engine bell from a puffing old "iron horse."

An era has vanished, and with it that hodgepodge of sounds bells once created in every hamlet and town and along every byway and pike between. Yet, thanks to our craving for Americana, countless bells remain in both private and public possession. Whether mute or still, in comparatively rare instances, in active service, these bells constitute a fertile source of stories about the happenings that make up our heritage. Closely involved in the mainstream of early American life, they are uniquely qualified to document historical events and social customs during the nation's formative years. The stories they can tell range from quiet little local anecdotes to rollicking nationwide celebrations, from amusing to sorrowful, and from undeniable to unbelievable. All, however, are in some manner informative, often offering fresh insight into that elusive element called the American spirit.

First of all then, this book is admittedly about bells. It is also about the people who made, who used, and who heard these bells through times both trying and joyous in the American past. Furthermore, since no one had previously assembled all this bell lore, it is a book that needed to be written. There ought to be at least one account relating the important role of bells in the America our forefathers knew.

1

OUR DEBT TO SPAIN

In any popular poll taken at random, our Liberty Bell would undoubtedly rank first as the bell best known to Americans—in fact, as the only one known by name to countless hundreds. That is perhaps as it should be, for the bell is emblematic, cast at the special request of a fledgling nation for a very special purpose. It has no equal.

Nevertheless, from a historical viewpoint, it is worth noting that nearly two centuries before the Liberty Bell was heard, other bronze-throated voices were ringing out from Spanish missions thousands of miles westward. The story of how these first church bells came to America is a unique one not found in the history of any other nation. We are indebted to the Franciscan padres, who were instrumental in acquiring bells for their first missions across Spain's frontier, now New Mexico. As each band of Spanish conquistadors fanned out to the north of Mexico City in search of gold, one or more missionary priests marched along. They were to found the missions that would spark the beginnings of many new colonies for Spain.

Although there might be policy clashes between the conquistadors and the priests, for the most part the military actively supported the padres in their requests for bells at all missions. Though for differing reasons, both recognized the efficacy in their tones sounding over remote lands. To the padres, their sound was unequaled for drawing together the Indians they hoped to convert and for regulating the mission's daily routines and special activities. To the conquistadors, their sound kept alive reminders of glorious Spain with its beautiful bells and fired the soldiers to renewed zeal in claiming new lands.

Lugging these early bells through the wilderness and over trackless deserts was a backbreaking task. By modern standards they were not large, weighing perhaps two hundred pounds, the earliest of all weighing even less and being just large

1

enough to mount and swing. Even so, they presented a problem on a thousand-mile trek by horse and mule, especially when added to the weight of military and living essentials and equipment for the animals. What is more, securing the bells in the first place was an undertaking entangled in red tape. There were papal and royal decrees affecting both the casting of the bells and their use. Interrelationships among the royal treasury and the crown and the bishops in Spain and the bishops in the New World and the governors—all had to be recognized and considered in making a request.

The earliest bell to reach New Mexico was carried on the colonizing train of Don Juan De Onate y Zacatecas, who founded the first capital in this country near San Juan Pueblo in 1598, nearly two centuries before the American Revolution. Eventually there were to be forty-eight missions dotting New Spain, each with one or more bells, most of which were cast in Mexico, usually at Zacatecas. Only a very few came from Spain, as shipping space on ocean vessels was at a premium.

Time and various uprisings have taken their toll of these structures and their bells. Only a fraction of the original number remains, and even where their bells still ring they are heard less frequently today.

Several missions that still retain notable bells are within easy access of Santa Fe and Albuquerque. San Antonio de Isleta is one of the best known, and particularly worth a visit because the belfry as well as the church is open, and here in one of the peculiar twin towers may be seen our nation's oldest dated bell (1632). It is remarkable to find at Isleta an original bell of such age. The mission was founded just shortly before that date and, though never entirely destroyed, was badly used during the damaging Pueblo Rebellion of 1680 when the Indians tried to overthrow Spanish rule. After the reconquest the mission church was restored but, centuries later, had to be entirely remodeled after a roof fire. The two bells remaining in Isleta's towers might well have been permanently damaged or destroyed as a result of either incident.

Mission Zia dates from the same period and, having escaped the rebellion of 1680, is one of the few original missions left in New Mexico. Its bell, similar to several others cast in Zacatecas, Mexico, is dated 1710. Characteristically, Zacatecas bells are shaped with a squared lip, ornamented with a diamond cross, and inscribed with modified Roman letters, each capital being on a separate raised block.

A highly treasured bell cast in Spain before 1680 may be seen in one of the mission towers at Acoma, that famous sky-high pueblo identified as the oldest con-

Mission San Antonio de Isleta, located south of Albuquerque, New Mexico, has the nation's oldest dated bell (1632) in one of the twin towers above its massive adobe walls.

Small proportioned replicas of the two bells in the twin towers at Isleta were made by a resident padre circa 1938.

tinuously inhabited community in America. There are said to be only three Spanish-cast mission bells in all of New Mexico. Because of their rarity and beautiful workmanship, they are proudly cared for.

With its fresh adobe stucco gleaming against an intense blue sky, massive Ranchos de Taos stands magnificent in a solitude of vast horizons and distant peaks. Its sparkling appearance is explained by a custom that requires restuccoing the exterior annually. Though often referred to as a Franciscan mission, and considered the finest example of Franciscan architecture in New Mexico, not all authorities consider it a true mission. Only those churches built to serve the Indians were so classified. Whether or not, its remaining bells are splendidly housed in large imposing twin towers. And in the sanctuary, among pieces of handcrafted silver from seventeenth-century Spain, is a set of three chime bells used to announce the entry of the priest at Mass.

Laguna Mission, dating from 1699, is also beautiful to behold, with its creamy exterior and two coppery bells hanging side by side over the great doorway. Only one of these is marked. So many of the bells cast in Mexico were crudely decorated, and the Indian custom of throwing stones to ring them has almost obliterated their markings. Laguna's, however, are less scarred; and the one that is marked has all the usual features of a 1710 Zacatecas bell clearly visible.

Church of Ranchos de Taos, New Mexico, seen as a storm approaches across the desert. One tower had lost its bell when this view was taken.

Penitente Church of Santo Tomas in the mountain village of Las Trampas, New Mexico. Both bell towers are now gone, one having been stolen along with its bell. *New Mexico State Tourist Bureau*

The Penitente Church of Santo Tomas in the village of Las Trampas was completed in the year 1761 by Spanish colonizers for their own use, and therefore it was never a true mission. It is interesting today in its state of semipreservation, its bell towers crumbled away. The bells that hung in the twin towers from the day the church was dedicated were named Maria del Refugio and Maria de la Gracia. Years ago Maria del Refugio and its tower were stolen, leaving its companion to toll alone until the second tower crumbled away. Today Maria de la Gracia hangs from a balcony beam near the entrance. Bells belonging to a Penitentē church are customarily ornamented with that religious order's special cross, a cross of quite unusual design.

Left
The remaining bell of the original pair at Santo Tomas, dating to 1761, is Maria de la Gracia. It is now rung from a balcony beam near the entrance. *New Mexico State Tourist Bureau*

Right
Two types of crosses found on old Spanish mission bells: *above,* starred diamond cross; *below,* Penitente cross. *Drawing by Dorothy Cole*

One other venerable bell in New Mexico, not to be overlooked, is the so-called San Jose bell in the chapel at San Miguel in Santa Fe—which, strictly speaking, was never a mission church. Tradition claims it was cast in Spain in 1356, making it, and not Isleta's, the oldest bell in America. Both claims have been challenged by experts in the field of Spanish history. But even if traditional claims are invalid, the bell remains a prized piece among other historic paraphernalia at beautiful San Miguel. Though silent now, it will continue to draw controversy. Has the inscription SAN JOSE RUGAD POR NOSOSTROS :: AGOSTO 9 DE 1356 indeed been tampered with, making it likely the casting was done in the 1800s? And is the workmanship more typical of Mexico than of Spain? Traditionalists say no. Some scholars think otherwise.

Larded with legend as parts of its story may be, this is the bell's biography as told to those visiting San Miguel today: It was cast in honor of Saint Joseph in the Province of Andalusia, Spain, in 1356. After ringing in Spain for over three hundred years, and one hundred years in Mexico, it was brought to Santa Fe by ox-cart for use in a private chapel. Later, it rang in the belfry of San Miguel until the storm of 1872, after which it was placed inside the church and eventually in the Bell Room, where visitors have the privilege of seeing and ringing it. This historic relic weighs 780 pounds; its metallic contents, when analyzed, showed mostly copper, considerable iron, some silver, and a little gold. The silver and gold are attributed to jewelry donated in thanksgiving for the triumph of the Christians over

Left
San Miguel Church in Santa Fe, New Mexico, built by Franciscan friars in the early seventeenth century, was one of the few mission churches to escape destruction in the Pueblo Indian Revolt of 1680. *New Mexico Department of Development*

Right
In the Bell Room at San Miguel hangs the old San Jose bell, more often called the Bell of San Miguel. It weighs about the same as the Liberty Bell, yet appears smaller because much of its weight is accounted for by its uncommonly thick metal. *New Mexico Department of Development*

the Moors in the 1300s when the bell was cast. Reputedly it is the sweetest-sounding bell in America.

The two most noted Spanish missions surviving in Arizona are San Xavier del Bac and Tumacacori, both built by the Jesuits near what is now Tucson. A Texas structure, Mission San Jose y San Miguel de Aguayo, is officially "Queen of the Missions," architecturally speaking, but San Xavier del Bac is nevertheless conceded to be an equally fine example of pure mission architecture. However, one of its twin Moorish towers with arcaded belfries was never completed, thereby destroying the otherwise perfect symmetry of the facade (at the same time, some believe, escaping taxes due the king of Spain on all completed missions).

Only three bells of the original four remain at San Xavier from its founding days in the 1700s. The inscription on the most sonorous of these suggests that it may have been part of the lost Peruvian-cast chime from San Juan Bautista Mission in California. Just how it came to be lost has always been a mystery. It is a known fact that the Jesuits and the Franciscans, insofar as possible, used native materials in building their missions. A less well known fact is that the Arizona padres made clapper replacements for their bells by shaping them from a huge meteorite that had fallen in the mountains.

Legend holds full sway over the empty bell tower of Arizona's once-imposing Tumacacori, pronounced Too-ma-ka-kori and meaning "Caleche Bluffs" in the Papago language. Only a shell of its former self, this mission still stands as an authentic and enduring monument to Father Eusebio Francisco Kino and the other Jesuit priests who labored there, beginning in 1691. The importance of each Spanish mission could be judged by the number and size of its bells, for there were strict ecclesiastical rules about this. Tumacacori was highly important, as evidenced by its four sizable bells.

The story of those now-lost bells goes back almost five hundred years, to the time when European bellmongers cast four perfectly harmonized tocsins that never

Beautiful San Xavier del Bac Mission, conceded to be a fine example of pure mission architecture despite the one belfry never completed. *Library, Archives, State of Arizona*

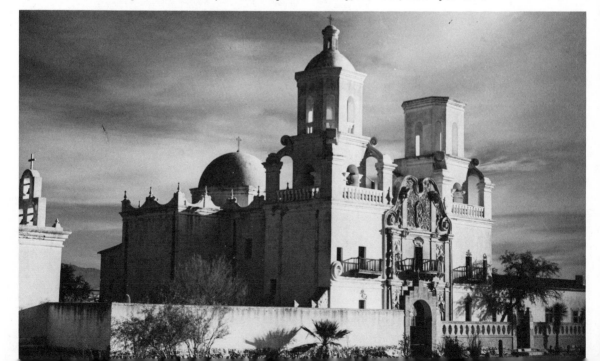

Mission Tumacacori, its belfries now empty, is only a shell of what it once was. Both Tumacacori and San Xavier were built by the Jesuits near present-day Tucson. Today it is administered as a national monument by the National Parks Service. *Library, Archives, State of Arizona*

rang in unison but always in melodious chime. For anyone standing today wrapped in the gentle charm of the mission's pastoral setting, it takes little imagination to call up musical visions of that chiming over the Santa Cruz Valley.

When Mission Tumacacori fell into the hands of warring Indians, the Spanish padres were forced to leave. Four treasures they could not possibly carry with them, nor could they bear to leave them behind. These were their fabled bells. There was only one thing to do—hide them. Two of the Jesuits, working alone and pledging themselves to secrecy, stripped the arcaded towers and buried the bells far off in the desert. Carefully they memorized important landmarks to make certain they could recover their treasures when they returned. But they left, never to return, their whereabouts unknown and the secret of the bells' location lost forever. Legends surrounding these bells have multiplied with each passing decade, and even today there are those who declare they have heard ghostly ringing in the Santa Cruz Valley; and more than one prospector has told tales of his futile search for the bells.

As elsewhere in the Southwest, the missions in Texas developed prior to the American Revolution and were flourishing when George Washington was born. So many have crumbled, and are impressive only in their desolation. Any number of their bells were despoiled during the Siege of 1836, when Santa Anna retreated and ordered all the bells in San Antonio dumped into the river. Eventually some of them were rescued by historic-minded Texans and restored—but not always to their original location. They showed up at sawmills, plantations, schools—almost anywhere. Nevertheless, in many instances among Texas's remaining missions, at least one original bell is extant.

Mission San Jose y San Miguel de Aguayo of the San Antonio Valley has long been looked upon as the "Queen of the Missions" in point of architectural beauty and importance. Its single bell tower dates from 1720, when the mission was founded, and is one of its chief architectural gems. The bell is reached by a circular stairway enclosed in a turretlike structure, the steps each hewn from a single oak log and grooved together in the shape of a fan.

One legend about the tower bells relates how they rang of their own accord at

Mission San Jose, San Antonio, Texas, as seen in a special night-time view, with its sculptural ornamentation highlighted and its bell silhouetted in the open belfry. Probably the most prosperous and beautiful of Texas missions, San Jose was known as "Queen of the Missions." It is now administered as a historic site by the Texas State Parks Board. *Photograph by Thomas J. Collins*

the death of Father Margil de Jesus, who founded the mission. He was a beloved figure throughout Texas and was to Texans what Fra Junipero Serra later was to Californians, an ardent teacher and leader not only in the mission movement but in the movement to equip each mission with bells.

Legends seem more plentiful than facts for these earliest of missions in the Southwest. But such facts as are available for those in Texas are painstakingly documented in the award-winning book *Bells Over Texas* by Bessie Lee Fitzhugh. Mrs. Fitzhugh devoted a quarter century to ferreting out historical accounts detailing the events for which each bell and mission should be remembered—lest they disappear from memory before being written down.

Along El Camino Real

Still another chapter of our history—and, again, one noticeably unique—echoes from California's Spanish mission bells. In the words of the poet, *The scroll of California's significant history/Unrolls to music of that sacred sound.*

The once vital importance of that sound has inspired countless writers and composers, with results too often romanticized. However, in the chronicles left by the first colonizing parties and later by the mission padres, we have a satisfying number of facts about the bells they brought with them. The bells were naturally intended to serve serious spiritual and practical needs. Yet in the course of events their use occasionally took a humorous turn, and even such little episodes were faithfully chronicled.

The earliest account relates how, in 1602, an exploratory party was sent by the king of Spain to determine the wisdom of establishing colonies along the California coast. Here for the first time bells are mentioned among the goods collected for the expedition. Three ships were outfitted and sailed together from Acapulco, Mexico, but one became separated from the others. While weighing anchor this lone ship was surrounded by numerous whales. To frighten them away before they capsized the ship, "a continual noise with bells, basins and other instruments was kept up."

Although there are other brief allusions to bells being brought into California on that first expedition, the first appreciable records are dated well over a century later when the king of Spain permanently claimed the ports of San Diego and Monterey. It was at these two points that California was "born to civilization" and here that the Indians first bowed to the humanizing influence of the padres at Mission San Diego and at Mission San Carlos Borromeo de Carmelo nearly five hundred miles northward on Monterey Bay.

The Indians did not always bow willingly to the new regime, marked as it was by the regular ringing of bells. In fact, the regularity of that sound summoning them daily to worship and to labor was a source of great annoyance to some of the neophytes. One morning soon after Mission San Diego had been established, its bells made no sound. When the padres investigated they found them stuffed with thorny weeds, the dry tumbleweeds of the mesa!

One name stands out above all others as the moving spirit behind this mission movement in California and the importance of bells to that movement. The name is that of Fra Junipero Serra, the eighteenth-century Franciscan who had been notably successful as a missionary among the Mexican Indians. Already fifty years old and suffering incurably, the devout Serra nevertheless welcomed his appointment in 1768 as head of Spain's ecclesiastical team to found a chain of missions linking the southern and northern reaches of her new claims, along a route that would come to be called El Camino Real.

In his *Noticias de California*, Serra's friend and chronicler enumerates with special care the bells gathered for their first evangelistic journey that resulted in

A much worn, pitted example of the small swinging bells early friars carried with them through the wilderness. A long career as a cattle bell so encrusted this one with grime that the applied silver conquistador figures were entirely hidden. *Stephen Foster Memorial*

Mission San Antonio de Palo, twelve miles from Temecula. With its great bell tower, adobe walls, and other buildings, it was founded in 1816 by Padre Peyri as the Asistencia, or branch establishment, to San Luis Rey. *California State Library*

missions for San Diego and Monterey: seven swinging bells and eleven altar bells of copper, brass, iron, and silver. Three of the swinging bells were lost en route.

Many, many years later Marie Walsh, while researching for her book *The Mission Bells of California*, found an old Spanish bell dated 1738 still hanging in the restored *campanario* at San Diego Mission. It bears a diamond cross and is of superior workmanship despite its crude lettering. She, of course, had no positive proof but was fond of saying, "I am inclined to believe this lovely bell is one of those brought up in the early days of Serra's labors in California. . . ."

The picturesque *companario* at San Diego with its only slightly asymmetrical arches cut to accommodate the bells.

Father Serra, according to early chronicles, was always accompanied on his journeys by several converts carrying one of the consecrated bells of the Catholic church and a golden cross. Wherever the party camped for the night, this bell and any others being transported became the center of an unvarying ritual. As one historian describes it, the venerable friar ordered the mules to be unloaded and the bells to be hung on the branch of a tree. The famous Franciscan then rang them himself and shouted, "Come to the Holy Church, come and receive the faith."

One day, the account continues, a fellow friar asked, "Why do you tire yourself when this is not the place where the church is to be built, neither are there any brethren about this region?"

Replied Father Serra, "I desire that the holy bells be heard by all the world, and in every desert. . . . At the least, I desire all the people in these mountains shall hear them."

Little wonder that a contributor to *The Overland Monthly* later commented, "I confess I get a better idea of that most earnest and eloquent Christian missionary, Fra Junipero, from the loud-ringing harmonies of the oak-hung bell, sounded at sunrise, noon and sunset, in the Monterey wilderness, than from the stately eulogies of his numerous biographies."

Earnest and eloquent Serra was, in pleading his spiritual cause with his superiors. As he trekked south and east from Monterey overseeing the founding and building of one mission after another, he was ever attentive to the matter of securing bells of quality and in proper size and number for each. The subject often appears in his correspondence, as in this portion of a letter quoted from Bolton's translation of *Noticias de California:*

> In view of the custom that His Majesty, whom God prosper, has of giving two bells to each one of the missions newly founded, a large and a small one, two are lacking at present for the already founded mission of San Gabriel, two for that of Santa Clara, and two more for that of Our Father, St. Francis, when it shall be founded. And if from these four cast at San Blas, the officer should appropriate one for the presidio, there should be one lacking for the mission of San Luis. For this reason I beg that Your Excellency may be pleased to order that the four bells which lately went to Monterey shall be delivered to me and that three be sent for the three missions mentioned. And if Your Excellency should be pleased to send one more to be placed in the presidio to ring the three Ave Marias for Mass, I would esteem it highly and would place it there without fail.

The Franciscans in general and Fra Junipero in particular were noted for their good sense as well as their spiritual zeal, which accounts for their success with the temporal aspects of life at their missions. In their prime these establishments were huge affairs, encompassing entire Indian villages in the shadow of the church proper. And their vast agricultural programs were a matter of great pride.

Consider, for example, San Juan Capistrano, one of the most prosperous of the twenty-one missions comprising the entire chain. Here in less than two score years the faithful padres gathered together and baptized more than 4,000 persons, garnered 243,000 measures of grain, and at one time owned 31,270 head of animals. The practical help of the mission's bells in regulating communal life on such a scale is easily apparent. Without them it would have been extremely difficult to call the community together and to regulate its activities.

Many of the missions also supported an agricultural outpost, or Asistencia. Like the missions themselves, these were extensive, admirably planned structures, with a bell tower dominating the scene at each one. Most famous and beautiful of the towers rose over the Asistencia of Mission San Luis Rey, located at Pala. This branch establishment of San Luis Rey, founded in 1816, became a gathering place for peaceful Indians living nearby. There are many romantic stories about the Pala bells, one of which was cast by the noted founder Cervantes and still hangs in the tower today.

It has already been mentioned that many of the Indian converts resented the programmed sound of the bells, particularly when the sound was calling them to frequent labor. For others there was always a certain feeling of mystery associated with the sound. An amusing tale is told about an enterprising padre at Mission San Juan Bautista, who took advantage of this feeling of wonder—thus, hopefully, banishing any further resentment: Over the pulpit hung a bell to which he fastened a white horsehair thread, unknown to the nephytes. This thread stretched to the outside of the pulpit, where the padre would pull it and cause the bell to ring at the very moment he entered. The Indians, it is said, were properly awed and could never explain the seeming miracle of the *campanita* ringing of its own accord whenever the padre entered the pulpit.

One of the most fascinating facets of Spanish mission architecture lies in the various means devised to accommodate the bells. No two missions display them in like manner. The genius apparent here is eminently worthy of the Franciscans' epic struggle in carting the bells to their destinations.

Basically there are four types of architectural support. There is the terraced bell tower, as at Santa Barbara, where Moorish towers rise two stories high above the roof. This feature also distinguishes beautiful old San Carlos Borromeo de Carmelo, the second mission Serra founded and the one he loved as his own.

Then there is the *campanario*, or bell wall, to be seen at San Diego and also at Santa Ynez and San Gabriel. The bell wall at San Juan Capistrano is one of the most picturesque and most photographed bits of California mission architecture. On one side it enclosed the famous Garden of the Bells, where the legendary swallows arrive and depart on their appointed days each year.

Gables and bell cotes are favored by San Jose, where the side wall is shortened into a deep alcove so the bells hang protected by the red-tiled eaves. The bells at San Francisco de Asis (Dolores) likewise hang in an improvised bell cote.

Finally, for those missions without any other way of hanging bells, there was always a stout beam available somewhere in the structure, or, nearby, a lacy pepper tree with limbs large enough to support a bell in much the same humble way the founding padres hung theirs.

And what is the present status of the missions and their bells? El Camino Real, or the Royal Road, still extends from San Diego to Sonoma, forty-five miles north of San Francisco, and more or less connects the twenty-one structures. The way is appropriately marked at regular intervals with tall guideposts, each with a pendant bronze miniature resembling a mission bell.

Most of the missions are in various states of preservation or restoration, but the same cannot be claimed for their bells. Some are still in fair-to-good condition, but

At Santa Ynez the bell tower is just an extension of the front wall, its arches completely symmetrical. *California State Department of Public Works*

Right
The bell tower at San Carlos Borromeo at Carmel shows distinct Moorish influence. Being the second mission completed by Father Serra, it was "one he loved as his own."

In the bell cote of Mission Dolores in San Francisco are three bells dated either 1792 or 1797. All three are original, the gift of the viceroy of Mexico. This is the trio that inspired Bret Harte's haunting poem "The Angelus."

many have been irreparably damaged by earthquake or fire; still others have been recast—rebuilt, as it were—but in the process losing their historic Spanish identity and becoming, instead, examples of the modern bell caster's art. As an illustration, among several removed from Santa Barbara's towers in recent years and sent to the Netherlands for recasting were two originally cast in Mexico in 1787 and two in Peru in 1818. Though they retain their original shape and their exact inscriptions, they are nonetheless modern Dutch bells now.

More than half the fine old Spanish bells were seized and carried off who knows where during the secularization of the missions around 1834. Many others were seized by the unscrupulous during those years the missions all stood in a state of disrepair. Miss Walsh's pursuit of such relics led her into many a dark and decrepit belfry where, under very difficult conditions, she copied timeworn inscriptions. On one occasion she found a bell from San Juan Capistrano hanging in the tower of a railroad station. Others she discovered in equally anomalous locations.

Those that have disappeared are by now considered lost forever; yet in the 1950s a heavily inscribed and dated bronze bell, centuries old and cast in Spain, was unearthed by a Kansas crewman laying pipelines through desert areas in California. Nothing else remained of what appeared to be a ruined and half-buried adobe village and mission.

Such original ones as do remain are not always found at the original mission site for which they were cast because there was considerable borrowing and exchanging of bells among the padres, a fact sure to confound and frustrate the bell buff attempting to reconcile present findings with earlier written records. Regardless, and though less frequently heard as compared with their once tireless proclaiming of daily hours and events, the old Spanish bells are rewarding to study simply as irreplaceable examples of a vanished art. For the most part, they and others each mission may once have owned have been documented to some extent by the padres. As a simple example, at the foot of the *campanario* at La Purisima is a small wooden slab with the following information:

> In 1835 five bells belonged to La Purisima. Two were cast in Lima, Peru, and dated 1817 and 1818. Two of the original bells remain in the *campanario*, two are at other missions, and one lost.

Some of the six Santa Barbara bells as they were being shipped to the Netherlands for recasting. The smallest one shown was a badly cracked Ruelas bell dated 1797, a poorly cast specimen to begin with.

Contrary to common belief that the bells along El Camino Real were cast mainly at the old armory in San Blas, Mexico, official references reveal that they were the products of numerous scattered founders and foundries. Taken as a whole, they prove somewhat more interesting than their counterparts throughout the Southwest, though their basic provenance is similar. By the time these others were being brought to California the art of casting had become better defined. Not only were founders now signing their bells; several were earning a reputation for individual styling and ornamentation of their work.

Notable names appearing on California's mission bells include those of Manuel Vargas in Lima, Peru, who cast at least fourteen of them; Paul Ruelas in Mexico City, who shipped about the same number; and Cervantes in Santiago, Chile, who sent very few that far.

Vargas was considered the most literate and meticulous in his work, and it is possible that he may have served his apprenticeship in Spain, where the finest bell casting was done. Or possibly he apprenticed at the renowned bell foundry on La Calera farm near Santiago. Misspelled words and imprecise ornamentations are unknown over a Vargas signature. His larger bells are often characterized by a sizable diamond cross with an eight-petaled daisy in each diamond. Nine of those he cast for California missions were accounted for in a single chime at San Juan Bautista. They ranged from a treble of one hundred pounds to a deep bass of several tons. Today few Vargas bells remain. Only three or four missions have even one. Santa Barbara owned two, dated 1818, among those recast.

Ruelas was the least literate of these three founders and the most careless in workmanship. Perhaps he delegated much of the work to Indian helpers who had no apprenticeship training. Two of his bells, dated 1797, were also among those recast for Santa Barbara and both had been badly cracked for years. His work is usually identifiable by a double inscription, one part of which contains the words *Ave Maria,* with or without an ornately unique cross.

Working first in Chile and, as some believe, later in Mexico, Cervantes was another founder noted for his exacting workmanship. Only two of his bells have been located in California today. The one at Pala has already been mentioned; the other is at San Buenaventura, the last mission personally planned and built under Fra Junipero's supervision. Known as "St. Mary of Zapopan" because of its inscription, the bell is a beautiful example of Cervantes's superlative skill. For the devout

San Buenaventura Mission is the only mission having wooden bells. This wooden bell hangs in the Mission Museum and was made about 1809.

it is a tangible reminder of Our Lady of Zapopan and the role assigned her after the great conquest of Cortes. According to its inscription, it must have been cast for the church at Zapopan, only a few miles from Guadalajara, Mexico, then later sold to San Buenaventura when hard times lay upon the dwindling Mexican village.

AVE ° MARIA ° PURYSYMA
MARIA ° D ° SAPOYAN ° ANO ° D ° 1825 °
[Hail Mary Most Pure. Mary of Zapopan Year of 1825.]

San Buenaventura owns a select variety of early bells, the one by Cervantes, one cast by Ruelas, two from Zacatecas, and in its museum two large old wooden bells—the only ones of their type to be seen along El Camino Real. The intervention of California's Native Daughters is credited with saving these wooden bells (originally a trio). When the group took steps to preserve them, one had already tumbled from its tower, riven beyond repair and consequently scrapped. Another was half worm-eaten and had been left in its tower to rot. The third was waiting at the depot for shipment elsewhere.

Of unspecified purpose, these wooden bells have led to considerable speculation. Presumably they were made from native oak trees that abound around Ventura. Some authorities label them as pseudobells, to be used like the wooden *matracas* during Holy Week while all church bells are traditionally silent. As each has a metal plate inside, apparently to serve as a sounding plate for the clapper, others believe they were intended for actual use in lieu of bells missing for one reason or another.

Aside from Spanish-cast bells in the missions along El Camino Real, there were several atypical ones of far different provenance. The English firm of Vickers and Company in Sheffield, noted for their steel bells, received an order for two from General Vallejo during his reign over Sonoma at the northernmost tip of the chain of missions. The American foundry of Holbrook and Sons in Medway, Massachusetts, cast an order for six, one of which went to San Gabriel. One other New England firm, Henry N. Hooper and Company, filled at least one order for a California mission bell, as did several foundries in Saint Louis and San Francisco.

Another unexpected type of bell comes to light in records at San Fernando Mission, which show that two Russian ones were received there between 1806 and 1815. History having assured us that the Spaniards always feared the Russians would come down from Alaska and gain a foothold on the California coast, it seems unbelievable that any such bells would have found their way into Spanish structures. The explanation is simple: In 1806, the Grand Chamberlain of the Czar came down from the impoverished colony of Kodiak, seeking a supply station for Russia's needy settlements in Alaska. The Spanish *commandante* proved sympathetic, and thus began a brisk trade. At the copper foundries in Kodiak, and later in Sitka, many large bells were cast purposely for trade in California. They were designed for missions and churches, but today most of them are silent showpieces either privately or municipally owned.

A much neglected footnote to El Camino bells involves the humble neophytes who faithfully performed the duties of ringing them at each mission. We have only minimal recognition of the Indians who fulfilled this singular role demanding such energy, repeated punctuality, always an attentive mind, and of course long years of practice. The bells numbered from three to nine, so it follows that crossing and recrossing that many rawhide ropes required a certain proficiency if the resulting music was to be more than a jangle.

The names of at least four skillful ringers are known. There was old Acu, the gentle ringer at San Juan Capistrano, whose task it also was to exercise Lola, the parrot, around the Garden of the Bells. There was Don José, the colorfully garbed ringer of bells and genial guide at Carmelo, who had journeyed there from the land of the Aztecs with Father Serra himself. Then there was Gregario, the official ringer of San Luis Obispo's great Peruvian bells, who lived to be not only the mission's last living link with its Spanish past but also the last practicing master of the complex ringing patterns originally learned in Mexico by the early padres.

It was a remote noontime, in the year 1889 to be exact, when eleven-year-old Gregario arrived at San Luis Obispo, where he immediately succumbed to the chiming of the mission's bells and where eventually he was to assume the ringing duties of ninety-year-old Naja. Naja had been there since 1820, when he had helped hoist into place the five new Vargas bells arriving that year.

According to a tribute paid him on his sixty-second anniversary as bell ringer, Gregario waited two years to be called as Naja's apprentice. He busied himself with all manner of humbler tasks until he heard the words, "Learn the bells, boy."

Learn them he did, practicing six months just for his solo performance of sounding the Angelus, mastering the weight of each tug, the amount of slack to allow, the direction and speed of each hand's movement—to evoke the precise tones with which the Angelus was meant to greet each dawn, noon, and dusk. Years more were needed to perfect his technique for the more elaborate patterns such as that for Mass, where all the bells came into play.

Gregario maintained his position even when advancing years made the climb up the thirty narrow steps painful. Fortunately, the very full old ringing schedule was diminished in 1925, but this in no way diminished his devotion to his task. He continued to preside over his bells, as one observer described him, like a veritable Toscanini in proud action.

2

STORIED STEEPLES

At the time Franklin, Massachusetts, incorporated itself as a town in 1788, a friend of Benjamin Franklin wrote to him in Paris that, a town near Boston having chosen his name, the writer presumed a present of a bell from Franklin would be very acceptable, not only because they had no bell with which to summon the people to meeting on the Sabbath, but especially because they were erecting a new meetinghouse. Franklin replied that he assumed the people in Franklin were more fond of sense than of sound, and accordingly sent them a handsome donation of books.

Had many colonists subscribed to Franklin's viewpoint, fewer bells would have enlivened the airways over the early republic. As it was, church bells were in great demand during those formative years. Congregations vied with one another in seeking the first or the largest or perhaps the sweetest-sounding bell.

One of the most amusing stories in this connection centers in New Hampshire, where Portsmouth's Strawberry Bank was rivaling Boston Harbor for foreign trade in the mid-seventeenth century. Upon hearing that several bells had been imported for new meetinghouses around Boston, Portsmouth's citizens began to fume. To permit Boston to surpass the Bank was unthinkable. Captain Peter Jackson, one of the wealthiest citizens, resolved that the Bank's new meetinghouse must have a bell. He offered to purchase one on his next voyage. (During the first century of colonial life, before American bell foundries were established, many ship captains obligingly brought back European bells, glad to have them for ballast on their return trip because American-bound cargo was scarce.)

Strawberry Bank's minister led the opposition to a bell, saying it savored of popery, and the proposed gift was rejected by vote of the congregation. Captain Jackson was not dismayed by his apparent defeat, for he knew his influence among the roisterous sailors of the town. Soon the minister was gratified to see a small group of seamen attending his Sabbath services, and gradually their number increased. When the captain was ready to undertake another voyage he again offered to bring back a bell, and this time a majority of the congregation accepted his offer.

The sly captain departed, in search of a bell, unaware that back in Portsmouth a tipsy seaman was spoiling his little joke by revealing how Jackson had paid each fellow a pound sterling for his vote. On hearing how they had been tricked, the indignant minister and his more devout followers decided not to permit a bell in the meetinghouse, after all. In England, meanwhile, Jackson had located a loud-voiced fog bell that he felt would outring any bell in Boston. When he returned to New Hampshire, however, and learned how unpopular he and his bell were, he had no choice but to dump it on the wharf, where it lay until a more broad-minded pastor arrived in Portsmouth.

Though the chief desire of emigrating Puritans apparently was to leave behind every reminder of the Church of England and all ritual connected with it, one exception seems to have been the meetinghouse bell and its turret (which would later evolve into a steeple). Apparently overjoyed by their new-found freedom to worship, most of the colonists felt it a privilege to proclaim that freedom by ringing a bell mounted on their very own place of worship. In England, as dissenters from the church, they had been denied the use of both a church bell and a churchlike structure. But some, like the Strawberry Bank preacher, did not share their feeling; to them that rhythmic ringing sound still smacked of the very ritualism and popery they had struggled to escape.

Both viewpoints are reflected in the architectural changes as austere boxy meetinghouses evolved into more gracious spired churches. The start of this evolution can be conveniently traced in the seacoast town of Hingham, Massachusetts, where Abraham Lincoln's progenitors first settled in America. When the town's earliest meetinghouse was erected in 1635, there arose the question of a bell. A negative Puritan vote concluded with these words: "A church bell is a contrivance of priests, not suitable for our meetinghouses. We will continue the use of our drum."

Unique among early meetinghouses and churches in Massachusetts is the one in Hingham called Old Ship. It was built by ship carpenters in 1681 and has always had a bell in its turret. The present one, the fifth, was hung there in 1822. It is rung by pulling on a rope that drops to the middle of the broad aisle in this square structure, since the turret rises from the center of the roof.

Old Ship is the oldest church building in New England; the oldest wooden one and oldest in continual use in our nation. Not only is it unique architecturally, but also historically, as the only example of a primitive meetinghouse that has been restored to its original condition. The hipped roof slopes up to a central "deck walk" skirting an open belfry and surrounded by a balustrade to protect those who watched for returning ships in stormy weather. Rising above the belfry is a spire topped by a weather vane—a practical reason in itself for erecting a spire. Altogether, there is a degree of structural grace here foreshadowing some changes that would flourish a century later.

By the time of the American Revolution meetinghouse plans were giving way to church plans, most of them including either a cupola or a steeple, the latter often surmounted by a spire. As a result, more than a few early meetinghouses began remodeling their structures and adding one or the other of these features. A number of the church plans after 1800 were influenced by youthful Charles Bul-

19

Old Ship Meetinghouse, Hingham, Massachusetts, is designed in the square form typical of earliest meetinghouses, far removed from the English Gothic style. The Hingham belfry is unique in having a compass rose painted on its ceiling, there being no cardinal points on the weathervane itself. A National Historic Landmark. *Photograph by G. Harris Danzberger*

finch, who was doing innovative things in the way of transforming colonial meetinghouses into churches as we know them today. His work drew attention to the possibilities in a church's crowning architectural detail, its belfry.

By then it was commonly agreed that a belfry, whatever its form, was useless without a bell. The market for the whole business of ringing apparatus mushroomed, and out of this heavy demand emerged a great American industry, that of bell founding. Any lingering puritanical critics of the new trend (and they had always been in the minority) were likely to have been taunted by this sassy jingle.

> Build a church without a steeple,
> Cussed church and cussed people!
> Raise a steeple with no bell,
> Who for you can toll a knell?

If anyone believes that religious groups in the "gude auld days" were less factious than in our own time, let him examine early town records. They are reliable sources, certainly, and represent our forefathers as sometimes expressing their convictions with a bluntness that ignored courtesy and even Puritan piety, especially when it came to their meetinghouse. Second only in importance to its location was the "weighty" problem of its bell.

A new one was needed for the 1700 meetinghouse in Newbury, Massachusetts, and Captain Sewall was entrusted to "procure a good and sufficient meeting house bell for the town of Newbury, suitable for our towne considering the remoteness of our dwellings." One large enough to be heard at a distance meant a more expensive bell, for they were sold by weight, and therein lay the point of dissension. Disputes lingered on and on until the sexton was "ordered" to hang the old bell in the new turret. Later a Colonel Pierce, Esquire, came into favor and, along with Tristram Coffin, Esquire, was "impowered to procure a bell of about four hundred pounds weight."

By contrast, little expense was spared to equip each Bulfinch cupola or steeple with the finest bell money could buy. In some instances this meant one cast by Boston's eminent and gifted patriot, Paul Revere. The Fifth Meetinghouse of Lancaster, Massachusetts, now owned by The First Church of Christ, boasts this priceless combination of a Revere bell and a cupola regarded—like the church itself—as Bulfinch's masterpiece. It is said to have been inspired by Saint Mary-le-Bow's in London, the most beautiful Sir Christopher Wren ever built in that city.

In Maine can be found two other Bulfinch churches of matchless beauty, their call to worship ringing out from a Revere bell: one in Kennebunk, one in Castine. The bell at Kennebunk once served not only to call worshipers but to sound the hours and mark the days of the week. Three times a day it was rung—at seven o'clock, at noon, and at nine for curfew. After curfew echoes had faded away came measured strokes indicating the day of the month. Today it is heard only for Sunday morning services.

Probably few American churches enjoy greater popular distinction than Christ Church of Boston, now more familiarly known as Old North. It is the city's oldest existing place of worship; its first stone was laid April 15, 1723. It too has associations with Paul Revere, not because one of his bells hangs in the steeple, but because he once rang the changes on Old North's historic chimes, and because the signal lanterns he arranged to have hung in the steeple April 18, 1775, warned of

The Fifth Meetinghouse of Lancaster, Massachusetts, now owned by The First Church of Christ, is regarded as Charles Bulfinch's masterpiece, said to have been inspired by Saint Mary-le-Bow in London. In the belfry hangs a 1,067-pound bell marked REVERE BOSTON 1822. A National Historic Landmark. *The Reverend Alexander St.-Ivanyi*

"Redcoats" marching to Lexington and Concord as he himself rode off to spread the alarm.

The steeple today is not the original, but an accurate replica of the one that went down in 1804 and *its* replica blown down in 1954, thanks to Hurricane Carol. The chimes, however, are still the full original peal of eight and are justly considered the finest and sweetest-toned in the nation. Inscriptions on them reveal their story, those on the third and the eighth saying:

WE ARE THE FIRST RING OF BELLS CAST FOR
THE BRITISH EMPIRE IN NORTH AMERICA, 1744
[and]
ABEL RUDHALL OF GLOUCESTER CAST
US ALL. ANNO, 1744

The story of why Paul Revere wanted to help ring those chimes is an interesting one typifying colonial Boston of the 1750s. One year when his Puritan parents forbade any observance of Christmas, as was their custom, the boy and his friends longed more than ever to share in the music and color of the Anglican celebration. In enterprising boy-fashion they devised a plan for offering their services to Christ Church as bell ringers. Their contract is still preserved in the church archives—it bears the boys' signatures below an agreement that guaranteed Paul and his friends "the whole care of the Bells" so long as they attended to ringing them one evening each week for two hours and at any other time the wardens of the church "shall desire it." The contract was in effect for one year and officially established the young ringers as the newest members of the Society of Bell Ringers.

The number of historic steeple bells in Boston, including many chimes, is probably without equal anywhere in the United States. Even in colonial times "the skyline was dominated by steeples and the whole town by bells," comments Esther Forbes in her biography *Paul Revere and the World He Lived In.* A high concentration of history-laden steeples characterizes all New England, in fact, and to a lesser degree all the eastern seaboard southward. It was here where our history began, where religious and patriotic zeal reached its greatest fervor, and where colonists could find no better way to intensify feelings than to make their bells resound on every possible occasion. A century later this means of expression still held sway, as the diary kept by the rector of New York's Trinity Church proves. It shows his joyful entry dated April 3, 1865:

At about 10 o'clock they brought the news that Petersburgh had been evacuated. I rushed out to see if it was true and there to my great amazement and ectasy read the overwhelming words "Richmond ours!"
New York went off at once into fits. There was an immense gathering in Wall Street, at which between 5,000 and 10,000 people sang the Doxology, and the bells of Trinity clattered and clanged as loud, as hard and as fast as three raw hands could make them go, for the bellringer, Ayliffe, was absent from town.

Although a considerable number of bells remain in ringable condition and a fair number are still sounding periodically—usually before church services—our perfunctory use of bells today is in great contrast to the almost daily use once given them. Their ever-diminishing refrain over the past century became most noticeable first along the open countryside, where other old familiar calls once heard beyond woodland and meadow gradually vanished. Besides the Sermon Bell summoning the congregation, there was the Pardon Bell rung before and after the sermon for the pardoning of sin; the Gabriel Bell that woke the people; the Pudding Bell telling all cooks it was time to prepare dinner; and the Passing Bell for the dead.

The Passing Bell was the last of these to be abandoned. Not too many years ago some oldsters in the northern tier of New England could still recall from their youth the sexton's three measured strokes for a child, two groups of three strokes for a woman, and three groups for a man. When a person of prominence died, a stroke of the hammer for each year of his age followed the Passing Bell's announcement. If the sexton tolled at the rate of two strokes a minute, a ninety-year-old person's honorary tolling extended over three-quarters of an hour.

It is our changing customs, of course, that have brought the sound of steeple bells almost to a halt in some communities; and it is also our changing attitudes, which—unfortunately—seem almost to border on indifference now and again. In the mid-twentieth century a national campaign was underway to revive the custom of ringing church bells on the Fourth of July. The mayor of Wilmington, Delaware, after making his appropriate proclamation, was approached by the city's ministers, perplexed as to how they could comply. Of the more than 150 churches, fewer than five had bells!

A study in Atlanta, Georgia, revealed that the people there had built over six hundred churches, but when all their churches and college campuses were surveyed, only twenty-five were found to have bells. So time there, too, has muffled the sound of steeple bells the city once knew. Writing in the *Atlantan*, Mrs. George Mayer asks why. Such sounds have not reached the vanishing point in all cities, she finds, in calling attention to the many still heard in San Francisco, for example. (Providence, Rhode Island, and Cincinnati, Ohio, also come to mind as cities still cherishing and using their historic bells.)

One explanation for Atlanta's loss may date back to the Civil War. War has always had its impact on mass confiscation of bells, not to mention voluntary donations to be melted down and cast into weapons. If in Atlanta there was any situation even approximating what happened in New Orleans, many of its large bells must have disappeared, never to be replaced during the long, difficult days of Reconstruction after the Civil War, with financial panics to follow.

Mary Taber recounts the New Orleans story in her *Anthology*, a quaint little volume of bell facts. In 1863 General Beauregard of the Confederate army issued a call to the patriotic South to contribute bells of all sorts and kinds to be cast into cannon for the Confederate army and navy. To this call there was enthusiastic response. Bells galore were sent to New Orleans from all parts of the Confederacy. In Marietta, Georgia, as in other communities, a tender of all its church bells was made up and signed ex-officio by the ministers.

When General Butler captured New Orleans and established his supremacy, all his plunder became "contraband of war," which he shipped north to be sold by the United States government. Here is a copy of his invoice:

Ship North America from New Orleans to Boston with 800 bells,
say 200 tuns, from cowbells, plantation bells, steamboat bells, to heavy

church bells, contributed on call from General Beauregard for material for brass cannon. Value $50,000.

This prize cargo, sold in Boston at from twenty-two to thirty-one cents per pound, netted $30,000, some of it being sold to melt down, some to be used as bells. The whole episode was a bitter one for the South. Apparently, however, the German Catholic Church on Shawmut Avenue in Boston felt no compunction at accepting as a gift from the general the finest chime in the lot. It was one "Beast Butler" had personally confiscated from a New Orleans church whose members had come under his displeasure.

The chimes of Saint Michael's in Charleston, South Carolina, have figured prominently in more than one war, and as a direct result are the most well-traveled of bells. Four times they have crossed the Atlantic, in addition to their maiden voyage from London in 1757. During the American Revolution they were carried away by British troops and sold in London as spoils of war. A former Charleston merchant living there heard of their fate, purchased them, and returned them to Charleston. Then for over seventy years the chimes regulated the social, civic, and religious life of the city, bringing each day to a close with a curfew.

During the Civil War the history of the already famous bells once again almost came to an end. They had been sent to Columbia for melting into ammunition, but not being used for that purpose, were placed in hiding. Here they were found by Sherman's men on their march to the sea and smashed into a hundred pieces.

Saint Michael's of Charleston, South Carolina, the most monumental of American Georgian churches. Its steeple, inspired by that of Saint Martin-in-the-Fields, London, houses a chime of bells that crossed the Atlantic Ocean five times. *Chamber of Commerce, Charleston, South Carolina*

There was at that time no record in Charleston of where the bells had come from. However, despite the great poverty in which the parish found itself, the rector wrote to a friend in London about the cost of a new set. That gentleman, after a thorough search of the city, found the company that had cast the original set, and in their books were recorded the exact proportions of the metal, the size of the bells, and so on. The company was immediately engaged to make a new set.

In the employ of this firm was an old founder who had been apprenticed under the very foreman who, more than a century before, had cast the original set. Spurred on by the whole unfolding story, he did not rest until he found the original molds for casting. Back in Charleston, the overjoyed parishioners saw to gathering up all the fragments and sending them to London to be recast in these molds.

Finally the set of chimes was ready for another of its journeys across the Atlantic, and it is this set that hangs in Saint Michael's today. It is considered one of the city's chief historic treasures—no visit to Charleston is complete without hearing its sweet chiming.

Bells naturally go where people go, and as our expanding population kept pushing westward, a few bells were traveling the same direction in their owners' covered wagons. Others would be ordered later and sent by canal barge and ox-cart. In general, money was not too plentiful among those settlers opening frontier territories, so it is not surprising that the soul-satisfying experience of presenting a church with the gift of a bell became a welcome practice. Actually, Old World royalty had set the precedent, and Queen Anne, ever a friend of the Episcopal church in the colonies, was one of the most generous donors. Saint Thomas of Bath, North Carolina, received a bell from Queen Anne in 1710. It hung in a separate belfry long since gone. During the Civil War the bell was contributed to the Confederacy, to become one of many cast into the four cannon of the Edenton Bell Battery. Today still another Queen Anne bell hangs in the present belfry beside the church. It too came as a gift, from her Bounty Fund, which she had bequeathed for charitable purposes before her death in 1714. It was cast in England in 1732, recast in New York in 1872, and is so inscribed. The bell in Saint Joseph's Procathedral, Bardstown, Kentucky, the first cathedral west of the Alleghenies, contains many beautiful pieces of art that were the gifts of Louis Philippe of France. The tower bell is supposedly his gift also.

At the old state capital town of Vandalia, Illinois, is a highly storied bell donated by the grateful parents of little Illinois Riggs, to honor her name. Romulus Riggs was a Philadelphia merchant with land holdings in Illinois. His liking for the state grew strong, thus his and Mrs. Riggs's choice of a name for one of their daughters. Their gift was presented to the Presbyterian Church at Vandalia with their letter of donation, dated August 27, 1830, stating, "If this dear child should be spared to us, it may be the will of an all-wise Providence to place her amongst you. . . . We therefore . . . ask that she may be remembered in kindness by you all."

Little Illinois did grow to womanhood, but "all-wise Providence" did not place her in Illinois; she married a Philadelphian and lived in her native city all her life. In 1856 she wrote to the Vandalia church saying she remembered her father's taking her to hear the bell before it was shipped to its destination. Though no longer in service, it is still prized as the first Protestant church bell in Illinois.

Even as the Vandalia bell was being cast in faraway Philadelphia, another was being donated to a church in California for quite different reasons. Presumably it

When this scene was pictured, the retired bell of the Presbyterian Church at Vandalia, Illinois, was still proving useful. During his pastorate, Dr. Coen found it helpful in keeping children aware of his congregation's proud heritage in owning the first Protestant church bell in Illinois.

still hangs in the belfry of Plaza Church in Los Angeles, keeping alive the memory of the first couple to elope from California. Their romantic story is given by Bancroft in his *History of California*.

Secrecy surrounded the wedding plans of a young American sailor from New Bedford, Massachusetts, Henry Fitch by name, to the charming Doña Josepha, a native daughter of California. There was likely to be interference from Governor Echeandia on the pretext young Fitch was a "foreigner," but actually because Echeandia wanted the Spanish beauty for himself. The couple's fears were realized when their wedding was indeed forbidden. They eloped to South America, married, and later returned to California, only to have the young husband immediately arrested, tried, and found guilty on charges of having forcibly abducted an innocent girl. The ecclesiastical court's vicar-in-charge read the punishment: "I condemn him to give as penance . . . a bell of at least fifty pounds in weight for the church at Los Angeles, which barely has a borrowed one."

Whether given in penance or out of a grateful heart or in a splurge of beneficence, donated bells have now and then helped reverse that waning trend in ringing them. Donors occasionally feel moved to ensure the use of their gift by stipulating that it be sounded at some specified time on a recurring basis. A 2500-pound prayer bell was given to a church at Troy, New York, with the request it be heard each evening at seven o'clock. The First Light Infantry Company of Providence, Rhode Island, donated one note to the sixteen-bell chime of Grace Church, requesting that it be rung "on the 10th of September in each Succeeding year Forever in memory of Oliver Hazard Perry of R. I. the victor of Lake Erie 1813." In between these extremes of daily or of yearly ringing, any number of options are open to donors for ensuring that their gift be heard.

A minister, if innovative, is also in a position sometimes to involve the sound of bells in the services of his church. When Thomas Cole and his wife Catherine were prevailed upon to donate a bell to a rural congregation struggling to "raise" a church, they could not have envisioned the unique role their gift would play, nor the nationwide fame it would one day bring Iowa's Little Brown Church in the Vale. But a future pastor was to see possibilities. That bell was the first to arrive in Chickasaw County and its coming from New York State was an event. It was rung almost continuously from Dubuque until it reached its destination near Nashua.

The Little Brown Church in the Vale, near Nashua, Iowa, where a romantic tradition grew up around the bell in the tower when newlyweds were asked to pull together on the rope that rings it.

The Reverend F. L. Hanscom, who went there in 1940 as the twenty-sixth pastor, was impressed with the hundreds of marriages being performed at the rustic little church in its idyllic setting. As a result, he introduced one last bit of symbolic ceremony for each pair of newlyweds leaving the entryway. He asked the bride to ring the bell. She could not pull hard enough on the knotted rope to make a sound. He requested the groom to help. It was then that the minister gave his advice: "Always remember the bell rope! You'll find married life much easier if you pull together."

Any very large church tocsins were a distinct luxury for congregations in the Far West of pioneer days, for they were extremely expensive because of shipping costs. Made in the East, they had to be sent on sailing vessels by way of Cape Horn, then transported by oxcart. Transportation being what it was, crude and slow, this was no small venture. Had anyone asked his opinion, Daniel Webster would heartily have disapproved all the energy expended in getting large bells to the west coast, for he was utterly opposed to developing that part of our land, "that vast and worthless area . . . those great deserts . . . those endless mountains . . . that western coast, rockbound, uninviting . . ."

Fortunately, the pioneers foresaw promise and even wealth in the West, and, despite the lengthy journey involved, their pioneer efforts to secure at least one bell in each community never wavered. Whether heard from a church, a town hall, or any other building, there was something about the booming voice of a bronze bell that fostered unity. With hordes of diverse groups rushing westward, any unifying force was highly desirable—so men reasoned.

The Wright Brothers' Bell in California made the typical journey that brought bells of any size to that state from the East. More than a century ago it was cast in a foundry on the Ohio River, then barged three hundred miles down to the Mississippi River, and another thousand miles to New Orleans. There the 500-pound iron bell was loaded on a schooner for its trip through the Gulf of Mexico, across the Caribbean Sea into the Atlantic Ocean, through the Straits of Magellan, up along the west coast of South and North America, until it reached Humboldt Bay. Here it was unloaded and carried by wagon into the wilds of Humboldt County. After several moves, the bell today hangs in Saint Luke's Methodist Church, Richmond, California. It has been renamed the Wright Brothers' Bell because at one time in its history two boys of that name, later world famous, were associated with it. Preacher Wright had Orville and Wilbur pulling the rope regularly to sound the bell calling his parishioners into the church.

Tower Talk

The infinite variety seen in the steeples piercing our American skyline for better than two centuries is almost a thing of the past so far as modern architecture is concerned. Yet hundreds of such architectural "signatures" that mark our early churches are still standing, and they afford us insight into the ethnic backgrounds of those who built them. Often there is a traceable relationship not only between the architectural style and the ethnic backgrounds of the builders, but between the origin of the bell and its owners.

New England meetinghouses with their simple "turrits" reflect only American Puritan influence, wholly unpretentious. But when meetinghouses were replaced with churches in the early Republic, varying European influences came into play, harking back even to the baroque style of the steeple with an octagonal lanterned belfry.

Easily recognizable Spanish influences have already been noted in the arched walls, bell cotes, and Moorish towers of California's missions. Something of that same Spanish influence still lingers in Florida, too, notably in the Cathedral of Saint Augustine, which marks the first Catholic parish in continental United States. The cathedral was not built until the end of the eighteenth century, although parish records date much earlier and one of the original bells in the Moorish tower bore the date 1682. Along with others in the belfry, it was silenced by fire in 1887, but a new chime was arranged in the four niches of the *campanario* rising above the roof in typical Spanish style.

Equally recognizable are the bulbous onion-shaped domes and carrot-shaped spires on remaining Russian-built churches in Alaska. One photogenic example is near downtown Juneau and another, until destroyed by fire a few years ago, was in Sitka. For the latter, known as Saint Michael's, seven bells arrived from Russia in 1844 at the same time as the first bishop to Alaska, Bishop Innocent. They gave continuous service until the fire in which they were all lost.

The Moravians brought with them to America their fondness for the flèches, or bell cotes, of the old country, capped by lofty traceried spirelets. In this new land those distinctive features were translated into arcaded cupolas with high ogival roofs. From such cupolas the congregations were called to services by the sound of bells or, in some cases, trumpets, both so much a part of Moravian liturgy. The

Spanish influence is seen in the bell cotes at Florida's Saint Augustine Cathedral, in a view showing the original structure as it looked in 1871 before a damaging fire. *State Photographic Archives, Strozier Library, Florida State University*

The restored Russian Cathedral in Sitka, Alaska—Saint Michael's—looks very much as the original did in this picture, except for the seven Russian-cast bells, all of which were lost in the fire of January 2, 1966. *Alaska State Historical Library*

Rare individual bell in storage at Saint Michael's at the time of the fire. It was saved, only to be stolen during the confusion and never recovered. Reputedly it was cast in Sitka. *Alaska State Historical Library*

The Moravian Bell House at Bethlehem, Pennsylvania, erected in 1746, was so named from the beginning because of the bells in its cupola of a somewhat stylized ogee form. *Historic Bethlehem, Incorporated*

Bell House at Bethlehem, Pennsylvania, erected in 1746, was named for its bell-shaped cupola with six arches of bells cast that same year by Samuel Powell, an English founder and the landlord of Bethlehem's Crown Inn. They cracked in April, 1776, presumably while ringing for independence, but were immediately recast by Matthias Tommerup, a bell founder who worked in the basement of Bethlehem's Brethren's House.

Another architectural idea underwent a different sort of adaptation in America —the detached belfry built apart from the church proper. Largely of Scandinavian origin, it has appeared in this country occasionally, not so much under Scandinavian influence as from individual preference and need—as in the case of the two sisters who were not on the best of terms but who both wished to donate a bell to their church. It would never do to mount the two gifts for ringing in unison, so one sister had hers placed in the church tower and the other had a separate belfry constructed to hold her gift.

A picturesque example of these detached belfries is the red brick archway at Pohick Church near Alexandria, Virginia. Though it is not historic, it is interesting for its construction. Presumably the foundation for it was laid in 1917. It was planned in memory of George Washington, who with his family worshiped at Pohick Church. Among the rectors preaching here was Parson Weems, whose stories of Washington's boyhood included the immortal cherry tree episode.

It is a matter of record that bell towers and steeples have sometimes served an additional purpose other than their intended one of housing bells. In the 1940s the bell tower at Maryknoll Seminary in Ossining, New York, as the highest point in Westchester County, became an ideal vantage point for "Operation Skywatch." Equipped with binoculars, the Maryknoll fathers joined ground observer corps across the nation in scanning the skyways for hostile aircraft.

Some coastal churches, if favorably located, permitted their steeples to double as signal towers. The Presbyterian Mission Church at Fort Wrangel, Alaska, has the distinction of being the oldest church in that state. For over half a century a beacon

Volunteer watchers for hostile aircraft used binoculars while on duty
in the 100-foot bell tower at Maryknoll Seminary, Ossining, New York.
Maryknoll Brothers joined other volunteers across the nation while
"operation skywatch" remained in
effect, in the 1940s. *The Maryknoll
Fathers, Maryknoll, New York*

burned in its belfry, warning mariners along the coast. Venerable Grace Church of
Yorktown, Virginia, on favorably high land, was one of the earliest churches to
have a signal erected in its steeple. Unfortunately, both here and at Wrangel, the
light signal and steeple and bell came crashing to the ground during a raging fire—
such being the chief enemy of every tower in the days before fire-fighting equipment came into use.

A mariner's light in a steeple could prove fatal to that structure in time of war.
Saint Philip's of Charleston, South Carolina, had already contributed its chimes to
the Confederacy during the Civil War when Union gunfire destroyed its steeple.
The mariner's light beaming from it had proved too tempting a target.

One tier of the handsome steeple on Boston's Old South Church was once put
to quite another use. This famous steeple, erected in 1729, consists of four sections:
an arched octagonal belfry holding a Paul Revere bell, a wooden lantern with small
windows on all eight sides, a tall spire, and a weather vane. Just prior to the Revolution, Parson Prince was in the habit of using the lantern section for his study
where he could house his priceless book collection and write his sermons. No doubt
the quaint little room made a soul-satisfying snuggery for the scholarly gentleman,
with soft light filtering through the small windows, the tower clock sounding the
hours, and, far below, the subdued tattoo of hoofbeats along Marlborough (today,
Washington Street).

The tower gracing Gloria Dei (Old Swede's) Church, Philadelphia's oldest, is
also "storied" in more ways than one, for it too is compactly designed in several
tiers and has looked down on many famous personalities entering its doors. Betsy
Ross was married here in 1777, and Jenny Lind sang from the organ loft in 1851.
The tower was erected in 1700, when the present church was built by the first permanent white settlers in Pennsylvania. Plans called for a room above the tower entrance for various religious articles belonging to the church; over that, a room for
the church library; and crowning the tower, a spire. The tower was calculated at
from eighty to one hundred feet, "if such a height would at all be ventured, considering the terrible hard windstorms of this country."

Among several priceless treasures brought by the first white settlers of Pennsylvania was a bell from Gothenburg, Sweden. As a result of fine custodial care
these treasures and the church remain beautifully preserved. Or is this due to the
fact that, after the laying of the cornerstone, Old Swede's pastor called upon a
noted mystic nearby to cast a horoscope to find a propitious day for starting construction, one that also boded well for the church's future!

31

In retrospect, it may seem that most of the pealing and tolling over our land in the past has issued from church steeples, and statistics support this thinking. Yet a small book could be written about the many fine and time-honored school bells. Scarcely a school of any kind or at any level of the educational scale lacked a bell during the late 1800s, even well into the 1900s; something more will be said of these in a later chapter. Then there were the heavy courthouse and factory tocsins booming forth day after day, as well as bells on some business establishments adding their voices to the metallic chorus.

Many were so installed that they not only could be rung at will but could function also as clock bells. If it seems strange to find early meetinghouses and churches equipped with clocks, it should be remembered that clocks and watches were far from common. If a church tower was prominently located, as it usually was, it offered an ideal mounting for a timepiece. Such was the case with the old meetinghouse in Wethersfield, Connecticut. Completed in 1754, the building waited twenty years for a bell; but then one was ordered, and a clock as well. Cash money was scarce at the time, though the town was rich in onions. Thus the church fathers' decision to levy an onion tithe on each citizen and so pay for bell and clock.

The clock was delivered without fanfare; but the bell, made in New Haven and transported to Wethersfield by oxcart, attracted a great deal of attention. Few towns along the route could claim ownership of a bell. Nevertheless, on the day bell and clock were to be raised to their tower, it was the newly uncrated clock that caused a wave of excitement. It had but three faces! The reason was not apparent until the spectators realized that the blank fourth face was to look down on the graveyard. The frugal church fathers had no intention of wasting onions on a clock to mark the hours for those sleepers to whom time was no longer important.

Browsing among tattered old news clippings, especially those from Boston dailies, usually uncovers at least one curious tale relating to bells. One paper devoted a full column to the odd story behind a Portuguese bell that arrived in Nantucket, far from its intended destination. The year was 1810, and because a plague raged in Lisbon a certain flock of parishioners prayed for an end to it, promising in return a set of six bells for the Church of the Good Jesus of the Mountains. The plague did cease, and the casting of the bells was duly entrusted to José Domingos Dacosta, the best founder in Lisbon.

No sooner had the set been cast than Captain Charles Clasby of the Nantucket whaling fleet chanced to visit the Portuguese city. He had long wished to buy a bell for his native town, so in company with another captain, who was a connoisseur of bells, he visited Dacosta's foundry. His choice of Dacosta's stock? The finest of the newly cast set. At first the founder refused to break the set by selling just one bell, but in the end he relented.

It is providential the captain's purchase ever reached Nantucket. The year was 1812 and war with England had been declared. On the way home the captain's ship encountered a British sloop-of-war with a crew that had not heard the news. The whaling crew took care not to enlighten the Britishers, who might have confiscated the bell. Once safely on the island, the bell was eventually paid for by the joint efforts of the Unitarian Society and public subscribers. The price, $500. Even some Quakers subscribed, reminding everyone that Friends do not believe in using bells for religious purposes; but since this one would be sounding alarms and calling town meetings, they felt it their duty to help.

Finally Dacosta's masterpiece with its long dedicatory inscription to a Portuguese church was echoing from a Unitarian cupola on Nantucket Island. Before long a letter arrived from officials of Old South saying they had heard about this fine new tocsin, and as they had a clock but no bell, they would like to know for how much it could be bought.

The Nantucketers replied they had a very fine tocsin but no clock, and they would like to know the price of the clock. Ignoring this reply, agents of Old South persisted, offering to pay one dollar per pound for the bell. Since it weighed 1,575 pounds, it would have brought the islanders a pretty profit. But they were already sentimentally attached to its tone. Today the church has its clock too, so the bell, as one of its duties, also rings the hours. Old South finally satisfied its need for a bell to mark the hours for its priceless old 1756 clock, the masterpiece of its maker, Gawen Brown.

Along Charleston's wide southern thoroughfare, from high overhead in Saint Michael's steeple, mellow chimes have announced the hour since 1764. Described as a primitive system of wooden cogs, ropes, and weights, the clock is today feeling its age and suffers occasional lapses. But, claims one writer, no modern timepiece would dare argue with it. In Charleston you are not late to an appointment unless you are late by Saint Michael's chimes.

Lacking a clock in some church tower, a community might decide to finance a public tower clock. Boston probably fathered this idea with the public tower clock the town began maintaining in 1650. Records accounting for expenses in keeping it running also reveal that a second came into use in 1718, made by the same Benjamin Bagnall who advertised the first "coffin clocks," known later as grandfather clocks.

The year 1966 saw one of the most widely recognized industrial clock towers in our nation pass into oblivion when the Elgin National Watch Factory, in Elgin,

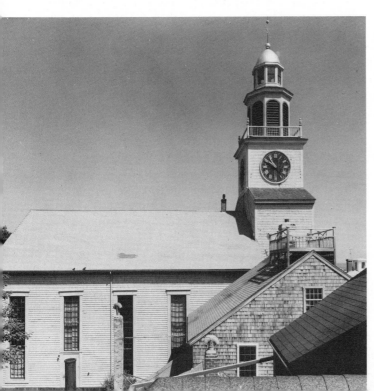

South elevation view of Second Congregational Meetinghouse Society Church, known as the Unitarian Church, on Nantucket Island. From its oaken tower sounds the Portuguese bell cast and inscribed for a church in Lisbon that never saw it. A National Historic Landmark. *Historic American Buildings Survey, Library of Congress*

On October 3, 1966, the Elgin National Watch Company's noted landmark came crashing down. Some 30,000 watchmakers had had their working hours regulated over the years by the sound of the huge tocsin in the tower. *Elgin (Illinois) Courier News Photograph*

Illinois, was demolished. Similar demolitions are commonplace, but not all are so dramatic. Far from the oldest of its kind, the tower was one of the tallest, and the clock, one of the largest. The numerals were a yard long, one foot longer than those on Big Ben. It took two railroad cars to transport just the clock from Connecticut to Illinois in 1906.

The bell, which predated the clock by nearly twenty years, came from the McShane Bell Foundry in Maryland. Originally it announced the factory's opening, noon, and closing hours, but that practice ended in the 1930s. It is interesting to note the very considerable use to which the "Big Bell" was put when first installed. As reported in the local newspaper at the time:

> At 6 o'clock, when the factoryites ought to be up and getting ready for a day with Father Time, the bell is struck seventy-eight blows with an eighty-pound hammer; at 6:50, 37 blows; at 7 o'clock, one blow; at noon, one blow; at 12:50, 37 blows; at 1 o'clock, one blow; at 5, one blow; after which it is silent until 6 a.m. the next day.

The "Big Bell" rang for the last time during the watch company's seventy-fifth anniversary of its founding in 1867. Happily, it was salvaged before the demolition and now rests in silence in the Time Museum, Rockford, Illinois.

Happily, too, the old American Tobacco Company bell has been placed on public display—but in a semisilent capacity, since it is rung only one day out of each year. When a North Carolina couple learned that the company proposed putting the bell in storage, they rescued it from that fate by purchasing it to mount on their lawn. For posterity they have built a cornerstone under the 2,400-pounder containing all available information, plus their canceled check given in payment. In its new home, a different role has been assigned the old factory bell. Each

34

Fourth of July its owners stage a neighborhood party, welcoming people from the area to ring it in honor of the day.

If not all factories boasted a clock bell, at least many (like the American Tobacco Company) had a bell installed somewhere on the premises. Especially in early New England mill towns, a familiar sound was the insistent five o'clock morning bell awakening workers. Then at seven o'clock the same relentless voice propelled them toward their machines.

Somehow, when steam whistles replaced factory bells they failed to endear themselves to the townsfolk. More than one petition was circulated urging a return to the old factory tocsin. A few did enjoy a brief return to service before being scrapped or merely silenced. But in the end changing times had their way.

There are always exceptions to generalizations, and indeed Robinson's of Newport Beach, California, is just that, with its airy windbells adjoining the store's ultramodern entrance; yet, by and large, today's stores and other places of business seldom consider using bells to call attention to their establishments. Nevertheless, time was when that idea was more popular. As recently as 1926 Wanamaker's of Philadelphia was ordering a fifteen-ton Founder's Bell from Gillett and Johnston, one of England's three remaining great foundries at that time. Its cavernous voice, pitched to a low D as it clocks the hours, is familiar to Philadelphians, though most of them are unaware of the story behind the bell, commemorating the store's founder, John Wanamaker, as well as the fiftieth anniversary of his "new kind of store."

The Boston Sunday Herald of November 13, 1903, reported the arrival of a beautiful and ancient bell for a local restaurateur, Mr. Rudolf Karwiese. His partner, traveling abroad, had bought it from a centuries-old church (dating to 667) in Munich, Bavaria, that was about to be destroyed. In exchange, he offered three new bells for a new church, but the owners demanded five, and these he had to give. The *Herald* described the ornate workmanship and the inscription:

JOSEPH J. G. DALLER ME FECIT, MUNICHU, ANNI 787

Mr. Karwiese proposed to hang the bell on his restaurant at 12 Hayward Place. One can only hope he enjoyed its silvery notes for some time, though his name

The fifteen-ton Wanamaker bell ready to embark for Philadelphia from the Gillett and Johnston Foundry. Since its arrival would coincide with American's Sesquicentennial, its weight had been purposely specified as one ton for every decade of independence.

disappears from city directories in 1906. The restaurant continued until 1915. Today that whole street has disappeared, and all efforts to trace the bell have proved futile. Were its whereabouts known (granting it even exists), it would qualify as possibly the most ancient in the United States.

Bells were customarily used in conducting one type of business that is best forgotten. The business of selling slaves was carried on in more or less open markets throughout the Deep South, and usually a bell sounded to mark proceedings. One of perhaps the only two remaining examples of such markets stands in the center of Louisville, Georgia, the colonial capital of that state. It is the original eighteenth-century structure, intact, modeled on similar ones seen in Portuguese Africa, but the bell tower is an American addition.

The bell, cast in France in 1772 for a convent in New Orleans, was stolen by pirates on the high seas, later sold in Savannah, and sent inland to the new state capital. Before assuming its heartbreaking role in the old market, it was rung to assemble settlers when Indians were raiding and also to celebrate many victorious occasions. Amidst the worn but still handsome embossings on its bronze surface, the bell bears an illegible phrase naming its maker.

By considering the number of counties in each state, it is not overly difficult to estimate the number of courthouse bells that must have existed a century ago. Naturally each county wanted to proclaim its importance with a substantial building crowned by a cupola and bell to announce court sessions. In some counties the bell also functioned in a wider capacity—ringing alarms for fires, signaling other alarms, pealing for patriotic occasions, tolling at the death of distinguished persons, and marking the passage of time if there was a courthouse clock.

Of them all, none is more renowned than the old Cook County Courthouse bell that tolled its own doom before crashing to the ground amidst the flames of the Great Chicago Fire. On that fateful Sunday night of October 8, 1871, the bell, even while engulfed in flames, sounded a solemn, continuous, final warning. The bellman did not abandon his post until the roof of the building was ablaze. Those who heard the tolling above the din of falling walls, the roar of raging fire, and the screams of frantic citizens said they would never forget the sound. Scarcely

The Old Market House, once known as the Old Slave Market, still stands intact in the center of Louisville, Georgia. The bell (lowered from its tower today) was being sent by the king of France to a New Orleans convent when it was stolen by pirates, who sold it in Savannah. *Drawing by Dorothy Cole*

Small watch charm souvenirs made from the metal of the old Chicago courthouse bell destroyed in the Great Chicago Fire. The metal in the bell had come from cannon used in defense of Fort Dearborn in 1832, during the heavy Indian massacre. *Private Collection*

had the shapeless mass of bell metal cooled amid the rubble when hundreds of souvenir hunters came with chisels and hammers, and two-thirds of the metal disappeared. What remained was sold at auction to Everhardt and Company for the making of souvenirs.

A courthouse bell still used to announce the opening of court is today a rare phenomenon in America. One of the very few, and more than likely the only one in North Carolina, can be heard in Duplin County opening each session of the district and the superior courts. This eighteen-incher is mounted on a post outside the sheriff's office, a rope and chain passing through the window to facilitate ringing.

Unbelievable as it may seem at this distant day and time, even some state legislators were once summoned to duty by the ringing of a bell. For the past ninety-two years North Carolina state assemblymen have managed to convene without being called in that manner. Until then the state had kept a bell in a wooden belfry in Capital Square in Raleigh.

Of passing interest is the way Vermont state legislators were for many years reminded of the day of the week—not by a tower bell, but by tunes from the chimes in a giant clock standing in their statehouse in Montpelier. The clock is now in the keeping of the state historical society and no longer in operation, but these are the tunes it once played: for Monday, *"Johnny's So Long at the Fair"*; for Tuesday, *"Auld Lang Syne"*; and for Wednesday, *"Home Sweet Home"*; then *"Annie Laurie"* on Thursday; *"Jennie Jones"* on Friday; *"The Minstrel Boy"* on Saturday; and, appropriately, *"Old Hundred"* on Sunday.

Magnified copy of the certificate issued with each tiny souvenir bell made from Chicago courthouse tocsin. *Private Collection*

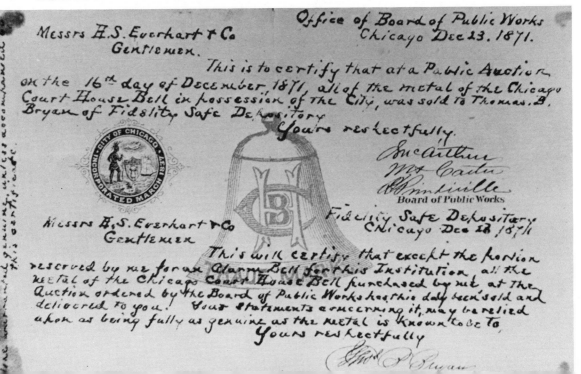

3

PORTRAIT
OF A BELL FOUNDER

Bellmaking has received scant attention in studies of the developing metal arts in early America. Though the reasons for this neglect are obscure, the fact remains that bells have been made here since the early eighteenth century. As an actual industry, however, bellmaking did not get under way until after the American Revolution. John Phillips of New York was one of the first founders to call attention to his craft. In the *Boston News Letter* of June 1717, he advertised "Cast bells at a reasonable price warrented for Twelve Months, if it crack or break, it shall be new cast for nothing. All new bells shall be made of better mettal than any other that comes out of Europe or Churches or Meeting Houses."

Little else is known of John Phillips, but judging by his advertisement he was well trained for his craft. It is interesting to note, and definitely to his credit, that this early founder guaranteed his bells because, until the birth of the Industrial Revolution, there was no lawful buyer protection. The rule of the day was the Latin *caveat emptor*—"let the buyer beware."

The next advertisement on record is dated June 5, 1738, and reads simply: "A Bell Founder, John Whitear of Fairfield, Conn., makes and sells all sorts of bells from lowest size to Two Thousand Weight."

John Pass, later one of the partners who recast the Liberty Bell, solicited orders through the *Pennsylvania Gazette* of August 17, 1749. Thereafter, similar advertisements appeared more and more frequently all along the eastern seaboard. A John Robertson was advertising in the *South Carolina Gazette* in 1760, as a brass and bell founder who "begs leave to return thanks to those gentlemen and others who have been pleased to favour him with their custom and at the same time informs them that he continues to make in the neatest manner . . ."—and here he lists over twenty-five various castings and mountings in brass.

A similar and equally lengthy advertisement appeared in the *Pennsylvania Gazette* in 1767 for a Daniel King, who—among other things—made house bells, horse bells, criers' bells, and many more of all sizes. As if this were not enough to keep him busy, the advertisement concludes, "He also rivets broken china, in the neatest manner." As with John Robertson, such diversity might suggest that both men were jacks of all trades and masters of none. Fine surviving examples of their work, however, disprove such an idea.

The first colonial bell foundry of note was established at Abington, Massachusetts, in 1761 by Colonel Aaron Hobart. A British navy deserter named Gillimore, who had learned the art of founding in England, went to work for Hobart and stayed until the foundry was ordered to produce cannon for the Revolution. After the war, the man who was to become colonial America's foremost bellmaker learned his art from Hobart. This, of course, was Paul Revere.

Granted, the quest for facts relating to early bell founding in America is an elusive one. So much has gone unrecorded. Nonetheless, there are notable exceptions, largely the result of founder's descendants who take pride in preserving such records as do exist. Paul Revere's family exemplifies the point. Records accounting for his many activities in the metal arts and certain other trades have been faithfully kept or presented to suitable institutions. Helpful as these are in reconstructing Revere's unexcelled ability in the metal arts, they leave to conjecture just how he became involved in bellmaking with Colonel Hobart. It may be that upon the colonel's approaching retirement he desired a successor and therefore initiated the relationship. Perhaps he thought of Paul Revere because he was already an established silversmith and metallurgist; his copper engravings were being widely exhibited; and soon after the Revolution he had established a foundry for casting cannon, bolts, copper sheeting, and the like.

If it is true that Hobart opened the door to having Revere join him in making bells, it is also coincidentally true that the latter was at this point seeking some additional outlet for his energies. He was only moderately enthusiastic about the hardware store he had recently opened, where he also sold small necessities like

Portrait of Paul Revere painted by John Singleton Copley, probably around 1768-70. *Museum of Fine Arts, Boston*

playing cards, spectacles, sealing wax, and wallpaper. When the congregation at his father's old "Cockerel" church wished to have their cracked bell recast, he supposedly volunteered his talents and soon sought advice in Abington, twenty miles from Boston, where he introduced himself to Colonel Hobart. He had no one to turn to in the city because, as yet, only cowbells and house bells were being made there.

The eventual business relationship worked out by the two men resulted in America's first large-scale bell foundry. Admittedly, Paul Revere's initial effort was no paradigm. Even his staunchest admirers commented on the "puny, harsh and shrill tone," but this is scarcely surprising. He may have worked in metals all his life, but bell casting is extremely specialized and, except for Hobart's advice, Revere knew not one iota about such casting. He nevertheless proudly placed these words on his first bell:

THE FIRST BELL CAST IN BOSTON, 1792
BY P. REVERE

After years of service, then thirty more in a dusty loft, this treasured relic rests today in the "patriotic corner" of the transept in Saint James Episcopal Church, Cambridge, Massachusetts.

Undaunted by less than perfect achievement at first, Revere continued experimenting and learning. Two sons joined him, Paul, Jr., and Joseph Warren, and the latter was sent to study firsthand the manner of casting bells in England and Europe. This is frequently referred to as the first authentic industrial research by an American manufacturer. With the information gained by his son and with twenty years' experience behind them, the Reveres could finally advertise with confidence bells that satisfied hoped-for standards: ". . . constantly for sale, Church and Academy Bells of all sizes, which they will warrant equal to any made in Europe, or this country . . ."

Paul Revere's moment of triumph came in 1817 when he cast his "great bell" for King's Chapel, Boston. Today it still resounds from its stone tower, summoning parishioners to worship. It weighs two and one-half tons and has the most brilliant tone of any Revere bell. On the paid bill for his work, Paul Revere was gratified indeed to write, "The sweetest bell we ever made."

Some of his contemporaries continued having reservations about the tone of Revere's other bells, but most thought them sufficiently "powerful and mellow." As to their quality, they compared favorably with, but never quite equaled, the finest from England. This was through no fault of the founder but simply because that more "elastic" quality of copper used for centuries was no longer available. The world's supply was depleted.

In all, nearly four hundred bells are listed in the Revere stock book, in order of manufacture between the years 1792 and 1828. The largest weighed 2,885 pounds; the average size, some 800 pounds. Of this total output, fewer than half have been located to date, some still ringing, some now silent. The identifying inscriptions on them vary, depending on the period when they were cast. As company ownership changed within the family from time to time, so did the company's inscriptions. Their first bells were marked REVERE; REVERE, BOSTON; REVERE & SONS, BOSTON; REVERE & SON, BOSTON—followed by a date in each case. Sub-

Early Paul Revere and Son advertisement featuring their cannon and bells.
Revere Copper and Brass, Incorporated

In the belfry of the Congregational Church at Topsfield, Massachusetts, hangs Revere bell #179, marked "REVERE & SON BOSTON 1817." Many other Revere bells are found in similar white-spired New England churches.
Edward C. Stickney

Revere bell dated 1818 (#185 in the firm's stock book) in Saint Michael's Church, Marblehead, Massachusetts.
Edward C. Stickney

sequent changes in markings continued after the senior Revere's death in 1818, with the last stock book entry appearing in 1828. His father's will had requested that Joseph Warren Revere remain in charge of the company, and this he did, officially incorporating the Revere Copper Company in 1828.

Statistics such as these, and other cogent facts, are interestingly presented by Edward and Evelyn Stickney through their writings and lectures. This Massachusetts couple is devoting a great part of their time and expertise to documenting the whereabouts and history of each existing Revere bell. They readily admit that more than half are undoubtedly gone forever. Still, their "discoveries" multiply decade by decade. In 1956 they reported locations for about ninety of the bells, all but two or three of them in New England. Two decades later they have approximately 120 located, one as far south as Savannah, Georgia; one as far west as Englewood, Colorado; and the most distant in Singapore, where Paul Revere's daughter made her home as the wife of Singapore's first American consul. Some hang in stately impressive structures, but the vast majority are found in those simpler white-spired village churches Americans tend to associate with New England.

Taken as a group, Paul Revere's bells have experienced a varied existence. Some have been engaged in important war maneuvers, the most important being

In this silver souvenir are particles from a Revere bell cast in 1798 for Minot's Ledge Lighthouse in Boston Bay. The lighthouse was swept away in an 1851 nor'easter, later rescued by the government, and sold to Faulkner Woolen Mill in Maine, where it served until fractured in a fire. Heirs of the mill family claimed fragments of the metal. A leaflet detailing the story was sold with each of the souvenirs. *Stephen Foster Memorial*

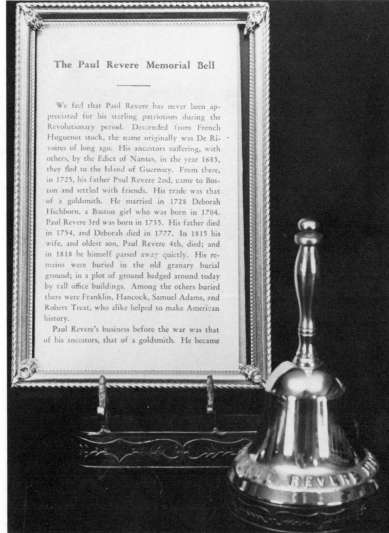

The Paul Revere Memorial Bell

We feel that Paul Revere has never been appreciated for his sterling patriotism during the Revolutionary period. Descended from French Huguenot stock, the name originally was De Rivoires of long ago. His ancestors suffering, with others, by the Edict of Nantes, in the year 1685, they fled to the Island of Guernsey. From there, in 1725, his father Paul Revere 2nd, came to Boston and settled with friends. His trade was that of a goldsmith. He married in 1728 Deborah Hichborn, a Boston girl who was born in 1704. Paul Revere 3rd was born in 1735. His father died in 1754, and Deborah died in 1777. In 1815 his wife, and oldest son, Paul Revere 4th, died; and in 1818 he himself passed away quietly. His remains were buried in the old granary burial ground; in a plot of ground hedged around today by tall office buildings. Among the others buried there were Franklin, Hancock, Samuel Adams, and Robert Treat, who alike helped to make American history.

Paul Revere's business before the war was that of his ancestors, that of a goldsmith. He became

the bell cast for the *Constitution*, which is rumored to have been under private—almost secret—ownership ever since its disappearance in the 1920s while that frigate was undergoing restoration. (Some, however, say the original bell was shot away in the battle with the *Guerrière* in 1812. At least one Revere bell has had a bounty offered for its return—the mayor of Concord, New Hampshire, proferred a twenty-five-dollar reward for a lead to the location of that city's first town bell. Several damaged in storm or fire have been melted down and made into souvenir bells that grace collectors' shelves. Another precipitated a riot—the famous broomstick riot of Lord's Hill, New Hampshire, when church members outside the district forcibly removed the 1,500-pound bell from Lord's Hill Church. Broomsticks wielded by the district's defiant women did not stay the thievery; but upon returning from a work project, their equally defiant menfolk went to court and reclaimed their Revere bell.

Four have combined to draw countless visitors and a measure of fame to Woodstock, Vermont. The residents of this Green Mountain town like to recall that theirs is the only community owning so many ringable Revere bells—all ringing despite the fact that the first one, purchased in 1818, was guaranteed for only one year!

The work of the Holbrook and the Blake foundries of this same general era warrants more than superficial comment, too. Between 1816 and 1880, when the Holbrook firm operated, more than ten thousand bells were made and shipped throughout the country. They rang at Harvard, Brown, Amherst, Yale, Dartmouth, and other large universities. Some, as already noted, found their way into California mission towers; some operated as lighthouse signals. Outside New England, not too many Holbrook bells have been reported in use today, but any found are readily identified by their maker's name and place of manufacture: East Medway, Massachusetts.

Major Holbrook had learned his craft well, having been apprenticed as a lad to Paul Revere, later working in partnership with Paul, Jr., after the latter withdrew from his father's firm. Being a gifted musician, the major had a tone-conscious ear and was convinced he could produce bells of a sweeter tone than any from the Revere foundry. Successive generations of Holbrooks who continued the family foundry, and were similarly gifted, shared his conviction.

Numerous important papers and catalogs from the Blake Bell Company have been preserved by direct descendants to provide fairly complete accounts of that foundry's productions. Somewhat paralleling Major Holbrook's rise in the industry,

A 1,300-pound Holbrook bell is pointed out by Alfred Sawyer, who is the "collector of collections" seen on the grounds of Silver Ranch. Bell was cast at the Holbrook Foundry in 1841 for the church at Sterling, Massachusetts, as stated in the deed and title to the church. *Silver Ranch, Jaffrey, New Hampshire*

Advertisement for William Blake and Company, from the Boston Directory of 1876. *Commonwealth of Massachusetts State Library*

William Blake had also come up from the ranks of Revere apprentices, to enter into partnership with Joseph Warren Revere. Begun in 1820, the work of this bell-making establishment spanned most of the nineteenth century under various mergers and partnerships, the last one forming in 1890 as the Blake Bell Company with William S. Blake as its manager. One short period of its existence, as the Boston Copper Company (1823-30), is of special interest to bellologists because of the relatively small number of bells marked with the name of that company. Incidentally, it had no connection with the Revere Copper Company of today, which was organized by Joseph Warren Revere in 1828.

Among the few bells marked BOSTON COPPER COMPANY is that in the 1821 meetinghouse at Acworth, New Hampshire. The fact that today it hangs in a structure listed in the nation's Historic American Buildings Survey is proof that even a single concerned individual can effectively spearhead a drive to preserve more than

Set on the highest elevation of all meetinghouses in New Hampshire, the church at Acworth is considered a remarkable example of turreted colonial architecture; carved spirelets decorate the corners of the turrets. Its fine Blake bell is supported by the original timbers, now carefully reinforced. A National Historic Landmark. *Historic American Buildings Survey, Library of Congress*

just "bits and pieces" of our heritage. The Acworth bell was in danger of crashing down from its timbers when Sarah Potter returned to her native village after a long absence. She found the metal covering on the steeple so eroded that moisture was seeping through and weakening the supports. Soliciting some funds and contributing even more of her own, she immediately hired Boston workmen to make the necessary repairs and give stronger support to the bell and the half-ton weather vane. Thanks to her vigilance, the Historic American Buildings Survey designates this one of "the best preserved of the larger meeting houses in the middle Connecticut Valley."

During the larger part of its existence, the Blake firm was known as Henry N. Hooper and Company (Hooper, Blake and Richardson from 1830 to 1868). A catalog cover carries this caption:

BELLS
Church bells in sets
Correctly tuned, any size required
Bells for factory, town, ships, R.R.'s
Hooper, Blake & Richardson

A later advertising catalog, sometime after 1890, states:

> Blake Bell Co. manufacture church, fire alarm, factory, steamboat, locomotive and plantation bells, made of copper and tin in the superior manner for which this establishment has been noted.

During its long existence the company was credited with many "firsts" and "largests," some of which are noted in this same catalog:

> We have invariably, at all public exhibitions at which we have entered bells, taken the first premium—either gold or silver medals or diplomas—over all competitions.

> We cast the first complete chime of bells ever manufactured in this country, consisting of eight bells, tenor weighing 2,000 pounds, and cast in 1825; also the second chimes ever made in this country, which are on exhibition at the Mechanic's Fair in Boston, in 1850, consisting of eleven bells, two weighing 3,000 pounds, and for which a silver medal was awarded to us.

> We have cast the largest bell ever manufactured in the United States, weighing 21,612 pounds, and made for the corporation of the city of New York.

Among Blake bells identified today is one in Saint Paul's Methodist Church, Lynn, Massachusetts, noted as the bell that inspired Longfellow's poem "The Bells of Lynn." It is inscribed HENRY N. HOOPER & CO., BOSTON, 1859. Below this is a Latin stanza beautifully executed:

LAUDAMUS TE, BENEDICIMUS TE,
ADORAMUS TE, GLORIFICAMUS TE,

GRATIAS AGIMUS TIBI
PROPTER MAGNAM GLORIAM TUAM

All during the eighteenth and nineteenth centuries, great numbers of bell foundries continued to spring up across the nation, increasing both in number and size as the nineteenth century progressed. *Zell's U. S. Business Directory* lists hundreds of such companies for the years immediately before and after the Civil War, when the industry reached its peak. Off-the-record estimates tell of companies producing all manner of bells from teacup size to 10,000 pounds, and at an unbelievable rate.

If bellmaking was not a top major American industry, it was definitely a competitive one, and that competition did not narrow until the closing years of the nineteenth century. New York City business directories list nearly thirty founders in the decade prior to the Civil War and the decade immediately following; by 1880 and 1890 no names appeared. The dwindling industry there is typical of what was happening in other areas of the East. Farther west, of course, production peaked somewhat later and the inevitable decline had not yet begun. Several leading foundries here and there continued well into the twentieth century; a few were doing business until the Second World War. Today, however, bellmaking as an industry has ceased to exist in America. Only one or two foundries of importance remain.

Wartime restrictions, depressions, the increasing use of sirens, the coming of small popular-priced electronic chimes more adaptable to changing concepts in architecture:—all these posed insurmountable problems for the American bell founder. To discourage him further, protective tariffs on bells from England and the Low Countries were lifted. With his high labor and production costs, he could not meet the new competition.

To compile a roster of American bell founders is impossible, as the names and locations of many are lost for all time. Nevertheless, even from a representative listing, their tendency to cluster in certain areas is noticeable. Some of these areas, in fact, gained enviable reputations in the art of casting. The *Journal of Fine Arts* for November, 1851, endorsed the work of the Cincinnati foundries in these words:

> Particular mention should be made of the bells manufactured in the Queen City of the West. There are two makers who deserve high mention for their skill and enterprise in the business. We allude to G. W. Coffin & Co. of the Buckeye Bell Foundry, and George L. Hanks, Columbus Street, Cincinnati, both of whom have attained a wide celebrity for the exceeding purity of their work. Chimes weighing three, four, and five thousand pounds are adjusted with perfect accuracy, blending in their tone delicacy with strength, and arranged with great simplicity as regards the means of performing on them.
>
> . . . Not only chimes and peals, but steamboat, factory and smaller bells, with their stamp, are noted for strength, durability and great melody and clearness of tone—the result of every experimenting in the different forms and compositions, with a view to constant improvement. These Cincinnati bell founders deserve eminent success, which they cannot fail to enjoy as a natural result of their skill and enterprise.

Fittingly enough, considering its fine tradition of bellmaking, Cincinnati has more than the average number of bells ringing, for a city of its size. Among them is a beautiful specimen cast by George L. Hanks. It is the 3,400-pound tenor named "Great Peter," probably cast in 1851 along with a chime for Saint Peter in Chains Cathedral there in the city. It is the epitome of all that Hanks claims for his work in his rather elaborate advertising. Four medallions circle the skirt, depicting the burial of Christ, the Madonna and Child, Saint Peter, and the Virgin. Wreathing the lip is a symbolical and heavily fruited grapevine in high relief.

The other Cincinnati firm alluded to in the *Journal of Fine Arts* tribute, G. W. Coffin and Company, was better known as the old Buckeye Bell Foundry, established in 1837. This foundry was not modest either in its claims, nor above a bit of competition in pricing. In an 1851 advertisement next to one of Hanks's, the caption notes, "Improved Church Bells Cast on a New Principle and 15 Per Cent Cheaper Than Any Foundry in the World."

The E. W. Vanduzen Company succeeded the old Buckeye Foundry, not only maintaining that firm's high standards but exceeding them when, in 1895, it produced a giant of a bell for Saint Francis de Sales Church in Cincinnati. At 35,000 pounds (including yoke and clapper), this remains the largest bell ever cast by an Ohio foundry and is still one of the largest free-swinging bells in the world. Six boys were needed to pull the massive 640-pound clapper by means of six hempen ropes. Actually, though, this monstrous creation rang only once, its thunderous voice so badly shattering windows and nerves that any further ringing was forbidden. Church bells shipped all over the world were the backbone of Vanduzen's fine reputation in the industry, but their name was also made famous around the world on the nation's fighting ships and commercial vessels equipped with Vanduzen bells. An extraordinarily handsome one was carried on the luxury liner the *United States*, at that time the fastest and most modern liner ever constructed. Rising costs, shortages of materials, and changing concepts in architecture resulted in fewer orders after the Second World War; the company was forced to suspend operations in the 1950s, leaving only three foundries of importance in America at that time.

One of the three was also fated to bring its work to a halt in the 1950s—the famous Meneely Bell Company of Troy, New York, which traced directly back to the Hanks family of bellmakers, the same family to which Nancy Hanks Lincoln belonged. Troy is another community long famous for its nucleus of bell-making firms, the oldest dating back to 1780 when Julius Hanks settled in Gibbonsville (later absorbed by West Troy and still later renamed Watervliet). He had learned the craft from his father in Litchfield, Connecticut.

Shortly after Andrew Meneely set up casting operations in Gibbonsville in 1826, he and Julius Hanks formed the Hanks and Meneely Company, a partnership that continued nearly a quarter century until Julius's son dissolved his interests. In a letter written only months before closing the doors of the Meneely Bell Company, Vice-President Clinton Hanks Meneely relates an event that understandably brought great satisfaction at an otherwise bleak period for this dynasty of bell founders. An abridgment of the letter stated:

> Another matter of great interest to us was contained in a letter just received from the First Presbyterian Church of Cooperstown, New York.

In going through old records they found an invoice and correspondence referring to their bell purchased in 1817 from Julius Hanks of Gibbonsville. We were not only able to advise them that Julius Hanks established the first bell foundry in this locality and that the writer is a member of the sixth generation of which he was the second, but also to confirm that the present bell at their church was furnished by us in 1898. This is undoubtedly something of a record to have one family responsible for a call to worship that was first rung one hundred thirty-three years ago and that involves six generations of American bell-founding.

Actually—and sometimes to the confusion of those attempting to identify a Meneely bell—there had been two foundries operating under this family name from 1869 until the operations of both came to a halt in the 1950s: Meneely and Company, Watervliet, and the Meneely Bell Company, Troy. The split from the parent company established in 1826 came after the Civil War, when Colonel Clinton Hanks Meneely returned home from the army only to quarrel with his brothers at the family plant in West Troy. He entered into partnership with a George H. Kimberly, and directly across the Hudson River they operated their own foundry in Troy from 1869 to 1879, when Clinton assumed ownership. Because of competition, relations between the two branches were strained for some time; but at the end they were working in normal accord, claimed officials from both sides of the Hudson.

Both foundries made notable installations that will keep their names famous in the annals of American bellmaking. At the World's Fair in New York during 1853 and 1854, Andrew Meneely's Sons won the coveted silver premium for the bells they entered in competition. The carillon at Valley Forge has twenty-nine Watervliet bells, later perfectly matched with twenty-seven Paccard bells from France to form one of the world's finest carillons. The Troy plant soon gained a reputation for its magnificent copies of the Liberty Bell. Its first of several was the 13,000-pound replica cast in 1876 to commemorate the country's hundredth anniversary. It now hangs in the tower of Independence Hall, where it strikes the hours daily. A very special copy of the Liberty Bell became the tenor in a chime the Troy Meneelys cast for Lincoln Memorial Tower at the New York Avenue Presbyterian Church, Washington, D.C. It was here that Lincoln often worshiped, and the bell symbolizes his efforts to perpetuate liberty for all. The chimes were given by the family of the late Robert Todd Lincoln in 1929. Clock chimes enjoyed a good sale at the Troy plant and frequently made newspaper headlines. Certainly those cast for the Metropolitan Life Insurance tower in New York City did—they were the highest bells yet hung, and the Cambridge Quarters played on them could be heard twenty-eight miles at sea.

As of today, only two important bell foundries remain active in America: McShane's of Baltimore, Maryland, and the C. S. Bell Company of Hillsboro, Ohio. The Hillsboro firm, however, changed ownership in 1974, and so it is no longer under the aegis of C. S. Bell family descendants, although it operates under the old name.

The McShane Bell Foundry has been casting bells continuously for more than a century, ever since Henry McShane came to Baltimore from Ireland in 1856. Like others before him, he began by setting up a small brass foundry for casting various

Advertisement for one of Cincinnati's most noted early bell founders, from *Musical World* of May 1, 1852.

The Meneely and Company factory at Watervliet, New York, as shown in an old catalog of about 1912. *Ed J. Barry*

Right
Cover from one of many informative brochures issued by Meneely's, illustrating their most popular installation years ago.

Below
Photograph of the Meneely Bell Company plant in Troy, New York, as it appeared about 1950. *Ed J. Barry*

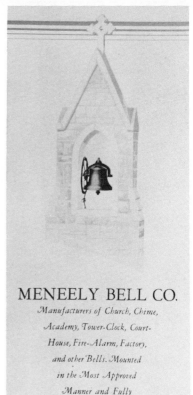

MENEELY BELL CO.
*Manufacturers of Church, Chime,
Academy, Tower-Clock, Court-
House, Fire-Alarm, Factory,
and other Bells. Mounted
in the Most Approved
Manner and Fully
Warranted*

items, mostly plumbing fixtures, with never a thought of making bells until fellow immigrant John Schmidt, from Germany, joined him and sparked his interest. Schmidt had worked in European bell factories and was expert in his craft. His expertise was invaluable and more than partly responsible for the statement, years later, "At all exhibitions, both state and international, wherever entered for competition with other bells, ours have received the highest awards."

The company's output included bells up to a top weight of 10,000 pounds—for church, academy, fire alarm, ship and steamboat, courthouse, plantation, and all other categories, even chimes. Their thirteen-bell chime for Machinery Hall at the 1876 Centennial Exhibition in Philadelphia was cited for its unrivaled clarity and mellowness of tone.

One of the most unusual castings by McShane's is the Mental Health Bell, a familiar symbol of the Mental Health Campaign. No other symbol could speak for this cause more dramatically, for the bell was cast from chains and shackles used as restraints on victims, until medical science proved them not only unnecessary, but cruel and detrimental to recovery. The metal that went into the bell came from mental hospitals in all parts of the country. It was stacked into a veritable "chamber of horrors" in the lobby of the Mental Health Association headquarters, until enough had been collected for a large bell to proclaim hope for mental patients. The stack was melted down at the McShane Bell Foundry on April 13, 1953. Serving as a foundry helper was Maryland's governor, who used a pair of tongs to drop into the bubbling crucible the last piece of metal, a pair of brass shackles.

For multiple reasons the C. S. Bell Company holds a unique place in the industry. In its century and more of existence, until 1974, it always remained under the ownership and management of the Bell family; from 1958 until her death, it was under the management of the founder's granddaughter, Mrs. Virginia Bell Thompson. Only three other women have played a major or even a semimajor role in American bellmaking.

This company's bells are not the traditional ones of brass and bronze, though they serve around the world in all the traditional capacities. Instead, they are made from a steel alloy under a formula perfected by Charles S. Bell, founder of the firm. It was on January 1, 1858, that he opened a foundry in Hillsboro to manufacture sorghum mills made of iron. He soon expanded to include evaporators and the *tortillas* used in Mexico to grind hominy. Perhaps it was due to his Scottish ancestry that he was continually experimenting to find a cheaper metal, to keep his products

Mrs. Dwight D. Eisenhower at the White House ceremony touching off the 1958 campaign of the National Association for Mental Health. The symbolic 300-pound bell (made by McShane's of Baltimore, Maryland) has this inscription: CAST FROM SHACKLES WHICH BOUND THEM, THIS BELL SHALL RING OUT HOPE FOR THE MENTALLY ILL AND VICTORY OVER MENTAL ILLNESS. *National Mental Health Association*

The second largest bell ever cast by the original C.S. Bell Company (it has a forty-eight-inch bowl) is in the possession of the Highland County Historical Society. Mrs. Virginia Bell Thompson is shown at left. *The C.S. Bell Company*

less costly for the farmer. At any rate, quite by accident, one day he dropped a piece of metal that rang with the resonance of a bell.

No sooner had he arrived at a formula for this metal than he decided to start casting bells, too. The first year the firm sold one thousand. By 1889 sales had reached 20,000 annually. "Old Charles," as he was affectionately called, would have been pleased with the tribute given his work on the eve of the firm's one-hundredth-birthday celebration: "Bells made in Hillsboro were shipped to all parts of the world. They pealed from schools and churches, called firemen to duty, farmers to dinner and Indian lepers to worship."

Surprise might best describe his reaction could he know the important part his steel alloy formula played in the Second World War, for Hillsboro produced thousands of bells for ships of both the United States and Russian navies. According to rigid government standards, brass and bronze are invariably looked upon as a requirement for navy bells, but emergencies breed emergency measures. The copper, tin, and zinc needed for brass and bronze were in short supply. Fortunately the Hillsboro firm could make quality bells without them.

Following the war, the C. S. Bell Company felt the same slump in business that affected others in the industry, but in this instance company officials were willing to diversify. The result? A return to making agricultural machinery, which solved their immediate problems. Eventually an unexpected new market for bells developed—the trend to country living brought a brisk demand for farm-type bells and, happily, Hillsboro is still shipping them out.

Before looking at West Coast activities in the industry, it is interesting to note the contrasting positions of Pennsylvania's two leading cities in the production of bells. It would be logical to assume that Philadelphia and Pittsburgh both had their nucleus of bell foundries. In reality, though Philadelphia did have its Pass and Stow, its Joseph Bernhard, the Wilbank Foundry in Germantown, plus others of similar repute, only one such company ever flourished in Pittsburgh. This was the Fulton Brass and Bell Foundry, dating back to 1832. Its long and colorful existence, through generations of Fultons, made the name almost a byword where steamboat, church, factory, and other bells were concerned in western Pennsylvania. The name was also preeminent throughout the South and West, as well as in distant lands, according to a Pittsburgh *Post-Gazette* tribute of 1859.

As early as 1835 a set of Fulton chimes received an award as the "finest sounding chimes," but the firm's greatest achievement came when it cast a two-ton tocsin for the Pittsburgh fire alarm system. This is undoubtedly the largest ever cast in the State of Pennsylvania. After years of service, its primary usefulness ended when the fire alarm system was modernized; then came the day in 1920 when its voice was heard for the very last time as it rang 1-8-4-5 strokes to mark the anniversary of Pittsburgh's disastrous fire of 1845. Today the huge tocsin rests before the Historical Society Building—a proud but silent symbol of the city's past.

In the Far West bellmaking centered chiefly in San Francisco, where such companies as W. T. Garrett and Sons, Globe Bell and Brass Foundry, and Weed and Kingwell were doing quality work around the turn of the century. It was in Los Angeles, though, that a most unusual type of casting was being undertaken by a dauntless lady who often joked about entering the bell-making industry through the back door, as it were. She was Mrs. Armitage S. C. Forbes, whose upbringing and early married life made it unlikely she would ever become involved in any enterprise of this nature. Yet in the early 1900s she opened the California Bell Company and became the first woman bellmaker in the nation and the world.

Advertisement for Andrew Fulton, Bell and Brass Founder, which appeared in the Pittsburgh City Directory for 1862. *Carnegie Library of Pittsburgh*

Cast by a Philadelphia founder who seems little known, this one-of-a-kind bell is inscribed in memory of Robert Fulton: T. W. LEVERING FECIT PHILADELPHIA A. D. 1816. NOW FULTON IS GONE. HE IS NO MORE BUT HE LEFT HIS GENIUS TO CARRY US FROM SHORE TO SHORE. UNION STEAMBOAT.

All this resulted from a rugged, colorful experience Mrs. Forbes had recently shared with her husband, a retired colonel, when the two of them literally dug up California history. The couple worked zealously to restore El Camino Real, traces of which had all but disappeared. Equipped with picks, shovels, tracings of old maps, and the blessings of less energetic citizens, the pair uncovered the old path of the padres traveling from mission to mission.

To fittingly mark their efforts, appropriate guideposts were needed. Mrs. Forbes's design of a bell hanging from a standard was chosen from many submitted as the most distinctive and emblematic of Spanish mission days. Cast in the Forbes's own foundry, the first of these was set up August 15, 1906, marking not only the restoration of a road important in American history but also the start of a unique career for Mrs. Forbes. People immediately clamored for replicas of the El Camino Real guideposts, and she suddenly found herself making bells.

The California Bell Company developed into a worldwide business, making all types of bells, ranging from little souvenirs of historic Spanish bells to large ones for ships and churches. Creatively absorbed in her latest venture, Mrs. Forbes did not permit herself to bemoan the fate of El Camino Real—vandalism, theft, deterioration, and rerouting of the highway were eroding the beauty and romance of the mission trail. In 1961 the California Mission Trails Association issued statistics on the dwindling number of markers, which originally had been located, one mile apart, the length of the route from San Diego to Sonoma: 400 of them had disappeared into private "ownership."

At eighty-eight years of age, after nearly half a century of superintending her company, Mrs. Forbes started searching for a successor who, she insisted, must be a woman. She found her in the person of Evangeline Aldrich, a career banker in Los

Left
Mrs. A. S. C. Forbes in the salesroom in conjunction with her Los Angeles foundry. On the shelf behind her are miniature replicas of the El Camino Real road markers she designed.

Right
This bell was designed by Mrs. A. S. C. Forbes to symbolize the Capistrano Mission bells and the swallows that nest around them. *Mrs. B. Ellsworth Young*

California Bells, Bears, Brackets

MISSION DE TAOS HAND BELL
Diam. 4¾"
Price_____

BRONZE BRACKETS
Hook - Roll - Scroll
Price_____

CAMPANA VIEJA
Diam. 4½"
Price_____

JESUS - MARIA - 1690
Diam. 10½"—Weight 28 lbs.
Price_____

"SABADA DE GLORIA" BELLS
Price_____

Dominguez Ranch Bell
Diam. 11½"—Wt. 25 lbs.
Price_____

California Bear Bell
Height 3"
Price_____

CALIFORNIA BEAR PAPER WEIGHTS
3 Sizes
Price_____

"CALIFORNIA" BELL
Diam. 8½"—Wt. 10 lbs.
Price_____

The wooden Gloria wheel in the center was a small copy of similar wooden accessories used in worship in early Spanish missions. (It was priced under twenty dollars!)

Angeles. Later Miss Aldrich was joined by a partner, Mae Franklin. This feminine duo devoted themselves to following the company's traditions and were producing 130 different types of bells when they were forced to close in the 1950s.

One of these traditions was the peculiarly lovely verdigris finish that had characterized Mrs. Forbes's bells, making them resemble the old mission bells with their natural patina from age and exposure to the elements. She had developed the formula for this by studying a bell from antiquity given her by an archaeologist uncle. To her knowledge, no other designer of Spanish replicas had been able to recapture that soft green finish quite so well.

Miss Aldrich once declared:

> The most exciting experience we ever had was provided by the Heart's Desire Bell. On the old radio program "Heart's Desire," the Columbus Community Church of Grand Junction, Colorado, broadcast that the dearest wish of its members was for a big bell to grace the church steeple. The radio program producer got in touch with me and ordered our very largest church bell. The next day he broadcast across the United States to the radio audience the story of this community's heart's desire and asked his listeners to help defray the cost of the bell by sending in just one penny apiece. Nearly forty thousand letters came in with pennies and currency, from people who wanted to help put that bell in the steeple of the Columbus Community Church. . . . In one New Jersey orphanage the small boys went without ice cream for a week so they could make a contribution! . . . There is still romance and a great deal of good-will involved in bellmaking.

Between East and West a nucleus of bell foundries were clustered in certain localities, and here and there were some isolated but no less important firms. If their stories could all be told, there would be exciting experiences for each. No great imagination is needed to visualize the sense of drama Gardiner Campbell and Sons must have felt on first seeing and hearing the famous Ringling Brothers Bell

Evangeline Aldrich at work in her foundry, as successor to Mrs. Forbes. *Independent Woman*

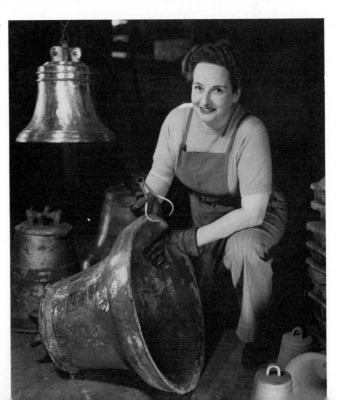

Wagon rolling along, making music with the big bells they had cast for it. The firm was one of several noted bell and iron foundries in Milwaukee during the final quarter of the nineteenth century.

Chicago bellmakers were a capable group and innovative in their advertising. E. A. Jensh, established in 1857, issued a handsome token calling attention to his work of casting bells as large as 50,000 pounds. H. W. Rincker, lately from Germany, pounced upon a more novel method of bringing his products to public attention—a method eminently befitting his first bell, since it was the first one cast in Chicago. It was made for a church in nearby Oswego, but not before Rincker had stipulated he should be permitted to hang the bell in front of his little establishment for a couple of weeks as an advertisement. Its melodious tones attracted crowds to the German founder's shop, and he probably realized many orders on account of it. The big half-ton bell was finally hung, and for forty-four years called people of Oswego to worship. Then someone set the parsonage on fire. When the church, too, went up in flames, the old bell melted and only one fragment was found. That, strangely, was the one bearing the name of the founder:

H. W. RINCKER FOUNDRY

Chicago, Ill.

1850

Eight or ten names of brass and bell founders drop in and out of Saint Louis directories over the fifty-year span between 1850 and 1900. The most enduring of these was the Stuckstede Bell Foundry, probably the only one of its kind west of the Mississippi River to celebrate a century and more of operation (1855-1962). Stuckstede went to great lengths to extol the merits of the many chimes it manufactured. In its giant catalog of 1896, not content with using mere words, the company worked out descriptions in a series of musical staffs showing the scale note to which each bell in a particular chime had been tuned, and its corresponding weight. At first glance, the result resembles a song book more than a catalog.

The bellmaking activities of another renowned Saint Louis founder indirectly led him into the ministry. This was David Caughlan, who was chosen to recast the famous old Spanish bell now known as the McKendree College bell, one of only three Caughlan-cast bells whose location is known today. Recasting the McKendree bell was one of Caughlan's last undertakings, for the year was 1858 and shortly afterward his strongly expressed belief in emancipation incited a mob to burn his foundry. This he interpreted as a "calling," so he entered the ministry and established the First Methodist Church in Saint Louis, East, as the town was then called.

As early as 1827, several brass and bell founders were at work in New Orleans. Their advertisements reveal them as skilled artisans in all kinds of metalwork. Samuel Ives kept constantly on hand a quantity of gutter spouts, boat chimneys, and "copper work from the largest sized Still to the smallest article." Durand and

Thiac advertised as a lock and blacksmith partnership executing with neatness all sorts of work in their line, including bells of every size, plantation tools, lightning rods, and iron helms for ships.

Were the mind's eye to conjure up a historical image of the typical American bellmaker, what manner of person would he be? Somehow time has rather stereotyped artists, carpenters, teachers, and others engaged in specific trades or professions. But bellmakers? Yet they share several characteristics in common, even though each was very much his own person.

So far as personal traits were concerned, founders tended to be men of recognized social position, with a strong sense of civic duty, staunchly patriotic. There apparently was not a summer soldier among them. In other branches of early American artisanry there are tales of those who preferred hiring mercenaries in time of war so they themselves might continue their craft without interruption. Unless there are tales as yet untold, not one of the known founders was ever reluctant to lay aside his craft and take up arms.

In pursuit of his trade, the average founder was not likely to be a busy entrepreneur the equal of Paul Revere or Daniel King. Very likely, though, he was extremely industrious, trained for and ably practicing more than one craft even while principally engaged in bellmaking. When he first set up his shop in Gibbonsville, Julius Hanks was "prepared to execute any orders in his line of business, viz: church bells . . . town clocks . . . surveyors' instruments." The Holbrooks entered into the business of manufacturing pipe organs as well as bells, and both made their name famous. Several other examples could be cited.

This same "composite" master craftsman was a person of strong convictions and almost unshakable confidence. He strongly believed in the worth of his chief product, for bells were a tangible part of the fabric of American life generations ago; and he had great confidence in his ability to perfect the finest bells—his advertisements leave no doubt about his determination to excel. Moreover, once the industry was established, an ironclad guarantee accompanied each sale, one no recognized bell founder ever defaulted. If his advertising was competitive, it was seldom abrasively so, seldom intentionally spiteful, for the bell craftsman was known as a man of principle.

Industrious, resourceful, strong-willed, confident, trustworthy in the performance of his craft—all these are the qualities of a sound businessman. Despite these desirable traits (or perhaps because of them!), the sincerest bell founder sometimes found himself on a collision course with partners, apprentices, or customers; nor, being human, was he always able to resolve matters to his satisfaction. The truth of this will become self-evident in even a rudimentary account of the actual process in casting a bell.

American Bell Founding

The whole process is, paradoxically, both chancy and extremely scientific. It is also complicated, involving an almost unbelievable number of systematic steps. The process begins on the drawing board, where a draftsman works out every detail of the bell's design and size with precise mathematical accuracy. Both the quality of the sound and the desired musical pitch are determined by the relative proportions of the bell's shape: its height, diameter, thickness, and weight. Even the clapper must be designed with its weight properly adjusted to the size of the bell. If it is too light, it will not draw a full tone; if too heavy, it will in time crack or otherwise injure the bell.

Customarily, American foundrymen adopted the tulip-shaped bell traditionally preferred by the English. However, in the case of Paul Revere, his namesake, and his partner George Holbrook, opinions were sharply divided. Apparently at the time Paul, Jr., and Holbrook withdrew from the senior Revere's firm to form their own, they did so because they refuted the idea that the English tulip-shaped bell produced the sweetest tone—as Paul, Sr., always insisted. Holbrook, being talented musically, felt that he was the better judge of tone and declared the French form far sweeter—the French bell was less elongated and had a broader diameter at the base.

Once the shape has been determined, next come those intricate calculations to correctly proportion height, diameter, thickness, and weight to give the desired pitch. For example, the deeper the pitch desired, the larger the bell; and always the thickness of the metal must be tapered to help achieve the necessary range of tones. Just as various notes are obtained from musical strings of differing lengths, so various notes are obtained from differing diameters ranging up and down the height of a bell. There are five notes usually. All these are touched off the moment the clapper strikes the sound bow, thus giving the effect of a perfect chord *if* the bell is properly in tune.

A great deal of attention is given the sound bow, for that is the all-important part of a bell where the fundamental (or strike) note sounds. It is this note that gives the bell its pitch. In addition, one eighth of the height from the lip, a minor third above the fundamental note is sounded; at three-quarters of the height, a fifth. The chord is completed by a note coming from the shoulder of the bell, a note a full octave above the fundamental. The hum note resulting from all these vibrations comes from the mouth of the bell, sounding a full octave below the fundamental.

After the bell has been designed, a model is created and two molds prepared that duplicate the contours of the model. Several weeks are needed to complete

The five partial tones in a bell that must be attuned to give it perfect pitch. *Drawing by Dorothy Cole*

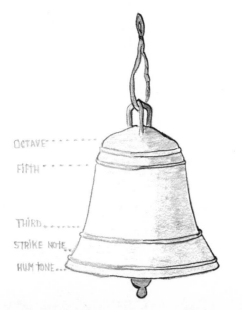

OCTAVE

FIFTH

THIRD

STRIKE NOTE

HUM TONE

these, so more than a month passes before everything is ready for the casting. Reduced to deceivingly simple terms, to cast a bell is to pour molten metal into a cavity created between two molds, an inner and an outer. The metal is traditionally bronze, the only material capable of producing a sustained ringing sound. Although each founder prefers keeping his specific formula secret, handing it down only to his successor, the basic formula is made from copper and tin in an *approximate* ratio of 4 to 1, sometimes with traces of minor ingredients—most especially zinc, for brilliance of tone, and nickel for sweetness.

There may be many stories of silver being added as a tone "sweetener," but these are largely legendary. True, it was once customary to toss tributary trinkets and coins into fiery melting pots; but, as American foundrymen have pointed out, these did not result in a high silver content and therefore did little to alter the tone. If they had, the tone would have been harsh—silver, like lead, has a dead tone.

Pouring the molten bronze takes only a few minutes, but they are crucial minutes. This is the chancy part of the casting process. There are so many variables, perhaps an inferior quality of copper, or slight impurities accidentally spinning into the fiery liquid as it is being puddled and poured. Even the most experienced foundrymen of earlier days had their disappointments. Everyone knows that Messrs. Pass and Stow had to re-recast the Liberty Bell; and Rincker, the German immigrant in Chicago, required two attempts to produce his first bell in his adopted land. His first try resulted in a bell with a peek hole in one side.

Although casting is more foolproof than it once was, master craftsmen of relatively modern times have admitted to being less than certain of the outcome until they knocked away the molds and tapped the bell to test its tone. That is perhaps the most anxious moment of all in the whole process, yet one that is anticipated for many days while the newly cast bell is cooling. One member of the industry used to relate a story about two supposedly identical bells poured at the same time from the same ladle of molten metal. One rang true, the other was a dud, or a "kettle," as it is called in the trade. No one ever knew why. ". . . just one of the hazards of the trade," he concluded.

If acceptable, the new casting is ready for polishing and tuning. The latter process is relatively simple now, with the aid of electric implements. Too, through long years of trial and error, foundrymen are now able to produce bells that are reasonably well tuned when they come from the mold, though seldom does a maker realize his dream of producing a "maiden" bell that needs no tuning before being hung. Electric tone detectors can indicate whether the pitch is just right, but *quality* of tone must be judged by ear. Any bellmaker is doubly blessed if he has a tonal ear; Chester Meneely, last president of the Troy Meneelys, was one of those rare individuals. At McShane's it was John Schmidt who had a perfect ear for pitch and double-checked each bell with pitch pipe and tuning fork. Lacking one of its own staff to perform this service, a company may have a professional musician on call whenever there is a bell to be tested for tone. Through improper usage, the quality of a bell's tone may be marred. However, once perfected, barring an accident, the pitch of a bell does not change. "Heat, cold, age, nothing will alter it," declares the I. T. Verdin Company of Cincinnati. This firm should know, for it is the country's largest and oldest establishment—now fifth generation—devoted to keeping bells in ringable condition.

In his day, Paul Revere preferred to let prospective buyers approve a new

In casting a bell, the first step calls for a thick layer of clay over the iron core of the bell mold.

Next, the bell-shaped outer mold is lowered over the core.

When the temperature is right, the huge crucible of fiery liquid bronze is allowed to cascade into the space between the outer and inner molds.

Below
Chester Meneely checks an approved bell, polished and waiting to be fitted to a yoke.

Here at the old Vanduzen Company a bell is on the tuning table being tested scientifically for tonal quality.

bell's tone. In fact, he was most insistent that any church wishing to purchase one of his bells must send a committee to hear it first. He would have the great bell carted from his foundry to his backyard, where deacons and vestrymen would assemble to listen while he sounded it with a hammer. Neighborhood small fry who wandered into this interesting little tableau could expect to be chased away by the master's cane, if they stood too close to his hammer.

Prices of bells today can scarcely be compared with those of other days. During the first century or so of their manufacture in America, bells sold for about 40¢ per pound. This added up to better than $300 for an average-sized bell of 800 pounds. To some it seemed a stiff price in a day when fresh meat still sold at only 3¢ per pound; yet it was not exorbitant for a piece of such exacting workmanship. On occasion, according to records, reputable artisans might sell a fine bell for as little as 25¢ per pound. However, in commenting on such a sale in 1850, one newspaper termed it an "unheard of low price," proof that it was far below the usual asking rate.

It is worth digressing briefly to note that the apprentice system was a decided asset in keeping down labor costs and, consequently, selling prices of bells. Hard as the system sometimes was on both boys and masters, bellmaking as a craft benefited. No other system has ever turned out such good workmen—unpaid ones at that, while they were apprenticed. Some chose to open their own shops eventually; not infrequently, thanks to their training, they proved more skillful than their former masters, thus setting new goals of achievement in bellmaking.

The foundryman's responsibility does not end as each bell is tuned, polished, paid for, and hauled from his shop. There is the matter of hanging gear and proper ringing equipment. If he is to guarantee his bells against cracking, it is obvious he must exert some control over certain factors governing their ringing. Today he has almost no problems in this area, but in other years very real problems plagued the industry until, first, the rotary yoke was devised, and, second, electric ringers were developed, making bells durable indefinitely. A rotary yoke permits the bell to be shifted so that the clapper does not always strike in the same place and cause a crack. Electric ringers, with their controlling mechanism, eliminate what was once the greatest threat to a bell's well-being—the irresponsible and the overzealous human ringer.

Craftsmen of colonial and later days were particularly eloquent on the subject of lazy ringers fond of "clocking," or tying a rope to the clapper and pulling that instead of the bell. Those quick, successive strokes hitting repeatedly in one spot were a surefire way to crack a bell, as were nonstop celebrations when ringers felt moved to exhibit their patriotism by sounding their bells as loud and long as they could. These same craftsmen felt, and rightly so, that some of their problems with the cracking of bells were directly attributable to townsfolk's taking it upon themselves to substitute a bigger and better clapper for more volume on special occasions, or even substituting a bell rope of a thickness other than specified—all this despite the craftsmen's efforts to educate their customers on proper ringing.

From such a cursory account of American bell founding it is readily evident the nation is losing—in truth, has all but lost—an industry that can never be adapted to speedy assembly-line techniques, even if there were a market for increased production. Therein lies one more reason for its gradual decline. It is likewise evident that the industry has been manned by individuals who were competent businessmen endowed with a rare mix of knowledge about science, certain of the arts, technology, and even teaching. Yet of necessity they relied on experience, not book learning, for their success. Unfortunately, neither their experience nor their competency could keep the industry afloat in the face of changing customs and concepts.

One more talent, their flair for showmanship, became especially evident throughout the nineteenth century whenever it was time for an important bell to leave the shop. Americans have always gravitated to anything resembling a parade, so here was the foundryman's unequaled opportunity to win applause for his work by parading his newest creation through the streets to its destination, or at least to the railroad station if it was bound elsewhere. Old company catalogs and records are dotted with accounts of important bells that made their festive debut in this way. A previously mentioned one, the largest ever cast in Cincinnati, was the center of attraction while being hauled to Saint Francis de Sales Church from the Vanduzen foundry where it was cast in 1895. "The bell," so a catalog relates,

> was removed to Government Square to be exhibited in public. . . . Later twelve magnificent horses hauled the bell through the streets of Cincinnati, while hundreds of people followed in procession, and the streets were lined with eager watchers to see the greatest bell ever made in America hoisted into its tower.

While the seven-foot-tall giant was on exhibit, people were charged twenty-five cents apiece to view it at close range, the better to appreciate the rich embellishments: the official seals of Cincinnati, Ohio, and the federal government, as well as medallions of the donor, six church wardens, and a group of civic leaders.

Houston, Texas, records of 1843 describe the pageantry and rejoicing that accompanied a beautiful locally made bell on its way from the Schmidt and Wilson Brass Foundry near Market Square to the Church of Saint Vincent de Paul. It was displayed on a flat-bottomed wagon gaily decorated with colorful flowers and paper streamers. Following it were national and city officials, horse-drawn fire engines, and the local band. No mention is made as to whether Messrs. Schmidt and Wilson were privileged to join the procession.

4

RING! RING FOR LIBERTY!

Were the Germantown, Pennsylvania, founder—John Wilbank—alive today, he would be dismayed to observe an endless stream of visitors (a million yearly) showering respect and affection on a bell he did not even consider worth hauling away. Wilbank had cast a new clock bell for the State House of the Province of Pennsylvania (known as Independence Hall today). While delivering it, he was offered the Old State House Bell (now the Liberty Bell) if he would cart it away. There are various versions of Wilbank's reaction to the proposition. According to one, he refused the offer, declaring, "Drayage costs more than the bell's worth." He did, however, accept the bell; then, in turn, he offered it to the City of Philadelphia as a gift. It was received with little enthusiasm.

Unbelievable as this episode seems, it is nevertheless true that despite its present exalted status, the Liberty Bell has not always been the nation's symbol of freedom and therefore has not always been as venerated as it is now. Possibly this old relic would have lain neglected still longer had its inscription not attracted the attention of abolitionists. It is somehow a significant historic coincidence that the bell should have been resurrected—and later named—by those concerned with the plight of pre-Civil War black inhabitants in America and was first used as a symbol of freedom in their behalf. After the publication of an antislavery pamphlet entitled "The Liberty Bell," other writers began adopting that new epithet, until earlier references to Old State House Bell or the Bell of the Revolution or Old Independence Bell gradually disappeared. Thus, not until it had been in America for at least one hundred years did the big bell begin to acquire its present and now official name.

As such incidents imply, the fortunes of the Liberty Bell have been varied. They have also been complex, so complex that many misconceptions and inaccuracies have crept into published accounts about its arrival in America and its subsequent use. When in 1751 the Pennsylvania Assembly ordered a bell for its State House, it was not, as too often assumed, being prophetic about an independence that would require another twenty-five years to win. Rather, both the bell and its inscription were chosen to commemorate the fiftieth anniversary (1701-51) of William Penn's charter granting religious and personal freedom to the Province of Pennsylvania. Only in relatively recent times has this fact been made clear, through the investigative efforts of the curator of Independence Hall in the early 1900s. He used to ponder over the significance of the date 1753 clearly visible on the bell. It had no association with the American Revolution, which event is of course always popularly linked with the bell. Not until 1915, when this same curator dug deeper into old records, was the original significance of the earlier date revealed.

From the time of its organization, the Pennsylvania Assembly had used a bell for official purposes and important public functions, a bell William Penn had supposedly brought with him from England. Before 1735, when the assembly acquired its State House, members had met from home to home, summoned by Penn's bell fastened to the limb of a convenient tree. This became the first bell raised to the modest tower above the State House. To the tradition-bound assemblymen, a new and larger bell seemed suitably necessary to mark the fiftieth anniversary of Penn's great gift, though there were Philadelphians who objected. Some felt the expense unjustified. Taxes were already too high, they complained. Some detested the idea of a bell from England, but from England it must come because there were no large casting facilities in the colonies.

Still, everyone argued, the occasion would demand some really bold, even majestic, bell ringing; so objections ceased, the assembly voted the necessary funds, and a committee of three was appointed to proceed with ordering a bronze bell of some 2,000 pounds having not only a voice to give out "a clap like thunder," but a "brave verse around the side" as well. Isaac Norris spearheaded the work of the committee, personally choosing the biblical inscription from Leviticus 25:10— PROCLAIM LIBERTY THROUGHOUT ALL THE LAND UNTO ALL THE INHABITANTS THEREOF. Anyone troubling to read Leviticus 25:10 in its entirety will see more clearly the appropriate intent of Isaac Norris's choice for celebrating fifty years of liberty in Pennsylvania (not for winning American independence in 1776). A biblical scholar, Norris could well have envisioned a parallel between the jubilee his copatriots were about to celebrate and the jubilee the Israelite were enjoined to celebrate.

Today the Liberty Bell no longer carries its original commemorative date. Because it cracked upon its arrival from Whitechapel Foundry in London, it had to be recast; so now it carries the date 1753 to indicate the year it was melted down and remade. Precisely why it cracked is a matter of conjecture. Possibly a congenital defect in the metal was to blame, although Thomas Lester, head of Whitechapel Foundry at the time, insisted it was their only bell in the past four hundred years to crack. Maybe the fault lay with an impetuous American workman who, to test its sound while hanging it, whipped the clapper too smartly. Whatever the cause, old Isaac Norris was about to return the bell when two young ironmongers undertook to recast it. The two were John Pass and Charles Stow, Jr., son of a doorkeeper in the State House. They broke up the metal, melted it, added a leaven of native copper to make it less brittle, then cast several small bells to test the sound of the new mix before finally pouring it into what was described as a "masterly mold."

Old Isaac Norris was elated with the noble appearance of the new bell, declaring, ". . . this is probably the earliest casting of a large bell in America." For "raising the bell frame and putting up the bell," Edward Wooley and his leather-aproned helpers were rewarded with a raising feast heaped along outdoor tables. This included:

> "Two pecks of potatoes, 44 pounds of beef, 4 gammons [hams], 100 limes, cheese, mustard, pepper, 3 gallons rum of John Jones and a barrel of beer of Anthony Morris." In addition, the bill included the cost of cooking, plus the use of earthenware dishes, and candles. The whole amounted to approximately twenty-eight dollars in present-day money.

All the joyous anticipating and feasting were premature, however, for when finally the bell was tested it gave forth an unspeakably wretched sound. As a result, Pass and Stow bore the brunt of much "tiezing" until they again recast the piece and this time achieved a deep, vibrant tone. Now at last the Pennsylvania Assembly had a bell that not only resembled the one originally ordered, but also gave forth that "clap like thunder" all assemblymen had hoped for.

The new bell performed for the first time August 27, 1753, when it summoned assemblymen; and in those days they heeded its call, incidentally, because any who were either tardy or absent must pay stiff fines! For the next twenty or so years the Old State House Bell rang for every imaginable purpose and occasion, and the occasions were many during those strenuous, rebellious days in the colonies. After proclaiming the nation's every important step toward its goal of liberty, the bell reached its greatest, most significant moment on July 8, 1776 (not July 4). On that day the first public reading of the Declaration of Independence brought Philadelphians flocking to the State House yard. Colonel Nixon, who commanded the City Guard, had been chosen to present the reading because he was an ardent patriot of powerful voice. As the last words of the document faded away, the crowds grew hushed, realizing the full impact of the declaration. Into that hush, from the tower of the building afterward known as Independence Hall, came "the jubilant crashing of a clapper on bronze." The sound galvanized listeners into action. Cheers, musket shots, and fireworks fractured the air. The crowds raced up and down streets and alleys, tearing wildly at the king's insignia wherever they appeared on doors or walls. That evening they would make a bonfire of them in the public square while the bell in the tower overhead rang still more exultantly.

If 1776 brought the bell its greatest moments, the year 1777 brought its most precarious, when it narrowly escaped becoming a casualty of war. On a tense and terrifying September night a courier rode through the streets of Philadelphia proclaiming to the stunned inhabitants, "Brandywine is lost! The British are marching on the city!" At once the assembly resolved to remove all bells from public buildings and churches before His Majesty's troops could confiscate them for making cannon. Most assuredly the British would want the Old Independence Bell, as it was often called after 1776, for by now they had heard how it officially heralded the colonies' public declaration to fight for freedom.

Under cover of darkness that night, the bell was lifted from its tower and concealed under empty potato sacks in one of the farm wagons hastily drawn up in the

Removing the Liberty Bell for safekeeping at the approach of Howe's army, Philadelphia, September, 1777. *Philadelphia Blend*

State House yard. This wagon was only one of 700 conveying military supplies and other bells to safety fifty miles away in Bethlehem and Allentown—and none too soon. General Howe, with a British force of 17,000 armed men, was only a few bullet shots away.

After its wild escape over the roughest of roads, with one accidental fall, the bell was smuggled—together with those from Christ Church—into a crypt under the floor in Allentown's Zion Reformed Church, where it remained for almost a year. Meanwhile, to decoy the British, a false announcement was circulated saying this bell had been buried in the water of the Delaware River.

Back in its tower eventually, it was a busy bell for another span of years. It rejoiced when the British surrendered, welcomed to Philadelphia many eminent colonial figures, tolled in muffled tones at the passing of others. Finally, on July 8, 1835, it was tolling as the funeral cortege of Chief Justice John Marshall passed; then, with no warning, it cracked and was silent.

Without a voice, the bell was more or less abandoned until 1846, when an odd incident again lifted it into the news. In that year, the church Washington had attended while living in Philadelphia claimed the exclusive privilege of ringing its bells on his birthday. *But* the church wanted the whole sum of thirty dollars usually appropriated by the city "for this service to the illustrious dead." Other churches demanded their customary share of the money and the honor. A squabble ensued. Quick to have their say on the matter, newspapers editorialized that since the churches refused to ring without pay, Old Independence Bell should peal that day and put to shame all paid patriotism.

Their suggestion appealed to the committee in charge of the day's celebration, so workmen hurriedly drilled the crack in the bell to widen it, hoping to prevent any vibration that would cause it to spread. The experiment at least made possible a few last notes from the old bell—until noon, when it suddenly went dumb, never to ring again.

Although unsuccessful, the drilling resulted in two fallouts important enough to be recorded in history. One is made clear in a report from the superintendent of the State House steeple:

> By direction of his Honor, the Mayor, I caused the fracture in the old "Independence Bell" to be drilled out for the purpose of ringing on Washington's Birthday, and have succeeded in saving the drillings, I had a small bell cast from them, which I have the honor to present to your Committee.

Other particles from the boring were saved, and afterward made into signets mounted in gold rings, to be presented to several people of importance. One went to Captain Lipscomb of Richmond, Virginia.

Permanently silenced now—with a compound fracture zigzagging up one side —the bell might have slipped into lasting obscurity had not the abolitionists already recognized the potential in its biblical inscription. As previously noted, it remained for those crusading for the freedom of black slaves to give the bell its present name, when they published their pamphlet *The Liberty Bell.* Still, this newer cognomen was slow to win general acceptance, largely because of indifference. To paraphrase a familiar adage, out of sound, out of mind. In the average mind, a bell has always been synonymous with sound, and one incapable of sound is worthless.

It took the Centennial of 1876 to catapult the bronze relic to the high place of esteem it holds today and to name it officially, for all time, the Liberty Bell. As the nation was being swept into a flurry of preparations for its centennial celebration, Victorians began viewing the bell in perspective. They found it relevant to the historic occasion they were to celebrate, ideal as *the* national symbol of American independence. Hanging mutely in a place of honor for everyone to see, the bell— crack and all—served to rekindle a spirit of patriotism. It seemed suddenly to gain status in the American mind, to draw unto itself a certain charisma that visitors sensed. At the close of the exposition, great popular demand to see the bell in other cities started it traveling around the country.

In all, it traveled more than 20,000 miles between 1885 and 1915, visiting seven great expositions from California to Carolina. At each it was acclaimed in the grandest manner. While it was en route at night, country folk built bonfires along the railroad tracks as they waited to glimpse the big bell rolling by in its lighted car. Wherever it stopped and at all expositions, the great as well as the near-great mingled with the masses of plain people to pay tribute. It was while the bell journeyed first to New Orleans in 1885 that Jefferson Davis, who had been president of the Confederacy, left his sickbed to view the patriotic relic. And while it was on its way to the Cotton States Exposition in Atlanta in 1895, in a Virginia town, a seventy-year-old great-grandson of Patrick Henry came to the train, asking to touch the bell.

Each exposition outdid itself to give an impressive showing. At Saint Louis in 1904, where it was invited by the petition of 75,000 schoolchildren, its arrival day was designated Liberty Bell Day. The city turned out en masse to see it riding majestically behind thirteen stout gray horses. Then, in a great rotunda, multitudes stood in awe to look upon it "lying without yoke or support . . . upon an American flag as background . . . never more impressive in its simplicity."

Scene photographed from an aquatint showing
the Liberty Bell on exhibit, presumably at one
of the expositions.

On July 5, 1915, it was readied for what was to be its last journey, this time to
the Panama-Pacific Exposition in San Francisco. To the strains of patriotic tunes,
including Sousa's "Liberty Bell March," it was carried to the "Liberty Bell Special" in a truck smothered in laurel and red gladioli, followed by a motorcade of
thirty cars, through Philadelphia streets packed with well-wishers.

After its return, the huge bronze crier was installed in Independence Hall
much as it is today, in the main corridor, suspended from its original yoke, the
whole display unprotected by glass or railing. Before that, for some reason, it had
always been moved about from one spot to another. For years it was in a glass
cage; once it had been suspended from the building's high ceiling by a chain of
thirteen links; and when first brought down from the tower chamber, it had been
shown with a stuffed eagle on top.

Even the timbers in its yoke draw attention, for they are the original ones from
which it was suspended in 1753. The yoke has several times been overhauled and
strengthened, yet authorities are still not in agreement as to the kind of wood used.
Is it elm? Walnut? Oak? Opinion was weighted just slightly in favor of walnut for a
time; more recently, experts have decided it is slippery elm.

No living person has heard this bronze crier's voice, of course, or ever will,
because no further attempts will be made to repair its now famous crack. That
crack has become a cherished and significant feature, a reminder of the Liberty
Bell's demanding role in the nation's troubled infancy. On rare occasions a few taps
with a special mallet are permitted, but there is no ring to the sound. A mallet was
used on the bell in this way to mark the country's Sesquicentennial in 1926, and to
initiate a United States Bond drive in 1950.

Silent or not, as a national symbol of a free America Pass and Stow's famous
piece of casting still wields considerable influence. It was highly popular in replica
form during the Centennial of 1876, the replicas ranging from little charms to small

68

The Liberty Bell in Independence Hall.

table pieces, mostly of the nonringable variety, with only a few large-scale copies in demand. During the intervening years, demands have increased for larger, ringable replicas, however, even some full-scale ones. To mark the bicentenary of the American Revolution, the prestigious Whitechapel Foundry of London was chosen to produce official copies of the Liberty Bell as originally cast by them. These are scaled to one-fifth the size of the real one and are purposely limited to 2,400 numbered copies, representing the number of months since the Revolution. The order, the largest ever received by this centuries-old company, has resulted in brisk sales since it was initiated in 1968. Newspapers have given wide coverage to the popular demand for these commemoratives, pointing out that in such tangible reminders institutions and individuals find renewed significance in their dedication to individual liberty.

Save for size, the commemoratives differ in two particulars only from the bell now in Philadelphia. Each has inscribed on it founder Thomas Lester's name plus

To the scale of one-fifth the size of the original Liberty Bell, Whitechapel Foundry cast 2,400 replicas to mark America's Bicentenary. Each is mounted on a plinth of hand-carved oak and tuned to exact E flat of the original. *Copley News Service*

the year 1752, and there is no crack in the design. Also, each rings to a true E-flat, just as the original did when Lester tested it before it left London. In this way the historic pre-Revolutionary contract between London and Philadelphia is now fulfilled, Whitechapel executives feel.

A surprising number of full-scale replicas of the Pennsylvania-province bell can be seen from coast to coast, with many only recently installed in municipal parks, university rotundas, and the like, for the Bicentenary. One of the more unusual cast especially for this occasion was commissioned by the American Freedom Train Foundation, with specifications that it be twice the dimension of the Liberty Bell itself. Along with hundreds of historic artifacts, it toured on the red, white, and blue Freedom Train, visiting eighty or so cities in forty-eight states, being viewed by more than 10,000,000 Americans. The bell was the work of the I. T. Verdin Company, through their partly owned foundry in Holland; according to company officials, it is to become a new national monument at the conclusion of its tour.

A single earlier installation made newspaper headlines in Los Angeles in 1967, when an insurance company purchased a full-scale replica to place in Liberty Park on Wilshire Boulevard. The bell journeyed to California on the *Queen Mary*'s final cruise from England. The Whitechapel Foundry that made it arranged to have it occupy a place of honor on the promenade deck during the entire voyage.

When the insurance company order was placed with Whitechapel officials, they supplied some comparative price statistics—always a newsworthy item. Officials stated that the original bell ordered by the Pennsylvania Assembly cost about $280, including shipment. The duplicate ordered in 1967 cost about $3,540, plus shipping charges. The increase of twelve times in a little more than two hundred years, the firm declared, was not too bad. Further statistics cited by the firm proved that the cost of metal had gone up twenty times, and that of manufacturing about eight times, in the last fifty years alone.

Possibly the most newsworthy among duplicates made of the Liberty Bell were those given each state, territory, and the District of Columbia at the close of the United States Savings Bond drive in 1950—fifty-three in all. These were designed by Professor Arthur L. Bigelow, bellmaster of Princeton University, and cast under his direction at Annecy, France. They are identical to the Liberty Bell in size, each meeting original specifications of "a cloth yard from lip to crown, and a full 12 feet around the circumference." One of the most gratifying aspects of the huge undertaking was the truly fine tonal quality achieved. Long painstaking research went into duplicating the metal content of the original to help achieve the desired timbre. Not to mar the results, the crack was merely painted on each duplicate. Even the most critical of bellmasters agreed that while listening to any one of these it was not difficult to imagine oneself hearing the long-silent Old Independence Bell.

Funds for this project were contributed by six copper companies, with other firms cooperating in various ways to make the huge patriotic drive a success. Savings Bond volunteers in each state made arrangements to parade that state's bell, with Ford Motor Company supplying red, white, and blue trucks, and the American Bridge Company providing the necessary hardware fixtures for mounting. At the conclusion of the bond drive, the United States Treasury, official owner of the bells, presented one to each state, allowing local officials to decide where it could best be permanently displayed. Almost all have been given places of honor—in a

Indiana's state replica of the Liberty Bell on parade during the Savings Bond Drive of 1950.

Front view of Puerto Rico's replica of the Liberty Bell, prominently shown in San Juan, the oldest city under the United States flag. *Estado Libre Asociado de Puerto Rico*

Side view showing the beautiful garden setting given Puerto Rico's bell at Muñoz River Park Museum. Traditionally, the islanders have always helped the United States fight its battles and are extremely proud citizens. *Estado Libre Asociado de Puerto Rico*

park, in or near the capitol, or at the entrance to some other prominent building. Virginia decided to house its replica at Thomas Jefferson's Monticello; North Carolina's is kept at the capitol; Puerto Rico's was given a handsome parklike setting.

Other Liberty Bells

From the beginning, the fortunes of the Liberty Bell have been closely entwined with those of Independence Hall. Also from the beginning—as few realize, even ardent students of American history—there has been another liberty bell associated with Independence Hall. Only chance prevented the second from becoming the nation's symbol of freedom, for it too was in place and ringing on July 8, 1776.

Today this second bell, a sister to the real one, rests in the Villanova University Museum, after a history almost as exciting as that of its more illustrious sister. But its biography did not come full circle until 1942, when the Reverend James Griffin, O.S.A., of Saint Nicholas Church, Jamaica, Long Island, returned to Villanova its "Old College Bell" as part of the celebration of that school's hundredth anniversary.

The whole story had its beginning back in the days when Isaac Norris and others pondered over what to do with their new Pennsylvania Province bell, now that it was cracked. Before Pass and Stow submitted plans to recast it, the Pennsylvania Assembly had grown impatient and ordered a second bell from England, identical to the one that was cracked. By the time the second order reached Philadelphia, the recast bell was already hanging in the steeple, so it was decided to keep both, attaching the second arrival to the Thomas Stretch clock already planned for the building.

Only this odd chain of events saved the present Liberty Bell from starting life

Villanova University's sister of the Liberty Bell. Folvey Memorial Library, Villanova University

in the colonies as a clock bell. Her sister bell bonged away the hours faithfully until about 1824, when a new clock was needed, with a larger bell. Eventually it was sold to Saint Augustine's, a Catholic church in Philadelphia toward whose building fund George Washington had contributed $50 in 1796. Here it remained until the "Know Nothing" riots of 1844, when it was badly damaged by fire as rioting mobs surged through the streets and burned the church.

The damaged bell was salvaged, to be later recast by Joseph Bernhard, who in the process made no attempt to reproduce the original inscription; instead, only the simple inscription CAST BY J. BERNHARD, PHILA. 1847, appears around the top of the barrel. The bell was then presented to Villanova College, where for the next fifty years it hung in a tree on campus to call students to classes. By 1917, its history forgotten, it passed to the Church of Saint Nicholas being built at Jamaica, Long Island. Then, shortly before World War II, historians of the Augustinian Fathers of Villanova traced the bell and brought it back in time to hang on the altar when Mass was celebrated for the college's hundredth anniversary.

In surveying a few liberty bells other than the most important one, mention should be made of the third clock bell installed in Independence Hall when renovations were undertaken for the 1876 Centennial Exposition. The largest bell ever to hang there—a 13,000-pounder—was designed as a copy of the real Liberty Bell. On one side, however, these words were added:

PRESENTED TO THE CITY OF PHILADELPHIA
JULY 4, 1876, FOR THE BELFRY OF
INDEPENDENCE HALL BY A CITIZEN

The citizen was a wealthy Philadelphian named Henry Seybert. He donated $1,800 for the cost of the bell and $20,000 for the giant striking clock. An ardent pacifist, Seybert instructed that the bell be cast from metal made up, in part, of melted-down cannon used by the opposing armies in the American Revolution, the War of 1812, the Civil War, and the Mexican War.

Of major historical interest and importance is the Little Liberty Bell of the Old Northwest Territory. In its recast form, it hangs now high in the belfry of the present imposing Old Cathedral of Saint Francis Xavier in Vincennes, Indiana. The original that proclaimed the birth of a new Vincennes, free forever of British domination, pealed its joyous announcement from a more modest steeple on a log chapel furnished only with crude split timber benches.

The bell, cast in Paris, reputedly from valuables contributed by several monarchs, arrived in the New World about 1742. For years it called the inhabitants of Vincennes to Mass; then came that memorable day in December, 1778, when it called them together for another purpose. Father Pierre Gibault, patriot priest and friend of Colonel George Rogers Clark, had already persuaded his parishioners to join the cause of the American Revolution; now he was about to administer to them the oath of allegiance to the new congress. Two months later, the bell would again peal triumphantly from its modest steeple while in front of the log chapel the Northwest Territory was formally surrendered to George Rogers Clark by the British Commander.

A parallel to the Vincennes story is found at Old Kaskaskia in the neighboring state of Illinois. There, just a few months earlier, on July 4, 1778, the so-called Lib-

Early view of Independence Hall (1778) showing one face of the first clock, to which the Liberty Bell's sister was attached.

Independence Hall (1779) after removal of its steeple. Liberty Bell is in tower. Its sister is seen on roof, at left of the tower.

The Little Liberty Bell of the Old Northwest Territory, recast, is housed high in the belfry of the present Old Cathedral of Saint Francis Xavier in Vincennes, Indiana. A replica of the original small log chapel the bell served stands alongside. *Old Cathedral Basilica*

Independence Hall today.

erty Bell of the West had pealed forth "loud and long." The occasion? A very, very special Fourth of July victory celebration. Colonel George Rogers Clark and his band of 150 wet, hungry, mosquito-plagued Kentucky Long Knives had just captured Fort Kaskaskia from the British, after one of the most improbable and important marches of the Revolutionary War, through mile after mile of flooded bogs and swamps. The colonel had been commissioned by Governor Patrick Henry of Virginia to conquer a series of British forts, thus claiming for the Commonwealth of Virginia land that today is the five states of Illinois, Indiana, Wisconsin, Michigan, and Ohio.

The bell that celebrated the liberation of so vast a territory experienced a career almost as dramatically varied as that of the bell in Philadelphia. It served under three flags; was washed away in the fierce floods of 1844, to be found again decades later only by sheer accident; has been eulogized in verse and song; and not too long ago was the center of a courtroom controversy.

This Liberty Bell of the West, donated to the Catholic church at Kaskaskia by King Louis XV of France, was cast at Rochelle in that country in 1741, by I. E. M. Norman. Two years of travel were required to bring the 650-pounder to Illinois. After reaching New Orleans, it was towed up the Mississippi River by bargemen walking along the bank, pulling guide ropes fastened to the raft. At Kaskaskia it was placed in a mission established by Father Marquette in 1675, where it made history as the first bell to be heard in the Upper Mississippi Valley. Poets were fond of sentimentalizing its effect on native settlers:

> Wrapped in wonder stood the red man
> As his ear caught up the sound,
> Rolling out to camp and wigwam
> From the Bell of 'Kaskia town.

Its mellow tones continued to please Illinois colonists until 1844, when one of the worst floods in history all but washed away the village. The bell was lost and not found until 1918, when workmen spied it still partly hidden in river silt but being gradually exposed by changing levels of the river.

Like its more famous relative in Philadelphia, the Liberty Bell of the West has not been used since it developed a crack. It is handsomely preserved and cared for by the state of Illinois, as the last remaining relic of the French frontier that once commanded an important spot in American history. The brick shrine housing it was built beside the Church of the Immaculate Conception in New Kaskaskia, which is actually an island formed when the rampaging river washed out the old mainland town and cut a new channel that resulted in the 14,000-acre island.

Its island location has created a problem or two for the bell. A legal dispute recently arose between Missouri and Illinois as to rightful ownership of such a valuable historic attraction. The court upheld Illinois's centuries-old claim. Because the island is not easily accessible to main-traveled roads, too few people are familiar with this significant symbol inherited from the country's struggle for independence. One side of the Old Kaskaskia bell is ornamented with the royal lilies of France in relief. The other bears a cross and pedestal, the top and the arms of the cross terminating in grouped fleur de lis. The beautifully executed French inscription has been variously translated; one version reads: "For the Church of Illinois by the gift of the King across the water."

The Liberty Bell of the West, a gift of Louis XV of France to the church of Kaskaskia in 1741. The State of Illinois now maintains a handsome chapellike shrine for the bell on the island of New Kaskaskia. *Illinois State Historical Library*

In contrast to Kaskaskia and Vincennes, Williamsburg has an eighteenth-century bell still in use today. It hangs in the steeple of Bruton Parish Church, where it is recognized as Virginia's "Liberty Bell" because it pealed when independence was declared, as well as on other momentous occasions. It was cast at London's Whitechapel Foundry in 1761 by Thomas Lester and Thomas Pack. An inscription reveals that it was the gift of James Tarpley of Bruton Parish, a prominent mercantiler whose store has been reconstructed at Colonial Williamsburg.

Evidently a purposeful future was forseen for the bell, as the first Vestry Book of the Reverend John C. McCabe notes:

> A new bell and a new steeple were to usher in a new order of things, and his Sacred Majesty George III was to be decidedly "rung out" of all authority, right, title, or interest in these Colonies; colonies destined in a very few years to bind themselves into a glorious league against oppression and tyranny, civil, military, or religious, and to endure, as we trust, as "THESE UNITED STATES," when kingcraft shall be remembered only among the stories of the past.

Its initial years in Williamsburg were indeed busy ones for the Bruton Parish bell. In 1775 it led the clamorous public rejoicing that met Peyton Randolph, president of the Continental Congress, on his return from Philadelphia. During the period that followed, until proclamation of peace with Great Britain in 1783, it was rung so loud, so long, and so often that the vestry was concerned. They feared it would crack from repeated blows of the clapper in the same place.

Fortunately their fears were not realized; the bell still survives to remind all who hear it of those cornerstones of freedom so firmly laid by Virginia's galaxy of patriots, among them George Washington, Thomas Jefferson, Patrick Henry, and George Mason. Though no longer rung so frequently, it summons parishioners and signals many special observances. It signaled, for example, the two-hundredth anniversary of that June 1, 1774, "Day of Fasting, Humiliation and Prayer" decreed by the Virginia Assembly in sympathy for the port of Boston, closed by the Crown as punishment for the Boston Tea Party. One year its solemn tones lent ceremony to an Armistice Day tour of Williamsburg by Her Majesty, Queen Elizabeth. In deference to American tradition, the Queen chose to kneel for her Armistice Day prayers in Bruton Parish Church. As she and her party knelt in the simple, straight pew of the nation's first President, Virginia's historic "Liberty Bell," high in the steeple overhead, tolled the seconds.

If the facts were known, it is fair to assume that a few other states and municipalities can also boast of bells that "rang in" American Independence in 1776, that, in one form or another, continue to voice the cause of freedom today. Though not as emblematic as the Liberty Bell, they nevertheless summoned indignant citizens to protest the same British edicts that riled the Quaker City during Revolutionary times. Later they ushered in the same spirited victories over British rule that prompted Philadelphia to celebrate.

In the 1940s the dominie of the Holland Society of New York put together the story of a heretofore unheralded Dutch bell in the city's Saint Nicholas Collegiate Church, a veritable Methuselah with a history reaching back to days before the Republic was founded. *The New York Times* was quick to pick up the story, announcing to the city in bold headlines:

NEW YORK HAS A LIBERTY BELL
ST. NICHOLAS COLLEGIATE CHURCH TOWER HOUSES
TOCSIN OF EVENTS IN 1731

The venerable old tocsin is marked AMSTERDAM, HOLLAND, 1731, where it was made by De Gravoe and N. Muller on order several years earlier from Colonel Abraham De Peyster. Before his death, he had instructed that it be hung in the new church at the corner of Nassau and Liberty streets "a legacy to the Low Dutch Church of New York," according to a translation of the last line in its Dutch inscription.

Early in the Revolutionary War, when the British converted the church into a riding school for their dragoons by removing pulpit, pews, and gallery, permission was obtained from Lord Howe to take down the bell. It was carted to Carlisle, Pennsylvania, remaining there until after New York was evacuated, the church restored. One Dutch Reformed Church historian has listed some of the occasions on which this bronze beauty was first rung. Among the earliest were 1739, during services of gratitude at the first major victory for freedom of the colonial press, brought about by Peter Zenger, a member of the congregation; 1756, to mark the disaster of Abercrombie at Ticonderoga; 1764, when patriots gathered for their first open discussion of taxation without representation; and 1775, for the good news of Ethan Allen's capture of Fort Ticonderoga.

In The First Baptist Church in America, Providence, Rhode Island, once hung a very special bell dedicated to freedom, but one not destined to survive in its original state. Three times cracked while ringing, and three times recast, it no longer resembles the original, which had a quaint inscription definitely marking it as a symbol of Roger Williams's principles, laid down earlier for his colony—civil and religious freedom for all men "of distressed conscience."

FOR FREEDOM OF CONSCIENCE THE TOWN WAS FIRST PLANTED.
PERSUASION, NOT FORCE, WAS USED BY THE PEOPLE:
THIS CHURCH IS THE ELDEST, AND HAS NOT RECANTED,
ENJOYING AND GRANTING BELL, TEMPLE AND STEEPLE.

That last line needs clarifying now, two hundred years later. It refers to the fact that in England no nonconformist religious body could call its house of worship a church or temple; nor could it use either bell or steeple. In the colonies there was freedom to use all three, as the original bell declared.

The recast successor to that symbolic tocsin is prosaically inscribed with the founding date for the church (1639) and the name of Roger Williams, "its first pastor, and the first asserter of liberty of conscience." Though it is not the original bell, the steeple housing it is the very one looked upon by colonists of the Revolution. Completed in 1775, the structure is one of the nation's most notable colonial landmarks. Historically, it has a long record—the first church of any denomination in Rhode Island and the first Baptist church in America. Architecturally, its graceful lines, with an especially fine steeple, evoke admiration and surprise—surprise that on the eve of the American Revolution, so to speak, such a deliberate copy of a famous London steeple would be raised in Rhode Island. It is a copy of designs used for Saint Martin-in-the-Fields. The three successive bells that have served The First Baptist Church in America have always remained safely housed in the 185-foot steeple, but with three narrow escapes: in 1815, when it "wavered and bent to the beast, but fell not"; in 1938, when Providence withstood a particularly severe hurricane; and in 1944, when it withstood another.

North Carolinians look to a liberty bell of a different sort, one that merited its cognomen after a single vigorous performance in the year 1771. It is a large brazen-tongued handbell six inches in diameter, used by the American Regulators, who had no drums to call their forces together to fight Royal Governor Tryon's troops at the Battle of Alamance. The original handle was burned; the present one is of walnut from a tree on the battleground. The bell has done quite a bit of traveling, for it was shown in 1880 at the dedication of the monument at the battlefield, at the

In its present form The First Baptist Church in America, and the first church of any denomination in Rhode Island, dates to 1775. It is an unsurpassed example of colonial architecture; its 185-foot steeple once housed a bell inscribed to the "liberty of conscience" Roger Williams preached about. *Photograph by Norman S. Watson; The First Baptist Church in America*

Tennessee Centennial, and at the Jamestown Exposition. Now it rests in a place of honor at the Museum of Cultural Resources in Raleigh.

Texas is not so fortunate as still to possess its original state liberty bell—of a size and type similar to North Carolina's—but a duplicate of the same age has been fittingly inscribed:

REPRODUCTION OF THE TEXAS LIBERTY BELL
AT OLD WASHINGTON-ON-THE-BRAZOS
MARCH 2, 1836

It was on March 1, 1836, that delegates assembled at Old Washington-on-the-Brazos to prepare the Declaration of Independence of Texas from Mexican rule. According to tradition, two daughters of a local hotel owner rang the hotel dinner bell upon a prearranged signal from a delegate, to announce the completed document. On seeing the girls parading up and down the long upper gallery of the hotel, sounding their bell, people rushed to the convention hall for a rousing celebration. Years later, a long search for that bell failed to locate it. Fortunately, however, a granddaughter of the hotel owner remembered the original, and one day when she came upon what she termed a perfect duplicate, she had it inscribed. Years later it was used to help celebrate the one-hundredth anniversary of Texas independence.

In Lexington, Massachusetts, the birthplace of American liberty, there was once another bell made famous by a single all-important occasion, on April 19, 1775. That morning it warned of the approach of the British, as it summoned the Minutemen to Lexington Common. The bell has long since passed into oblivion, the only vestigial evidence that it once existed being its tongue, preserved in Lexington.

Records reveal that the bell had been a gift to the town from Mr. Isaac Stone. The grateful townsfolk constructed a "Bell free," from which their gift could call worshipers and sound the curfew. During the Revolution the belfry stood on the Common, at a spot now marked by a bronze tablet on a boulder. In 1797 it was purchased by a son of Captain Parker and removed to his home, where he used it for a wheelwright's shop. In 1891 the whole structure was again moved, this time to Belfry Hill, where it remained until destroyed by a great gale in 1909. At a later date the Lexington Historical Society erected an exact replica on Belfry Hill, the one visitors see today.

In a little limited-edition Victorian booklet titled *Liberty Hall and Its Historic Bell*, the singular tale of another long-forgotten bell comes to life. This once famous tocsin was another of those purchased from a Nantucket sea captain (in 1796, for the town's new Congregational Church). Reportedly New Bedfordites were an impatient lot, eager not only to own a bell but also to occupy their rightful place in the partly finished church—some say to observe and hear their bell in action. One pew holder was so anxious to occupy his place that he bribed the carpenter with a quart of brandy to saw open his pew door, as yet not hinged.

Money for the bell—it cost $255—came in briskly from subscriptions, the second largest amount coming from a black citizen named Aaron Childs. In retrospect, this contribution seems almost prophetic of the special role the bell was destined to play in the cause of freedom, before its untimely end in the big New Bedford fire of

A replica of the old belfry near the Battle Green, Lexington, Massachusetts; the bell it housed summoned the Minutemen to action. *Carey Memorial Library*

Quaint cover of a Victorian booklet relating a singular tale of the liberty bell belonging to New Bedford, Massachusetts, published by New Bedford Fireman's Mutual Aid Society. Undated.

1854. During the excitement following the passage of the fugitive slave law in 1851 came a rumor that United States marshalls were coming to New Bedford, accompanied by United States Marines, to recover certain fugitive slaves hiding there, awaiting transit to Canada by the "underground railway." This ominous news was brought by New Bedford's express rider after an all-night gallop from Boston. Only moments after his arrival a strange vessel was sighted in the bay. No time was lost in sounding the alarm on the historic bell. It had a voice of thunderous timbre, and to the slaves its message was unmistakable: their enemy was near. That time, fortunately, the rumors were unfounded and no confrontation developed. There were to be other equally frightening occasions, though, when this same tocsin warned of impending danger to the slaves.

The bell was supporting the abolitionist cause from its original location, no longer a church, however, but a public building known as Liberty Hall. The name had been chosen to commemorate the many lyceum lectures being given there by advocates of freedom. The bell's mighty tones heralded such orators as William Lloyd Garrison, Frederick Douglas, Henry Ward Beecher, Wendell Phillips, and Stephen Foster. Then, on November 9, 1854, disaster struck and Liberty Hall crumbled in flames, melting the old bell beyond recognition, its "notes of warning to the poor, trembling fugitive" to be heard no more. The melted mass of metal was gathered from the ruins and several townsmen had tea bells or other objects made from it. Where these still exist, they are cherished last relics of New Bedford's liberty bell.

The widespread ringing of bells during the turbulent days of the American Revolution quieted to a degree at the end of the war; but once each year the young republic echoed with explosive sounds reminiscent of those heard when the British surrendered at Yorktown. Undeniably the Fourth of July was a time for celebration, with cannon and bells affording the best expression of liberty-loving emotions. In fact, that date on the calendar was sometimes nicknamed "bell day" because bells rang at any hour or even all day. In 1790 New York City appropriated $35 to keep theirs sounding all day. On the very first July Fourth, all bells in the churches of Marblehead, Massachusetts, were rung for an entire week. Nor were these isolated cases.

There was only one unfortunate fallout to such jollifications: too many good colonial bells were cracked irreparably in the name of patriotism. Much of the prolonged ringing was done in relays of two men each. It is understandable that some would be inept, far from expert at their task. Then there were always those impetuous souls who desired more volume from each bell. Out came the clapper and in went a larger one, with calamitous results. Given an outsize clapper, no bell has been known to endure hard, relentless ringing very long.

The popularity of bells for patriotic jollifications ebbed slowly until the days of the Civil War, when the sound of guns and firecrackers became the order of the day. Independence Day bells more or less disappeared from the American scene. Then, a little more than a century later, something remarkable happened. In 1963 Congress passed a resolution that proclaimed bells a part of Independence Day again. An early American custom was to be revived, thanks to congressmen who listened well; thanks to Eric Sloane, an expert on Americana, and his neighbor-writer Eric Hatch, who shared Sloane's strong feelings about America's heritage of this traditional way of celebrating freedom; thanks also to any number of individuals who had been agitating for this very thing and had personally been perpetuating the old Independence Day custom by ringing bells in their own community, sometimes right in their own backyards.

A brief digression to pinpoint just one instance of a long, uninterrupted observance of this custom: A magnificent Clinton Meneely bell weighing 3,000 pounds has been ringing each July Fourth since 1894 in Sherman, Texas. It was a gift from a winter resident of Sherman, Zenas E. Ranney, presented to Old School Presbyterian Church with the stipulation that it always be rung on July Fourth. On one side, the bell is symbolically embellished with a five-point star having large thick

Independence Day ringing is a tradition at the home of Oliver Elliott. Shown with him is his daughter, Mrs. Harry Long, ringing a few large ones from the Elliott grove of bells. *Front left, top:* 1886 McShane church Bell; Baltimore and Lake Erie Railroad bell; fire engine tocsin with two tolling devices; ship bell cast by Regester and Webb, Baltimore; 1838 engine bell from old Buckeye Foundry in Cincinnati. *Mrs. Harry Long* and *The News and Dispatch*

letters arranged between the points to spell T-E-X-A-S. Around the rim are forty-four stars representing the number of states in the Union at that time. In 1893 this bronze beauty was on exhibit at the Chicago World's Fair as an outstanding example of bell casting. Until an electric ringer was installed in 1970, sextons had to clamber up into the lower bell chamber to manipulate the bell rope, fastened to an ironbound wheel almost seven feet in diameter. It was an especially welcome climb, however, at least on July Fourth—according to one sexton—for the bell's throaty tones can be heard for miles, and never more joyously than when voicing the call of freedom.

Under his long-range plans to revive July Fourth ringing on a national scale, Eric Sloane found the time right in 1962 for broadcasting his idea on radio. Americans were in need of some unifying, patriotic force, and the idea of having bells chorusing across the land appealed to them. The response to Sloans's radio program was overwhelming, as were the questions it prompted. People were eager to know immediately when, where, and how to initiate such a program. Today community patterns for the observance, always at two o'clock in the afternoon, E.D.T., are fairly well established. Countless organizations helped; state legislatures and nearly all state governors added their official support. Bells that had not seen action for generations have been polished to sound again. Others about to be sold for scrap have been salvaged, especially for the annual "Let Freedom Ring" celebration.

This is a celebration that unites Americans of all colors and creeds in commemorating their nation's independence, without either words or bias, and in a manner that would delight our founding fathers. It was John Adams who remarked, at the adoption of the Declaration of Independence, "I am apt to believe that it will be celebrated by succeeding generations as the great anniversary festival. It ought to be solemnized with pomp and parades, with shows, games, sports . . . bells . . . from one end of the continent to the other from this time forward and evermore."

5

BELLS ON THE MOVE

At a signal from the dimly lighted, nearly empty station, the Wabash "Cannon Ball" pulled out of Detroit on its last trip. The engineer—forty-odd years on the run—sounded his bell, eased his throttle. Then on toward Saint Louis rolled the "Cannon Ball," last of the trains carrying that historic name. It was being eliminated at the end of this run.

The sound of its bell had become almost legendary to generations, as successive trains of the same name roared westward across Indiana year after year. Today as the train moved along, an Amish farmer heard its bell at a nearby stop and brought his team of six brown plow horses to a halt to listen. As the engine drew alongside his plow, he dipped his broad-brimmed hat in a farewell salute. At Danville, Illinois, the conductor coming aboard—forty-eight years with the railroad—reported that some old folks were weeping because they could no longer mark the passing of each day by the engine bell's familiar dong-dong as the "Cannon Ball" ground to its daily stop. Regardless, the train sped across the Mississippi River, under the big archway, into Saint Louis. There the engineer sounded his bell for the last time.

Scenes like this were occurring all too often along America's rails during the mid-twentieth century. The discontinuance of many big-name trains accounted for the retirement of uncounted locomotive bells. Of course, the rapid dieselization of coal-burning locomotives throughout the '40s accounted for the piling up of even more bells on each railroad's scrap heap.

By and large, in retirement these have fared better than some types of discarded bells. They have suffered fewer vicissitudes because rail executives were quick to recognize in them a remarkable means of gilding the railroad's public image. By donating their discarded bells to churches, schools, and other nonprofit organizations, preferably in the area served by their trains, they reaped more goodwill than even the cleverest advertising could generate.

The idea of giving away an occasional locomotive bell was not wholly new, for the Pennsylvania Railroad gave away its first, to a museum, as early as 1872. However, as a result of two happenings in 1946, Southern Railway takes credit for initiating the idea behind large-scale donations. About that time, Southern's president was freshly impressed with John Hersey's prize-winning novel *A Bell for Adano*, the story of a ship's bell presented to a war-ravaged church in Italy. At the same time, a little Moravian congregation in Bethania, North Carolina, sent out a plea for a bell to replace theirs, lost when fire swept their church. Touched by the plea and sensing the goodwill inherent in such a gesture, Southern's president ordered a fine specimen removed from the road's scrap heap and presented to the Moravians. Soon afterward, the story of "A Bell for Bethania" appeared in one of Southern's regular advertisements. A deluge of requests for similar donations kept the railway busy salvaging, polishing, engraving, and shipping their retired bells to deserving groups. Within five years all of three hundred had been given away, leaving an equal number of unfilled requests.

Though some railroads were chary of giving away their discarded bells, preferring to sell them for scrap, others were eager for a share of the goodwill Southern Railway was reaping. As a result, the distinctive sound formerly associated with locomotive bells is heard from unexpected quarters around the country. A Texas and Pacific bell sounds from a church in Midland, Texas; one from the Atlantic Coast Line, in Bellwood, Georgia; and when those two Indiana colleges, Wabash and De Pauw, clash in their annual gridiron classic, a Monon bell is rung by the victors. Up in the rural Jug Hill section of Maine, visitors are surprised to hear a farm bell that sounds like an old steam locomotive bell—which it is, from the Maine Central Railroad. It was made available as a prize on a television program in 1958, and 10,000 people competed for it!

A fair number of old locomotive bells have been put to new use in remote mission stations. Typical are Lackawanna's gift to a post in the African jungles near Tanganyika, or Norfolk and Western's sounding over a West Indies mission. Among the interesting tales that could be told by train tocsins traveling to serve in distant lands is the story of the beauty that once graced the locomotive pulling Missouri Pacific's "Sunshine Special" from Saint Louis to Mexico City. How many who knew its mellow tones ever imagined it would be called out of retirement to ring over a lonely Eskimo mission two hundred icy miles above the Arctic Circle! In 1953, when Pelly Bay Mission needed a bell, a Saint Louis family made it their personal search to locate one. The Missouri Pacific responded to the need. En route to the Arctic, the "Sunshine Special" bell traveled by rail, plane, and finally by dogsled, well photographed by the press on each lap of its journey.

An educated estimate puts the number of locomotive bells cast in this country at something under 150,000, produced by at least 120 companies. In the Altoona, Pennsylvania, yards alone 30,000 were cast. A considerable uncertainty surrounds the exact date the first locomotive bell was cast either in America or elsewhere. One is shown in almost all drawings of the "Royal George," built in 1827 for the Stockton and Darlington, pioneer English railway. But, as pointed out by a former director of the French National Museum of Transport, no other English or European engine for many years afterward had a bell. The first one in America was ap-

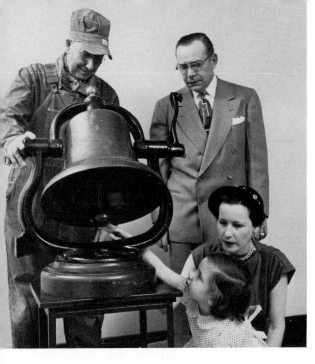

Engineer who formerly rang the Sunshine Special's bell sounds it one last time before it leaves for Pelly Bay Mission above the Arctic Circle. Listening at right is the Saint Louis family instrumental in securing the bell. *Missouri Pacific Lines*

parently placed on the famous "John Bull," imported in 1831 and rebuilt on this side of the Atlantic two years later, when certain features were added—notably a cowcatcher and the bell.

Another claimant for the honor of being the first belled locomotive was the "E. H. Miller," built in 1834 by Baldwin Locomotive Works, Philadelphia, for the South Carolina Canal and Railroad Company, then the longest rail line anywhere on the globe. Nevertheless, though the "E. H. Miller" is pictured with a bell, it is anyone's guess whether it was part of the original equipment. In any event, the next engines built by Baldwin, in 1835, had no bell. Garrett and Eastwick of Philadelphia are known to have built an engine with a bell in 1836, for a Massachusetts railroad; the "Lafayette" of 1837, a Norris-built engine for the Baltimore and Ohio, also had one. A few more years would pass, however, before such items were standard equipment. Thus, give or take a few years, the sound of locomotive bells was heard over the American countryside for only a century before vanishing.

Most engine builders, like the Baldwin Locomotive Works, cast all their own parts, including bells, and railroaders agreed that each builder's had a special tone. There was, in fact, considerable competition to see which could produce the most pleasingly resonant sound. Claimed one old-timer, "The prettiest toned bells of all came from the New York Locomotive Works, while the homeliest were Dickson's." A California gentleman insisted that Cooke's (Danforth, Cooke and Company, Paterson, New Jersey) had the nicest tone, and he applied to the Southern Pacific for one of their Cooke bells. This of course was in the days when a persuasive individual could occasionally induce a railroad to sell a discarded bell. The Southern Pacific obligingly worked over its scrap heap, tapping the forty or fifty on hand until a Cooke casting was found. The bell whose sound was dear to Death Valley Scotty had rung on the first railroad to steam into Colorado. He acquired it to place atop one of his buildings, where he used it to summon his horse and his forty-year-old mule.

There seems to be some disagreement as to whether locomotive bells were actually tuned. Many authorities generalize that they were not. *Railroad Magazine,*

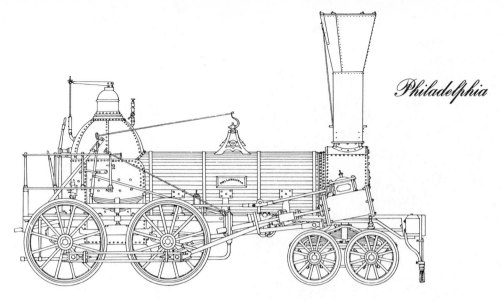

Philadelphia

Drawing of a Norris-built engine of 1843, showing bell in a graceful cradle on top, in the center. *Yung-Meyer Collection of Railroadiana*

however, states that in many cases the bells were expertly tuned by a musician with a tuning fork, and points out further that the Norfolk and Western, as well as some other big roads, arranged to have all its steam-engine bells sound to the same pitch. This naturally necessitated that each bell be machined and checked repeatedly with a tuning fork.

After 1890 a certain standardization crept into these bells, in both tone and design, as more and more railroads began buying bells from commercial suppliers. Some had been doing this all along. The James Nuttall Foundry of New Orleans had been advertising "Engineers' Signal Bells Made to Order" since 1858. Henry N. Hooper of Boston also advertised them prior to the Civil War. The Buckeye Bell Foundry in Cincinnati did not receive its first order for locomotive bells until 1873, but thereafter cast them on a regular basis.

The locomotive bell had usually been mounted toward the rear of the engine near the cab, convenient for the engineer to tug on its rope, which passed into his cab. While the rope method remained in vogue, the bell could be swung in a full arc and, if desired, held in one position long enough to vary the rhythm of its voice,

The *Betsey Baker*, Cascades, C. R. #1251, photographed in 1867. *C. E. Watkins Photo; Oregon Historical Society*

thus permitting each engineer to develop his own style of ringing. By 1899, however, steam and air bell ringers were coming into general use. In a volume published that year, *The Locomotive up to Date*, author Charles McShane stated that at first these new devices were used only on yard engines but were gradually to be applied to all steam engines, obviating any need for a bell rope. Of the 100 patented ringers already on the market, McShane described only two: The Breitenstein model, adopted by the Union Pacific, employed a piston to give a forceful, positive tone; the Gollmar type, adopted by several leading roads, gave a less forceful note but a note designed to be heard only when the whistle blew!

On the positive side, these new devices allowed more flexibility in positioning the bell on the engine. On the negative, they foreshadowed the end of any tonal appeal in locomotive bells. The 1940s saw still another forbidding change, the introduction of an automatic device to swing the clappper against an immovable bell. This innovation removed the last shred of whatever romance and music were left to locomotive bells. If in general the public missed the more rhythmical music, feelings among the trainmen themselves were mixed. Some were intrigued with automation. A young engine watchman at the Gunnison, Colorado, roundhouse was so intrigued he could not resist hoaxing his superstitious night partner. He put the poor fellow in a properly jittery mood by concocting a spook story about a headless machinist who sometimes returned about this time of year, "ringing a bell," he insisted. Then one murky, dark night he somehow set an engine bell to ringing while he kept himself out of sight—scaring the wits out of his partner.

Definite rules evolved for the engineer's use of his bell, as opposed to his steam whistle. The whistle was intended as a warning at distant crossings, the bell as an operating signal when coming into or leaving a station, or approaching a grade crossing within city limits. Individual states enacted their own laws from time to time. Typical is the one passed by the California legislature in 1949, requiring locomotives to sound bell or whistle at least eighty rods in advance of a crossing. Old right-of-way signs with the letter *R* were used along some routes, indicating to the engine crew when to ring their bell. A few of these can still be seen along the old Delaware, Lackawanna and Western right-of-way, according to Frank Reilly, writing for the National Railway Historical Society.

There were also rules, both written and unwritten, governing the use of station bells to assist trains in signaling their arrival and departure. In an old stationmaster's guide dated 1853, one rule states: "A bell will be rung five minutes before a train is to start, or at a roadside station as soon as the train is in sight. The station master shall intimate to the conductor when a train is ready to start, by ringing a bell. . . ."

One of the last remaining examples of early station bells hangs at the freight depot in the coastal city of Wilmington, North Carolina. Purchased by the old Wilmington and Weldon Railroad in 1856 at a cost of $286, it was made by J. Bernhard and Company of Philadelphia, "makers of fine castings." Perched atop the station shed, it gave warning five minutes before and again at the time of train departure. Grownups and children alike, so the story goes, enjoyed strolling along the cobblestone streets to gather at the station whenever a passenger train arrived. Life was leisurely in this southern city, and prolonged adieus to friends who were boarding the train often delayed its departure. Thus management's decision on a bell to announce the time in no uncertain terms. Sixty years ago when the station was remodeled, railroad officials considered scrapping the bell. Sentiment was against it, so it remains even though passenger service does not.

Station bells are known to have antedated locomotive bells by several years. One of the earliest, now in the Baltimore and Ohio historical collection, hung at the Endicott Mills, Maryland, depot about 1830. Reference to another early one appears in the 1836 annual report made by the first president of the Winchester and Potomac (later the Baltimore and Ohio). He wrote: "No disappointment has occurred in the regularity of our transportation. . . . The depot bell has failed on but one or two occasions. . . ."

Throughout New England almost every station had such a "timepiece" anchored atop its roof. After all, not everyone in those early days had a watch, but the station usually had a bell, and travelers depended on it to notify them of train time. Stationmasters continued to accommodate travelers in this way throughout the 1880s and beyond, in all parts of the country, wherever trains were operating. The Central Pacific station at Sacramento, California, was just opening in 1879; the stop was served by a musically toned bell cast that same year by Central Pacific.

For nearly a hundred years there was a big bell atop the Osyka, Mississippi, station, Illinois Central Railroad's first stop out of New Orleans. For a time it was also used by the fire department and by the local butcher to notify townsfolk when fresh meat arrived. In later years it served as a community time signal, ringing regularly at eleven o'clock each morning. When it was decided to demolish the obsolete Osyka station, the railroad gave this antique bronze fixture to the town, and it was removed to the McComb shops for cleaning, polishing, and restoration. The iron hanger and swivel were so pitted with rust they had to be sandblasted. The bell was not new when the railroad originally received it from a Pike County, Mississippi, settler who had been using it to call field hands. Finally, on April 17, 1970, local celebrities, railroad officials, and townspeople (many of them descendants of the original owner) gathered for the presentation. "We had a big ceremony in the public schools," recalls Illinois Central's manager of public relations. It seemed fitting to everyone involved that in its new role the bell's first notes should announce good news—the safe landing of Apollo 13 astronauts.

Typical of the smiles seen in Osyka, Mississippi, upon the Illinois Central's presentation of its station bell (April 1970) was that of the great-great-grandson of the bell's first owner. *Illinois Central Gulf Railroad*

Some larger and more pretentious depots added the sound of yet another bell, a clock bell to strike every hour and half hour, the better to keep travelers time-conscious. When it was erected in 1886, the Union Depot at Milwaukee, Wisconsin, was heralded as one of the finest in the country, from both an architectural and a practical standpoint. Its huge brazen-voiced clock bell was cast and installed that same year, the product of Meneely and Company of West Troy, New York. It weighed nearly 3,000 pounds and stood almost four feet high. Its sonorous voice remained a familiar one to thousands of downtown Milwaukeeans until the year 1912, when it was suddenly silenced.

There are conflicting accounts as to why its ringing was stopped. One relates that those mighty bongs interfered with the sleep of guests in downtown hotels. Whatever the reason, from 1912 until it was scrapped in 1942, Milwaukee's depot bell was heard only once, and then not officially. On Armistice Day, November 11, 1918, a hysterical railroader, intent on celebrating victory, climbed into the tower and whanged the bell "not wisely but too well." The hammer broke under the incessant whanging. Came World War II, Chicago, Milwaukee, Saint Paul & Pacific rail officials decided their mute bell should again serve some useful purpose. Slowly, impressively, it was lowered from its lonely tower and trucked to the road's shops for analysis before being donated to the government scrap drive. An assay indicated that all that sound had come from a combination of 2,271 pounds of copper, 659 pounds of tin, 14 pounds of lead, and 9 pounds of zinc.

There was a certain ritual attending the arrival and departure of trains in nineteenth-century America, and a few other types of bells played a part alongside those that signaled from engines and depots. For example, at urban street crossings, in the days before red flasher lights, there were bells to be rung by the crossing guards as they lowered the gates. In sections of the Midwest, where both the Chicago and Northwestern and the Chicago, Milwaukee, Saint Paul & Pacific tracks ran across the same town, manually operated crossing bells were in evidence through the 1930s. Residents in one Illinois community can recall how, whenever a Milwaukee train approached along the river, a guard at the main street crossing emerged from his shanty and with one hand tugged the iron bell atop a post outside while he lowered the gates with the other. Several blocks away, on the other

An issue of the railroad's official publication carried the story of the decision to remove the road's long-silent station bell from Milwaukee Union Depot, Milwaukee, Wisconsin. *Chicago, Milwaukee, St. Paul and Pacific Railroad*

side of the river, were the Northwestern tracks, also crossing the main street, on a rather steep hill. Here a woman guarded the crossing, using a brass handbell to warn vehicles and pedestrians. She would lower the gates first, then pace between them, across the street and back, constantly wielding her handbell.

In Victorian days, before the blare of loudspeakers filled every depot, it was standard practice to announce the opening of the dining room by sounding a musical brass gong. This inviting and gracious custom persisted the longest at the Fred Harvey restaurants on the Santa Fe line.

Some of these aspects of railroading take on reality with a visit to a collection of locomotive bells or to one of the many historic railroad exhibits, complete with engines and all manner of railroadiana. Locomotive bells from forty or more American and Canadian railroads are on display in the Schilling collection of Northfield, Minnesota, making it one of the largest collections of its kind. A large bronze Statue of Liberty centers the display, with most of the bells arranged below it on a star-shaped base.

The Morris County Central Railroad headquartered on Green Pond Road in Newfoundland, New Jersey, affords a scenic setting for actually riding behind one of the old steam engines and listening to its bell. There are several different locomotives, the oldest being #385, built in 1907 for Southern Railway. This North Jersey steam operation is the undertaking of hobbyists, including retired rail employees, who have restored old engines and refurbished old coaches so that they can carry riders on weekend excursions—riders who come with tape recorders to catch the sounds of bell ringing and whistle blowing; luckily, rural surroundings permit plenty of both. The normal run is a five-mile-and-return trip along the banks of the Pequannock River, where the New York, Susquehanna, and Western Railroad pioneered the first train service west of Newfoundland in 1873.

As opposite as they could possibly be to the polished beauties that echoed from American locomotives were the dark and toneless little horsecar clunkets that went *dang, dang* with every step of the horses that pulled the cars. Despite their unassuming appearance, these clunkets represent a type of transportation with a most honorable lineage. The very first American horsecars began operating in New York City in the 1820s. They were fancily contrived omnibuses that concentrated more on extravagant scrollwork than comfortable seating. None of the New York City horsecars ran on rails until 1832, when the city's first street-railway line was

The Schilling collection of locomotive bells, Northfield, Minnesota. *Schilling Hobby House*

Left

On an old locomotive bell atop Mount Roubidoux, California, Ike Logan sounded the hour of seven each morning for over thirty years. His first bell, cast in Manchester, England, had been used on a Southern Pacific engine. After vandals stole that one, the Santa Fe contributed one of theirs, only to have vandals steal its clapper. Thus, Ike carried a hammer with him on his 900-foot climb each day.

Right

Engineer Frank Larkin polishes the bell on old #385 built in 1907. The bell rings by air pressure, permitting its forward position well removed from engineer's cab. Train is one of several restored to take visitors on short excursions through the New Jersey countryside. *Morris County Central Railroad, Newfoundland, New Jersey.*

opened as a Manhattan extension of the New York-Harlem Railway. On rails, they were able to creak along at the unheard-of speed of four miles per hour.

These cars, from the 1830s well past the middle of the century, pushed their way into metropolitan life and gradually evolved into something resembling a trolley, although there were many variations. The small bells worn by the horses varied only in their inscriptions naming the particular city and railway being served. In thick letters encircling the lip, the inscription on a typical one reads: "Louisville, Kentucky, Central Passenger R. R. Company."

At the height of the horsecar business in the United States, over 100,000 horses

Horse-drawn streetcar, Somerville, Massachusetts, 1884. Typical horsecar bell dangles from collar of horse at far right. *Bradley H. Clarke*

and mules were required to pull the 18,000 cars then operating. Even if bells were used on only a fraction of the creatures, what an endless *dang, dang, dang* must have resulted. In some communities the cars remained in service almost to the end of the century. Apparently, later models replaced their horse bells with rope-operated types fixed to the car itself. Marian Lawrence Peabody, in writing of her girlhood in Boston during the winter of 1891, relates:

> Julie and I had been put in different schools. Julie walked to Miss Winsor's but I boarded the little horsecar that ran from Hereford Street down Marlborough, around Arlington to Beacon and then to Charles, where I got off and walked up Chestnut Street to Miss Folsom's School. . . . At one I went home again in the same car. It had straw on the floor to keep your feet warm and a little old driver and an old conductor, both bearded, who took the fares and pulled the bell rope to "stop" and "go." It looked like the Toonerville Trolley.

Eventually all horsecars were outmoded by electric trolleys, with their flat clangorous gongs. A trolley gong was a trolley gong, or so it would seem. To inventors, however, there must always have been room for modification and improvement, for there were gongs made to a great many different specifications, judging by old illustrated supply catalogs. The *Electric Railway Dictionary* of 1911 illustrates platform gongs, roof gongs, foot gongs, multiple-stroke gongs, single-stroke gongs, seamless gongs, and so on. Different tonal effects would result from each, of course. Among the more musical and memorable in this category are those still to be heard on San Francisco cable cars. Their clear, resonant notes, which have been floating over the hills of the city since 1873, are, as someone has remarked, like San Francisco itself, "sharp but not strident, insistent but not overbearing, enthusiastic but not compulsive, diverse but not chaotic." Each motorman, like the locomotive engineer of yesterday, works out his own distinctive rhythm as he jigs the bell cord. San Franciscans sensitive to the gong of the cable car can distinguish each motorman's tattoo as he plies up Powell Street and California Street, past exclusive Nob Hill, then downhill to Ghirardelli Square and Fisherman's Wharf.

If the call of the cable car gongs is not compulsive, the call of every fire bell is —or was—even though the term *fire bell* denoted different things to different people. To firemen catching forty winks in the upper dormitory of the station house, it was a signal on the wall ringing wildly to hurry them down the jiffy pole, onto the truck. To those living within earshot of the station house, the term meant a large rooftop tocsin used as an alarm signal. To every oldster who recalls seeing an early fire truck speeding to a blaze, the clanging bell that rode right along to that blaze was most memorable. Its demanding, even frightening, tones had an urgency today's sirens lack, effective as these may be in clearing streets of traffic.

The wall-mounted alarms were, to a degree, expendable; few seen anymore even in collections of firematics. Tower-type tocsins, like those on the wagons or trucks, were more likely to be salvaged. The 1950s were an especially vulnerable decade for old fire bells—even a city steeped in tradition like Charleston, South Carolina, ordered sirens to replace its two historic alarm bells that had signaled fires and hurricanes for as long as anyone could recall. Of those that have been salvaged here and there, some have merely been converted to a rather ignoble use as flower planters at the local station house. Others have been better honored in one

Scene photographed from an aquatint dated 1886, titled "The Municipal Fire-Alarm Telegraph Room, Boston." According to the only information available, the bells in the telegraph
room rang their alarm from high under the dome on City Hall. A floor plan of the building
in 1866 showed the fire-alarm room in the attic.

way or another, some incorporated into permanent memorials to fire fighters who
gave their lives in the line of duty.

Bonham, South Carolina, is typical of communities that feel a certain civic
pride in an old tocsin whose no-nonsense voice faithfully alerted the town to
danger. After seventy-two years of service, Bonham's bell was removed from the
roof of the old station house, cleaned, polished, and placed on a pedestal in a place
of honor near the town's new fire hall. "It was felt the bell was too much a part of
Bonham history to be sold for junk or lost," the city manager commented. "We
feel it will be a suitable memorial for the men who have fought our fires throughout the years."

An Atlanta mayor is credited with saving that city's now century-old fire alarm
from the scrap heap, according to Mrs. George Mayer, writing in an issue of *Georgia Magazine*. The origin of the bell itself is tinged with romance, for it had its
beginning during a dark period in Atlanta history, while the city was painfully
recovering from almost total destruction by the fires set by General Sherman's
army. New fires continued to break out despite the purchase of a hand pumper to
replace the Volunteer Bucket Brigade. It was a slow business notifying and organizing Atlanta's thirty volunteer firemen, and by the time the new vehicle was on its
way, fifteen working each side, the blaze was usually out of control.

The city council decided to place an alarm bell in a specially constructed
belfry on high ground, with a watchman in attendance. The cost of the bell,
though, was beyond their means, until a group of civic-minded ladies decided to
raise the money by giving "A Grande Ladies Fair." To stimulate attendance, they
announced the choosing of Atlanta's first beauty queen at the fair, her name to be
carved on the new bell. It was a brilliant affair, with throngs crowding the hall by
ten o'clock in the morning to cast their votes. Chief attraction was a magnificent
candy belfry. Inside swung a bell, also of candy, decorated with colorful candied
letters saying, "I'll sound the alarm and the noble firemen will respond."

When the votes for Atlanta's queen were counted, beautiful Miss Augusta Hill had won the honor, so her name was carved on the new bell before it was hoisted into the new fire tower, amid loud hurrahs and spirited band music. In her absence, it was rung for the first time by the presidents of Atlanta's four fire companies grasping the rope in unison. Local newspapers wrote of the whole affair in glowing terms, with others as distant as Nashville, Tennessee, taking note of the excitement.

Like others of its kind, the old fire alarm in Corpus Christi, Texas, was extremely important to its community. Used first in 1873, it was the signal that brought volunteer fire fighters whenever it rang ten rapid strokes, followed by a pause, then a number to indicate the ward where the blaze was located. It was always a busy bell, signaling not only fires but also the hours, morning, noon, and evening, as well as many civic occasions—including "ashings." This odd term was used during early days in Texas when many families had an ash hopper; water that dripped through ashes was used as the lye to make soap. When the ashes had cooled after a fire, a volunteer fireman would ring the signal for all who wanted ashes to come gather them.

After being retired from civic duty in 1919, the Corpus Christi bell remained an honorable city symbol until 1942, when it was suddenly asked to switch identities. On its way to be melted for its usable metal in the war effort, it was snatched up by the Navy Department to install on their newly built U.S.S. *Houston*. All this did not come about easily, but through the combined efforts of many loyal Texans who contributed to the building of the new U.S.S. *Houston* to replace the one bombed in the war; and through the particular efforts of Mr. Tom Cahill, a charter member of Corpus Christi Volunteer Firemen. When the city's old fire alarm was patriotically donated for war scrap, he exclaimed, "This is blue-blood scrap—too fine for just a scrap pile." To their everlasting credit, the Navy Department agreed. As a result, this cherished bronze voice was to be heard again, but with entirely different connotations, in accordance with navy protocol.

Just once did Texans have the thrill of hearing the full-throated bronze voice in its new role. In 1945, after the fighting ceased, "their" U.S.S. *Houston* returned home for a Navy Day visit. Thousands lined the Gulf shore and cheered as the bell tolled and bluejackets saluted while the Republic of Texas flag dipped in honor of the occasion. Wherever this storied bell is now, Texans hope its biographical legends are noted:

Original inscription:

MENEELY & KIMBERLEY
FOUNDERS
TROY, N.Y.
1873

On one side in black letters, painted by the navy:

USS
HOUSTON
1944

On the other side:

PRESENTED BY
CITY OF CORPUS CHRISTI
TEXAS

What must surely be one of the few old fire bells remaining in its original tower may be seen in historic Madison, Indiana, overlooking the Ohio River. The high brick structure is a part of the station housing Fair Play Fire Company No. 1. It rises at one corner of the well-kept old building and is topped by a figural weather vane, which in itself has been a landmark for more than a century. Fair Play Fire Company No. 1, founded in 1841, is the oldest volunteer fire company in Indiana, having seen action first as a bucket brigade.

Fire fighting was almost a lifelong enthusiasm with George Washington, who greatly motivated the organizing of and the pride in volunteer fire departments. Along with other prominent citizens of Alexandria, Virginia, he himself was a member of the Friendship Fire Engine Company, organized in 1774. While attending the Continental Congress in Philadelphia that year, he purchased a fire engine as a gift for the Friendship Company. Today it is still a part of the company's museum display. No bell was used in conjunction with that early engine, but a pair

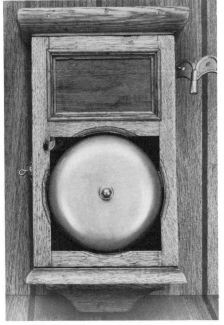

Indiana's oldest volunteer fire company was founded in 1841. The building with its tower, dating to 1850, still stands.

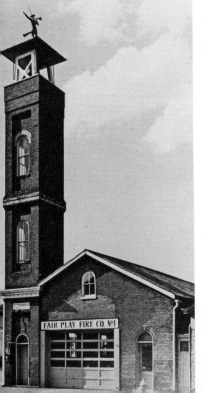

Above left
Firehouse bell used to summon sleeping firemen from the loft above. When the mechanism behind door had been wound with the butterfly key, the gong would clang automatically for a full minute if a chain attached to the side hook was yanked. This piece was reputedly rescued from the fire barn in Chicago at the time of the Great Fire. *Stephen Foster Memorial*

Above right
Fire bell of a type manufactured by New Departure Company (Bristol, Connecticut) from 1900 through 1910, designed to use either in a firehouse or on a fire wagon. It was rung by cranking the handle back and forth to activate clappers striking the outside of the bell. *Guy O. Davis Collection*

of them lent a certain advantage to a later hand pumper built in Alexandria in 1849, now also a part of Friendship Company's historic display. Bells were finally becoming standard accessories and were undergoing a weekly polishing with all the other pieces of equipment. On file in government archives, incidentally, are the oldest known letters of patent for a bell attached to a fire wagon. They are dated 1808.

The old hand pumpers had to be laboriously maneuvered over cobblestones; yet, even as they moved at the reckless pace of five miles an hour, the fires they were attempting to reach often got off to a rip-roaring start; but at least the clang-clanging of the bells as the volunteers pushed and pulled alerted townsfolk along the way. Once they reached the scene, the volunteers still had certain "arrangements" to make before they could hose the blaze. A bucket brigade had to be formed to keep the engine tanks filled—that is, until the day when suctions for the hose were perfected. During all this shifting of equipment, the bells again proved useful, clanging, urging greater effort—and fast. The speedy horse-drawn fire wagon was a great improvement over the cumbersome hand pumper. Its very speed produced a more insistent clanging of its warning bell, guaranteed to scatter dogs, children, and citizens in general, thus speeding up the firemen's work.

Bells that moved to a far different tempo and for an altogether different purpose were featured in circus parades in days gone by. Most popular were the melodic bells carried on richly carved, colorfully painted wagons. Best known of all in this category was the great Ringling Bell Wagon, acquired in 1892. The mammoth wagon was built by Moeller Wagon Company of Baraboo, Wisconsin; the bells,

Probably the oldest patent design on record for a fire wagon bell. The patent was issued to James P. Parke, December 19, 1808, for a bell to use on a hand pumper. *National Archives, Washington, D.C.*

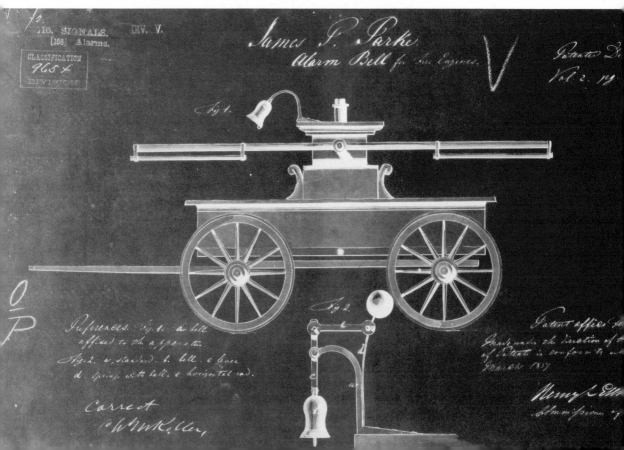

Detail of the bells on a fire hose carriage, circa 1855. *Museum of the City of New York*

cast by Campbell Foundry of Milwaukee. Nine in number, they were tuned to an octave, then mounted around the perimeter of the wagon, with one centered to hang above the others. The tunes played were largely dictated by the character of the instrument itself. Each bell was operated by a hand lever, and so it was not feasible to "flit" over the keys, as on a keyboard. Playing lighter, faster tunes was difficult, if not impossible. Hymns or majestic melodies, however, were ideally suited to this instrument.

Among other smaller bell wagons, Barnum and Bailey's Circus featured one that played tunes imitating those heard from famous Bow Church chimes in London. Gollmar Brothers Circus used a still slighter vehicle equipped with many small bells that produced a more lighthearted parade music. It is not difficult to understand the appeal of such showpieces, especially the great Ringling Bell Wagon as it

The speedy horse-drawn fire engine was a great improvement over the cumbersome hand pumper. Its very speed produced a more insistent clanging of its warning bell, as this scene of the Portland Fire Department would imply. *Hazeltine Photo, Oregon Historical Society*

The famous Ringling Brothers Bell Wagon. Its nine bronze bells comprising an octave were played by levers operated from the rear seat. *Ringling Museum of the Circus; photograph by J. J. Steinmetz, Sarasota*

paraded slowly along, with favorite hymn tunes rolling from its masterful chimes. Along with the calliope, they reflected in a novel way the aesthetic tastes of an age that wholeheartedly enjoyed melodic tunes and efflorescent ornamentation. Today their music is scarcely remembered; so few are alive who can recall it.

Seagoing Bells

Gone, too, are the sounds of many bells used on, in, under, and near the water. Majestic and important as ship bells have been in the course of American history, bells from the nation's inland waterways have been even more closely intertwined with their era. How many people realize, for instance, that beautiful Mount Vernon might very well lie in ruins today had it not been for the tolling bell on a little Potomac River packet one night long ago in 1853. "What is that?" asked a startled woman passenger as the bell continued its tolling.

"We're passing Mount Vernon, ma'am," a deckhand replied, "the home of George Washington. You can see the big white mansion up there on the hill. It's falling to pieces, though, and nobody cares. But all our riverboats still toll their bells when they pass."

In the moonlight the lady could see the sagging structure pointed out to her, and when she returned to her South Carolina home, she told her invalid daughter Ann of the impressive incident. This marked the start of Ann Pamela Cunningham's twenty-year struggle to unite women from every state in restoring Mount Vernon to its original loveliness, as Washington knew it. That was indeed a coup for women crusaders, a responsibility both the state of Virginia and the federal government had refused to assume. Unforgettably, it was sparked by the requiem bell tolling on a Potomac River packet.

For all practical purposes, the sound of the iron bell from Robert Fulton's *Clermont* has vanished; yet there are those who have heard it, for twice within remembrance it has rung its way up and down the Hudson River, as it did in 1807, resulting in as much notoriety as ever attended a steamboat bell on American river-ways. Despite the lost-again-found-again fortunes of its first hundred years, the bell is in existence, owned by The New-York Historical Society. It has been carefully authenticated, its various moves traced to everyone's satisfaction.

Labeled "Fulton's Folly" by skeptics, the steamboat *Clermont* was broken up after years of service, at which time it was lengthened and renamed the *North River*. There was no whistle on the *North River*, steam whistles being as yet unknown. Instead, its arrivals and departures were signaled with the same bell Robert Fulton had selected for his steamboat. It was not uncommon to transfer a bell to successive steamboats, as one after another was removed from service. The average steamboat rarely lasted more than five years, since travel in those days on undredged rivers was extremely hazardous, at best. The bells usually outlasted the boats.

By 1865, Fulton's bell was being auctioned, leading to a series of out-of-state owners, all recorded by name, until in 1908 it was taken to Troy, New York, where it was mounted on the counter in a hotel and used to call the bellboys. Finally it was acquired by the Hudson River Day Line, to use in their Hudson-Fulton celebration of 1909. For that memorable pageant, it was installed on a replica of the old *Clermont*, designed by two naval architects from inventor Fulton's original plans showing the bell mounted on deck, nearly midship, just forward of the smokestack. The bell was rung as this replica, along with a replica of Henry Hudson's *Half Moon*, was escorted in naval procession up the Hudson to Albany.

The same iron relic was aboard the *Peter Stuyvesant* in 1957, when she started her New York-to-Albany voyage commemorating the *Clermont*'s first trip in 1807. As a part of this ceremony, it was sounded as the boat passed the Livingston homestead, en route to Albany, the manor house where Robert Fulton stayed overnight on his upriver journey. As a major investor in Fulton's venture, Livingston was one of the forty passengers on that maiden voyage. His niece, Harriet Livingston, was later to become Fulton's wife.

Western rivers, too, have an important heritage in their riverboat bells. In appearance a badly damaged relic now, the one from the steamboat *Yellow Stone* nevertheless still symbolizes a most historic chapter in Texas history. Even in its mutilated state, it makes an impressive exhibit at the Alamo Museum. The *Yellow Stone* hauled cotton on the Brazos River until the San Jacinto Campaign of 1836, when it was pressed into service for the Texas army. During the campaign the bell signaled many history-making movements, climaxing on the day the *Yellow Stone* brought in the dictator of the Mexican government as prisoner. Shortly after the fighting, the bell was lost when the *Yellow Stone* sank in the river. Dredged up years later, it was used as a plantation bell—only to suffer another misfortune when its crown was crushed in a fire. It lay abandoned in the ashes for a long time before the plantation manager carried it up to the attic, where, years later, his grown daughters found it and recognized its significance. They presented it to the Alamo Museum in honor of the Texas Centennial in 1936.

A considerable number of assorted facts surround the steamboat bells once heard daily along the lower Mississippi River. When the *Robert E. Lee* and the

The *Yellow Stone* bell, now enshrined at Mission San Antonio de Valero, better known as The Alamo, San Antonio, Texas. The riverboat *Yellow Stone* played a significant part in Texas's bid for freedom in 1836. *Daughters of the Republic of Texas Library*

Natchez raced that stretch on June 30, 1870, they made riverboat history, since this was the race that won for *Robert E. Lee* the title of "Mississippi Queen." Mark Twain kept figures on the race, recording the winner's time as three days, eighteen hours, and fourteen minutes. Old prints of the Mississippi Queen show her bell in a prominent position on the forepart of her roof, and it is a fair guess that it came into play often during that historic race.

Ordinarily all such bells spoke to boatmen through a standard set of signals. When the boat was at the landing, six taps on the bell meant "Stand by." Three taps, "All ready." One meant "Let go," but when followed by one more it meant "All gone" (all fastenings released, the pilot ready to proceed). While the boat was moving, one tap meant "Heave lead on the port." Two taps, "Heave lead on the starboard." The rapid ringing of the bell at any time was a fire alarm. The language of bells also included a set of signals for foggy weather.

As a licensed Mississippi River pilot himself, Mark Twain was familiar with all the signals that steamboat bells could relay. In fact, he kept his own signals working overtime, according to opinions shared by river folk who knew him. His piloting instructor good-naturedly remarked that Twain "wrote a better job of piloting than he performed." He somehow lacked the decisiveness of a good pilot, and that often resulted in a flurry of signals as he maneuvered his boat.

Because of the sentiment they attached to their sound, many river people along the Mississippi have managed to acquire bells from some of the famous southern packets. They appear here and there on plantations or on civic plazas. One from the stern-wheeler *America* serves as a New Orleans grave marker for its captain, L. V. Cooley. Others have strayed into distant museums. Mark Twain's found its way to collections at the Stephen Foster Memorial in Florida. The Smithsonian has the bell from the famous *Kate Adams I*, and the Mariners Museum of Newport News, Virginia, owns the forty-nine-inch-diameter bell from *Kate Adams III*, this being the largest on record from any river steamer. For that matter, a bell with a flaring lip measuring forty inches across is large by any standards.

A bell with a similarly wide flaring lip was brought up by skin divers working Lake Michigan near Saugatuck, Michigan, in 1958. It had lain submerged for over a century on the hulk of a four-masted ship believed to be the lumber schooner *Milwaukee* that sank in 1842. Crusted with nearly an inch of rust, the relic came up intact, although an iron chain, when touched, crumbled apart. The 100-foot *Milwaukee* was large for her day—one of the largest in the lumber trade at that time, according to an old-time Lake boat captain. It would seem logical, therefore, that it be fitted with a sizable bell.

Retired bells from Great Lakes liners evoke their own particular memories among those who can recall their sound. In Henry Ford's Greenfield Village at Dearborn, Michigan, a bell is on display from the liner *Tashmoo*, of Detroit, affectionately called "The White Flyer" and once the pride of its owners, the White Star Line. The *Tashmoo* and the C and B Company's crack steamer *City of Erie* ran one of the most colorful races ever seen on the Lakes, back in 1901. Children are still taken to see the *Tashmoo*'s bell, to hear how—for their great-grandparents—its strokes signaled many a happy holiday cruise on the trim white vessel.

For seagoing vessels, whether commercial or naval, standards of composition, size, and use for bells gradually became better defined than for those on inland waters; in the case of the navy, they even grew to be inflexible, as they certainly were not in the days when Paul Revere cast a bell for the U.S.S. *Constitution*. Two hundred years of naval history have unrolled since then, showing the United States Navy the wisdom of specifying the exact metallic content as well as the size and pitch of the bell to be installed on each ship. Only in time of war are some of these specifications modified.

As for the uses to which they are put, bells on deck may not be quite so important as they once were because of today's many intercommunication systems. Still, they can be heard as a signal when ships are anchored in a fog, or as an alarm in emergencies. They also continue to be heard marking the time at regular intervals. A number of years ago the quarterly publication of the Great Lakes Historical Society featured a fine dissertation on ship bells, written by retired Lieutenant Com-

Below is the United States Navy bell especially developed under war conditions in accordance with the Bureau of Ships Specifications. Called the "Invasion Bell," it is made of a special cast-iron alloy to provide the tone that rang out signals on both landing craft and aircraft carriers during World War II. The deck bell at top was to be used on small water craft. The C. S. Bell Company manufactured both. *The C. S. Bell Company*

mander Irl V. Beall of the United States Coast Guard. In neatly capsuled form, Commander Beall tabulates the functions of such bells as warning signals, thus nullifying the idea that seagoing vessels need no longer rely on them:

> Now, Maritime Law requires ships to carry an efficient bell. Ships at anchor must, as prescribed by the International Rules of the Nautical Road, ring their bell rapidly for five seconds each minute.
>
> Vessels with a length greater than 350 feet must sound a bell as above in the fore part of the ship, and this must be followed immediately by ringing a bell of dissimilar tone for five seconds, in the after part of the ship. Thus an approaching vessel can estimate the size of the ship anchored in fog.
>
> The bell takes its place as an essential link in a ship's fire alarm system. In the event of fire, the bell is rung rapidly for at least five seconds, followed by one, two, or three rings to indicate the location of the fire—forward, amidships, and aft respectively.

Contrary to landlubber's notions, the naval tradition of "striking the bell" is not primarily intended to replace clocks for telling time. It nevertheless does indicate clock time by measuring the periods when certain members of the crew are standing watch. Every twenty-four hours is divided into six watches of four hours each, beginning at midnight. To keep time, the end of the first half hour is announced with one stroke of the bell, the first hour with two strokes, the next half hour with three, and so on until eight bells is reached at four o'clock. Then the cycle begins again, with the watches always ending at four, eight, and twelve o'clock.

There is something unmistakable about the sound of a ship bell, some special indefinable timbre. Coupled with this indefinable quality is a specific tone indicative of the ship's overall size. According to official information furnished to Dorothy K. Hill when she was writing her excellent treatise, *Marine Bells:*

> Small boats from 16 to 30 feet used a struck up bell. . . . These do not contain any particular tone. Boats from 26 to 65 feet use A flat. Those over 65 feet use A natural. Tug boats and boats of that type use D flat. Large boats over 100 tons, like destroyers, used B natural. Those from 1,000 to 2,000 tons use G natural. If they are over 12,000 tons, they use B flat. Vessels such as fuel ships, supply transports, and hospital ships, use E natural. Thus the tone of the bell shows the size of the vessel, so that the boat may be distinguished in a fog.

Given this bit of information, it is possible for someone with a projective tonal ear to view a now-silent ship bell, to gauge the size of the ship to which it belonged, then to hear—figuratively, of course—its exact pitch.

Bells from scrapped or abandoned vessels have been quickly acquired by museums or, in many instances, appropriately returned to the city or state for which their ship was named. Such was the pleasant fate of the bell from the U.S.S. *Washington*, in 1962, when her ship's twenty-four-year career ended. A half dozen or so of her relics were selected for permanent display in the rotunda of the state capitol in Olympia, the centerpiece being the ship's bell, which the governor himself unveiled.

The fortunes of the bell now at the impressive capitol entrance parallel the thirteen "slam-bang" battles in which the U.S.S. *Washington* won her thirteen battle stars, ending with her honorable discharge from service. Every year of the bell's quarter-century life is accounted for—including 1942, the year of its first ocean crossing, when it signaled what must have been its most mysterious emergency. While the *Washington* was steaming along in moderately heavy seas, one day out of Portland, Maine, the man-overboard alarm sounded. An intensive search of the sea revealed nothing, but a muster of all personnel showed the only absentee was the commander himself, Rear Admiral John W. Wilcox. According to the ship's official annals, his body was never found.

In the case of the bell from the U.S.S. *South Carolina* of Revolutionary days, the story is vastly different. Though it now enjoys a prominent position in the library at the University of South Carolina, much of its history will remain a closed book. This fact in itself makes it all the more remarkable that after nearly two centuries it ever found its way back to the state whose name it bears. According to naval records, two frigates being built in Amsterdam (and intended for France) were purchased by the Continental Congress. One, already named *L'Indien*, was eventually purchased by a Commodore Gillon and rechristened for his home state of South Carolina. She took part in the capture of the Bahamas, but was herself captured by the British in 1782. After that her whereabouts were uncertain. There were only unconfirmed rumors that her bell had been heard along trade routes in the Indian Ocean. If perhaps those rumors were true, there is less puzzlement over the fact that an American army lieutenant in New Delhi, India, came face to face with a bell marked SOUTH CAROLINA—this after the close of the Second World War. In due time he brought the bell home, where he learned that it had indeed belonged to the U.S.S. *South Carolina* of Revolutionary days.

In keeping to a safe course, vessels along the coast are (or in some cases, were) aided by buoys, lightships, and lighthouses; and the histories of each are just as distinct, one from the other, as were the sounds of their bells. In *Anchor to Windward*, Edwin Valentine Mitchell describes so aptly that eeriest of the various maritime bell sounds:

As seen in the reading room at the South Caroliniana Library, USC campus: the bell from the first U.S.S. *South Carolina* of Revolutionary days. She was a ship of 1,350 tons, had a crew of 550, and carried 46 guns. *University of South Carolina*

Of all these, the sound of the bell buoy is the most unearthly, perhaps because it is not rung by any human agency, but is operated by the uncertain action of the sea. Not only the irregularity of the sound but the general mournfulness of the tone, the grave note of warning, and the utter loneliness of the thing itself tethered amid endless acres of water make it seem nonterrestial. It is neither a part of the land nor a part of the sea, but is like a thing existing sadly in limbo. No one, I am sure, ever heard a merry or joyous bell buoy. I used to listen to it at night, and could sometimes tell from it the state of the sea and the direction of the wind.

Doleful and unreal as they may sound, bell buoys have a very real history in Coast Guard annals, a history beginning in 1841 with the earliest attempt to increase their effectiveness by fitting them with bells "so fixed as to be rung by the motion of the sea." The first experiment looked promising; and bells had already been installed in lighthouses and on some lightships, where they had proved the most effective fog signals yet devised. The results on buoys, however, were not wholly satisfactory, and it remained for Officer Brown of the Lightship Establishment to invent the forerunner of modern-day bell buoys. Funds were authorized in 1852 for the first Brown-type buoy, which had a 300-pound bell rigidly fixed to the framework. Today the bells are struck by loosely hung clappers that hit the outside

Left
Bell buoys were no more than day marks for offshore dangers before Officer Brown introduced the first true bell buoy, forerunner of the modern type. It used a mini-cannonball as a rolling clapper. *Aids to Navigation Division, United States Coast Guard*

Right
Drawing of a nine-foot type of bell buoy currently in use by the Coast Guard. *Aids to Navigation Division, United States Coast Guard*

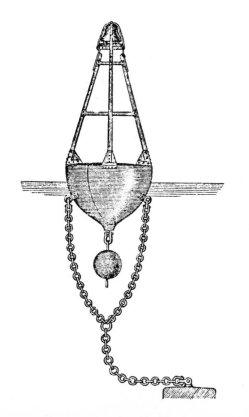

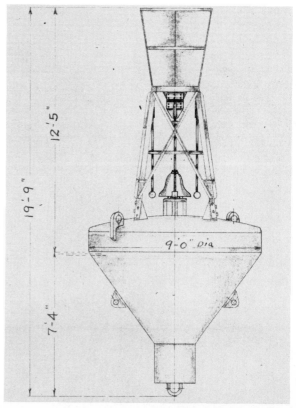

surface of the bell with every slight roll of the surf, whereas the early ones were designed with a small cannon ball confined by a plate over the mouth of the bell so that the ball could roll around and strike at any point. The sounds from these two different types were naturally quite dissimilar.

Gong buoys were not introduced until 1921, but a prototype used in New York Lower Bay in 1888 proved immediately successful, according to an account on record: "This buoy, which had been placed to mark the wreck of the bark QUICK-STEP, was called a double bell buoy, and produced a sort of chime as the bells sounded sometimes together and sometimes separately. Navigators of the day were well pleased with the distinctiveness of this signal."

The greatest advance came after 1904, when lighted buoys were adopted. Navigators soon realized the advantages in combining a light with a bell in a single buoy. Out of all these experiments evolved a system of buoyage that now includes approximately 700 lighted bell buoys and 250 unlighted, each equipped with an 85-, 225-, or 1,000-pound bell rung by the motion of the sea; a few have electric strikers. The Coast Guard Yard at Curtis Bay, Maryland, has a foundry for the manufacture of the bells, but because of the very limited demand it is infrequently used.

Lighthouse bells, used chiefly as warnings in thick weather, are much larger than any suspended in buoys, and today are generally sounded at regular intervals by a clockworks mechanism. Each lighthouse has its own special signal, such as two strokes every twenty seconds or one stroke every fifteen seconds, so that those who hear the sound can tell which particular station it comes from, then get their bearings. Bells of penetrating sound are needed; otherwise their call would never carry across a roaring sea.

One of the severest Atlantic storms of the nineteenth century was the gale of April 14, 1851, which totally destroyed Minot's Ledge Lighthouse off the Massachusetts shore. All during the height of the storm, the two faithful attendants kept the bell ringing and the lamps burning for ships in distress. Vowing to stay with the tower until it toppled under mountainous waves, the two men wished in some way to communicate their farewells to loved ones ashore. They seized heavy hammers and began pounding furiously on their bell. So penetrating was the sound that their signal was heard on shore, as they hoped it would be, even above the roaring surf.

Logs from the days of the first manned lighthouses are filled with such tales of man's misadventures with the sea. Many tales give proof that a bell was an indispensable part of the equipment, as does this one: On a bright, sunny day in 1839, the keeper of the Plum Island, Massachusetts, light rowed to nearby Newburyport with his wife to do a little Christmas shopping. In midafternoon a lashing wind prevented their return, and for the first time in its long history the Plum Island light stood dark, its bell silent. About midnight the *Pocahontas* hit the island and went down with all hands.

Bells at these stations figured now and then in lighthearted moments, too. This little vignette from Wood Island, Maine, points up the fact: The keeper's wife on Wood Island, Mrs. Thomas Orcutt, had a dog named Sailor that she had taught to ring the giant fog bell by holding the cord between his teeth. Sailor eventually became so famous that it was not uncommon during the summer for the family to hear a ship's whistle signaling their pet. Sailor would dash out to the bell, grab the cord, and give a lusty pull. The clang of the great bell would echo across the water to the passing boat, where the captain would give an answering salute, then start back toward Biddeford Pool, his passengers happy at having witnessed the Wood Island dog ringing the fog bell for their amusement.

In thick weather the fog bell was for years an indispensable warning device, since the beacon light was utterly useless in such weather. On a foggy night in 1919, a cruise ship carrying President Woodrow Wilson narrowly escaped the rocks at Cedar Point Light on Cape Cod—only the warning sound of the bell prevented disaster. The first mention of a fog bell at a lighthouse in the United States occurred in 1820 when an appropriation was made "for placing a bell near the lighthouse on West Quoddy Head, Maine." For beating a 500-pound bell with a hammer on all those frequent foggy days and nights, the sum of $60 was added to the keeper's yearly pay.

Not until 1852 was a bell attached to the Boston Light on Little Brewster Island in Boston Harbor, which, when it was built in 1716, was the first lighthouse established in America. Prior to having a bell, Boston Light had used a borrowed army cannon "to answer ships in a fog" by firing at intervals of a minute.

For a century and a half, then, lighthouse bells have played a part in keeping ships of all types on a safe course, providing a familiar and assuring sound. All that is changing now, and the end of the lighthouse era is in sight. Many factors have

Left
Lighthouse and fog-warning bell of West Quoddy Head, the northernmost light along the coast of Maine. The first fog bell in the United States was installed here in 1820. The one pictured is a replacement, cast by McShane's in 1900.

Right
Scene from an old color print captioned: "The first known fog signal in America was set up in Boston in July 1719. It consisted of a borrowed Army cannon placed on the seaward side of Boston Light. The gun was either used to answer ship signals or fired at intervals of a minute in heavy weather. It was replaced by Boston's first fog bell in 1852."

combined to bring about this change. After World War II, the importance of many light stations as aids to navigation began lessening because of their distance from newly dredged channels and the deeper waters needed to accommodate the newer oceangoing ships. Added to such irreversible facts, a whole new world of sophisticated electronic gadgets was surfacing in the mind of the newly trained technician. Those gadgets are now taking over the work of the lighthouse. Ships equipped with radar can feel their way along the coast in darkness and fog; seaborne instruments "interrogate" small boxes atop buoys and beach towers, triggering signals that reveal their position and provide other information. As a result, lighthouses, fog bells, and the keepers themselves are all a vanishing lot. According to a long-range program, the old structures are being gradually converted to automatic, unattended status. Of the several hundred lighthouses remaining, nearly a hundred are still manned along the Atlantic and Pacific coasts, the Gulf of Mexico, in the waters around Hawaii, the Caribbean, Alaska, and the Great Lakes. By 1978, Coast Guardsmen will be manning only about fifty.

What happens to a lighthouse and a fog bell that have outlived their usefulness? Some lighthouses remain in their old location to become maritime museums. Others the United States Coast Guard turns over to the General Services Administration, in charge of disposing of surplus government property. Interested individuals are allowed to purchase and remove the structures for their own personal use. For the bells themselves, there are graveyards where they are dumped. On a brighter note, there is a growing demand among private individuals for such storied relics as "conversation pieces," if for no other reason.

6

RURAL
TINTINNABULATIONS

Plantation bells have always held a somewhat legendary or romantic appeal, though usually they were cast as equals with the more lowly farm bells, all from the same melting pot. In writing of the South, period novelists have contributed to the romantic aura surrounding plantation bells by drawing on them for a bit of local color. "He went to the steps and pulled the great plantation bell," writes Gwen Bristow in *Deep South*. "The bell rang so rarely that it had the sound of oracular authority. It was there for great occasions or dire emergencies, and when it rang it meant that every soul on the plantation must drop his tools where he stood and come to the big house."

Some of the true stories behind identifiable plantation bells across the Deep South are in themselves tinged with romance of the past. One centers around a rusty, exceptionally old bell that announced George Washington's visit to Hampton Plantation in the picturesque Low Country near Charleston, South Carolina. The giant live oak from which it hangs would have disappeared long ago, had not Washington rescued it from the axe. Hampton Plantation was the ancestral home of America's famous poet, Archibald Rutledge, until his death a few years ago. He never tired of relating for visitors the history of the old oak—hundreds of years old, it is said—with its branches heavily draped in Spanish moss. The tree still obscures the view from the white-columned veranda, just as it did in the spring of 1791 when President Washington stopped. He had come to enjoy breakfast with his comrade-in-arms, Edward Rutledge, while on his way to a festive week in Charleston. As the President and the poet's great-great-grandmother strolled on the veranda after breakfast, she told him of her intention to have the tree removed in order to restore the view. The President remonstrated at such length that Mrs. Rutledge acquiesced. A small plaque put on the tree by the Daughters of the

American Revolution relates the incident. The bell, Archibald Rutledge always pointed out, is the same one that announced Washington's arrival at Hampton Plantation.

It is understandable that plantation families became attached to the sound of their bells, which may or may not have been chosen for their tonal quality. After all, these were made to give a loud sound but not necessarily a musical one. A century ago, Dasilide Conrad, the young daughter of a landowner at Bonfauca, Louisiana, felt a special fondness for the eighty-five pound bell used to call their slaves. By willing it to her descendants, she made sure it would remain as long as they lived on the plantation. Today it is still in the family, owned by her great-great-grandchildren.

Bells have always been looked upon as desirable loot in time of war, and during the Civil War plantation bells were especially vulnerable, easily subject to looting by Union troops. Twelve were brought up the Mississippi River to Illinois by one Union officer alone. Immediately after the Battle of Vicksburg, hilarious Union forces overran the plantation of Jefferson Davis. Spying a bell on its yoke near the homestead, the men decided it would make a fine souvenir for the folks back home. They packed it in a barrel, to be shipped up the Mississippi by boat. Eventually it was transported by oxen to Waukesha, Wisconsin, where it was placed in the belfry of a new one-room country schoolhouse.

To prevent similar looting on their plantations, some owners buried their bell along with the family silver. An unusually fine specimen of richest tone hung for many years in the hallway at The Oaks in Bloomington, Illinois. It had been found buried deep in shifting sands along the Gulf of Mexico. Its new owners could only guess at the pre-Civil War scenes it had witnessed prior to that terror-filled time when Ol' Massa must have ordered the bell well hidden. Captivated by its sonorous tone, a poet visiting The Oaks created an imaginary past for the antique piece in a verse, "Old Plantation Bell."

The omnipresent post bell, once a part of every farmhouse scene, began disappearing as machines began displacing hired hands. Except in isolated instances, post bells are no longer heard summoning field laborers to a noon dinner, sounding the end of a day's toil, or signaling the start of a barn dance. Yet there is a demand for them as an adjunct to suburban-style living, primarily as decorative pieces, but occasionally as signals calling children from play.

Those with a knowledge of the better-known companies that manufactured these bells enjoy searching for a farm-type bell carrying a recognized trademark. A few years ago a dealer in Georgia had accumulated a stockpile of several dozen. Among the better-known makers represented were The Goulds Manufacturing Company, and Downs and Company, both of Seneca Falls, New York; American Casting Company of Birmingham, Alabama, in operation only a brief time between 1904 and 1910; and C. S. Bell Company of Hillsboro, Ohio. Under their recent new ownership, C. S. Bell is still producing farm bells from old molds, the only one of this elite group of firms in business now.

The more commonplace of such types were of cast iron; the higher quality, of an alloy of cast steel and "crystal," the latter being defined as a hard mix of copper and tin giving off continuing vibrations. The largest ever made was listed in Goulds's 1874 catalog at 1,100 pounds, but evidently it did not sell because three years later it was no longer listed. One innovation at Goulds about that time, however, did boost sales. That was the "richly gilded" finish they began advertising for all their farm and plantation bells. Previously all had been made with a black japanned finish.

Farm bells are thought to have pushed westward into the Ohio Valley with Israel Putnam and his band of pioneers when they arrived to make Marietta, Ohio, the first permanent settlement in the Northwest Territory—or as the rhymster expressed it, when

> "In seventeen hundred and eighty-eight
> The white man came to the Buckeye State."

Despite British regulations against them, iron forges were already in operation throughout Pennsylvania by 1750, so it is reasonable to believe iron bells were being made. Such items were almost a necessity for any wilderness settlement, as a means of warning habitants of predatory Indians. Before long, though, wilderness clearings were tinkling, clanging, bonging, to the rhythm of many other bells. These tintinnabulations ranged from the negligible tones of weightless tiny goose and turkey bells less than an inch in size to the ponderous tones of noisy cowbells. Then there were middle-size sheep and pig bells filling in the chorus of metallic sounds. Frequently such barnyard bells served to protect the wearer from marauding animals. Chiefly they were of importance to the settler in keeping tabs on the whereabouts of the barnyard inhabitants.

Of these various tintinnabulations, the sound of iron pig bells is the one almost totally unfamiliar today. They never were widely produced, nor for very long periods of time. The settlement in east Tennessee known as Cades Cove fabricated such bells, along with those for sheep and cows. There, in 1827, Daniel D. Foute built the first iron forge. His was one of several in the area, and the noise of their hammers could be heard all over the Cove; but by 1845 the smoke-belching forges were already a thing of the past in that locality. Even though the Great Smoky Mountains were originally called the Great Iron Mountains, very little iron was found in that range; so, like the coppersmiths and brass founders, the Cove's ironworkers were always handicapped by lack of raw materials. Those who hanker to stand on the very spot where Daniel Foute made his small barnyard bells, and where homesteaders came to test their sound before choosing any, can easily do so by visiting the John P. Cable Mill in Cades Cove. Mill and forge stood side by side.

As to the matter of sorting over livestock bells for sound before buying them—there was good reason for doing so. It behooved each family to know the sound of its own bells, as well as of those belonging to near neighbors. This applied especially to cattle bells, for the task of keeping everyone's cattle separate was made easier when their bells did not sound too much alike. The tone of someone else's cowbells too closely resembling the tone of his own could prove a source of annoyance to a settler. There are even stories of bullet holes slyly shot into offending bells in order to damage their tone, thereby distinguishing them from others heard in the immediate neighborhood.

During the growth period of the young American republic, no groups were more important than the metalworkers skilled in providing tools, utensils, and related useful items such as bells. Blacksmiths were among the first of these to ply their trade in the colonies. By reputation, the blacksmith wore many hats in the operation of his shop. He was his own person, a proprietor; an expert in fabricating whatever a buyer needed, whether chains, hinges, pots, bells, or shovels; perhaps also a toymaker; and almost always a harness maker.

Individually, blacksmiths and other workers in base metals seldom had any claim to fame other than their skill (in contrast to some brass and bell founders, who were well known in other fields). Yet, as a group, they were seemingly men of decided personality and strong character, and by virtue of their trade, close to the pulsebeat of civilization advancing across a young America. It is unfortunate that so little is known of these artisans, except in some instances their names and the locations of their shops. Such a dearth of information does, however, double the worth of whatever accounts do exist. Edwin W. Mills of Missouri has to his credit many published narratives of Ozark pioneers, none more fascinating than the one describing pioneer bellmaking in southwest Missouri. Interestingly enough, his narrative constitutes a sequel to the Cades Cove story. A steady influx of pioneers from eastern Tennessee kept arriving in southern Missouri during pre-Civil War days. Fifty thousand strong they came in the year 1839 alone, bringing with them not only their household effects, their rifles, and cattle, but also the crafts in which they were skilled.

John Caskey was among the new settlers, a youngish man intent on setting up a forge to continue his trade of bellmaking learned back in Tennessee. He was destined to ply his trade in the Ozarks for forty years, to become one of the area's foremost artisans. Being an astute fellow, Caskey chose a site on the old Hartville-Springfield Road where endless caravans of covered wagons zigzagged down the James River Valley, and where he was neighbor to the trading post owned by Joseph W. McClurg (governor of Missouri 1868-70).

For many years before sheet metal was available, smiths had to create their own supply by reclaiming old metal. Caskey had easy access to wornout wagon tires, which he laboriously hammered into sheets. "He made hundreds of bells in this way," Mr. Mills points out, "and when one reflects on the vast number of blows of a hand hammer required to thus beat out the metal for a single bell, his industry appears colossal."

Bells of differing sizes had to be cut from the metal, then beaten into shape and riveted by hand. The largest, about six inches deep, were for steers, several graduated sizes slightly smaller, for cows. The sound of each was determined to some extent by the flare of its sides, a feature that could be altered as desired while shaping a bell. After shaping and riveting came brazing, an essential process in fabricating cowbells in order to prevent rusting and to strengthen the overall piece for long-lasting service. Swinging steadily from the neck of a steer or a cow, these bells had to be sturdy enough to withstand rough weather and, in the stompyards, frequent jostling and fighting. Brazing was also essential to the tone of the bell, for unless lap joints were properly joined and the whole bell covered with a coating of brass, a tone similar to that of a cracked bell resulted. George A. Kelly, who was making cowbells in Texas in 1850, traveled by horseback all the way to Tennessee to learn the truth of this. He was vastly unhappy with the clanking sound of the stock bells he had been making, but on his return he began brazing his with liquid brass to make them more "ringable."

Caskey had a unique method for testing the tone of his finished bells, one that revealed his thorough craftsmanship. As Edwin Mills re-creates the scene:

. . . To ascertain the carrying power of their tone . . . a man on horseback rode off in the distance, carrying a bell which he sounded from time to time. Another party remained stationary at the starting point. When the last faint tinkle of the bell almost ceased, the man at the starting point signaled the rider, who then returned, measuring the distance which the sound of the bell had carried. The bells whose tones could be heard for the greatest distance were of course the most desired and the most valuable.

Every time he had a wagon full of finished bells, Caskey himself peddled them to surrounding towns. His son estimates at least 2,000 as the total output of his father's forge—in addition to all his other items.

Daniel Foute and John Caskey were only two among uncounted numbers of artisans busy hammering out livestock bells for frontiersmen. Even though they have gone unchronicled in too many instances, almost every region had at least one recognized maker of such objects whose name has been handed down in documented accounts of his work. Eastern Michigan had its Orson Starr; southern Illinois, its Christian Gottlieb Blum; and Utah, its J. A. Robey.

Orson Starr had learned his trade from his father back in upper New York State, before moving to Michigan in 1831. He was proud to claim that his cowbells could be heard a distance of two miles because of his excellent brazing methods. That his bells were highly salable is evidenced by the fact that he readily traded a wagonload of them for a large farm north of Royal Oak. Today his carefully crafted bells, impressed at first with O. STARR and later with a seven-pointed star, are considered museum pieces. Christian Gottlieb Blum did not take up bellmaking until well after the Civil War. He was a tinsmith with an inventive turn of mind, who eventually perfected a stock bell of far-reaching tone, nicely finished with red and gold Holstein labels.

Eventually, as America became more and more industrialized, small shops operated by metal workers who could "turn out" anything a customer desired gave way to large factories. It was then that cowbells lost their personality, declares a Tennessee connoisseur. Factory-made bells all sounded somewhat alike, whereas each handmade one was individual—which explains why some people much preferred them even when manufactured ones became available. That is also the

Montage of old photographs picturing Orson Starr's cowbell factory at Royal Oak, Michigan, the maker's portrait (circa 1840), and one of his bells with a seven-pointed star. *Thomas Irwin Starr*

reason many artisans who worked by hand were able to continue. Though the start of Blum's bellmaking nearly coincided with the Industrial Revolution in America, his shop continued for three generations. Except for the introduction of a few time-saving tools, the entire production process remained unchanged. The demand for Blum stock bells from halfway around the world continued right up until 1955, when the last ones were made. In J. A. Robey's case, certainly no one wished to see his work succumb to assembly-line techniques. He prided himself on making various types of sheep bells to suit the ethnic backgrounds of Utah's immigrant herdsmen. His own favorite was for Greek shepherds, a cupped arrangement of chiming bells guaranteed, because of their uncommonly sweet tone, to relieve herdsmens' loneliness.

Factories that specialized in manufacturing quality stock bells used paper labels of their own design to identify their products. Now and then a stockman enjoyed purchasing an array of bells under a variety of labels, to satisfy himself as to the relative merits of their sound. Today, with Bevin Brothers Manufacturing Company the only major maker still in production, the need for labels has disappeared. The company discontinued them twenty years ago.

With a constantly diminishing need for cowbells, will they too be discontinued? The situation is problematic, according to Bevin Brothers. True, the day is over when every cowbell rolling off the assembly line is sold to hang from a cow's neck, but there is a healthy demand for them among sports spectators and other noisy celebrants. Reputedly they are still a must for every "chivarie," as practiced in remote southern mountains. In the hands of celebrants, however, the cowbell gives off a sound that little resembles the gentler, measured tones traditionally associated with it. Those are the tones that have awakened nostalgic memories in man for well over a century. Henry David Thoreau wrote in his journal under the date April 4, 1841:

> The rattling of the tea-kettle below stairs reminds me of the cowbells I used to hear when berrying in the Great Fields many years ago, sounding distant and deep around the birches. That cheap piece of tinkling brass which the farmer hangs about his cow's neck has been more to me than the tons of metal which are swung in the belfry.

Among the most scenic of the paper labels formerly used by manufacturers of cattle bells was this one used by Bevin's, until discontinued some twenty years ago. *Bevin Brothers Catalog*

Old cow bells are treasured individually not only for their nostalgic sound but for their history of ownership. *Mrs. B. Ellsworth Young*

Those Connecticut Jinglers

Sleigh bells were by no means confined to rural areas, though today the mind's eye tends to see them against idyllic country scenes. The Dutch of New Amsterdam were enjoying sleighing parties and races as early as 1700, making popular a social dictum adopted by other colonial towns: that the first jingling sleigh bells ushered in the season of gaiety. Such pleasures were contagious and soon spread to more rural New England. A young English visitor there wrote to friends in London:

> The pleasant custom of sleighing contributes much to enliven the country at that dreary season. . . . The frequent ringing of bells which are fixed to the horses of every sleigh seems quite in unison with the general gaiety around . . . .

It is an indisputable fact that both drivers and animals found added pleasure and exhilaration when sleighs and harnesses were plentifully decorated with jingling bells. As a natural result, the music of sleigh bells became blanketed with sentiment, obscuring the original reason for their use. In an age when sleighs were common on the road, some warning device was needed. Not only the high speeds attained, but the silent approach of hoofs and runners on packed snow created a public menace. With towering snowdrifts and narrow, curved roads, there was the constant danger of colliding either with oncoming traffic or with pedestrians temporarily deafened under heavy mufflers. Traffic during the winter nearly doubled, as a matter of fact. For every wagon a farmer owned, he had two or three sleds because all heavy hauling waited until winter, then moved easily and quickly over the packed snow. For reasons such as these, all northern states enacted statutes making it unlawful to ride in a sleigh not having bells. Strangely enough, the legislature at Bangor, Maine, did not repeal its sleigh bell law until 1953. Two years later residents of Michigan's Upper Peninsula were startled to learn it was still against the law there to sleigh without bells on the horses "or mules, as the case may be."

114

No matter which type comes to mind in thinking of them, whether closed crotals or open-mouthed bells, either riveted or toggled to horse collars, body straps, martingales, or rump pads; whether saddle, hame, shaft, or bridle chimes—all have gone the way of trolley cars and nickel fares. Their medley of sound, while it lasted, was an ever-changing one, depending on the range and combination of pitches. The lowest sound belonged to the large heavy bells, often used singly on sledges or pungs, or on the big muscle-bound Percherons and Belgians pulling them. The highest belonged to the small featherweight speeding chimes designed for fast driving, therefore fastened close under the shaft. Some of the racing sleighs weighed only forty pounds but everything about them was elegantly designed. Only light jingly bells were suitable for cutters such as these, going at racehorse speed. Fashionable drivers could order theirs made of silver or gold, richly ornamented, befitting the fine trotters that wore them. It is said that Gideon Welles, secretary of the navy under Lincoln, whooshed over Connecticut roads in a gunboat sleigh, with silver bells jingling.

The number of companies and individuals that were, at one time or another, involved in the manufacture of sleigh bells is quite staggering. Still more unbelievable is the knowledge that some thirty flourished in or near East Hampton, Connecticut, alone, producing a large percentage of the world's sleigh bells. From the beginning, the hub of activity in this industry centered around the Connecticut Valley. It was there, in East Hampton, that William Barton set bells a-jingling in 1808 when he founded the town's first factory devoted to producing them. The entire Barton family seemed especially skilled in this type of production. William had learned the craft from his father in Bloomfield, Connecticut. There were also bell-making Bartons established in Cairo, New York, with whom William associated himself for a brief time when he left East Hampton. Beelzebub Barton founded the first bellworks in Cairo, where he located on the Susquehanna Turnpike for the making of "church bells, sleigh bells, and other goods of character." There was also a J. Barton at Cairo, who was issued several patents for horse bells.

With his inherent Yankee inventiveness and his experience in cannon-making for the War of 1812, William Barton was the first to devise a speedier method of producing sleigh bells. In simple terms, his idea was to cast each globule in one piece, complete with pellet enclosed, as opposed to the old method of casting each in two halves, then dropping in the pellet and soldering the halves together. These little crotals (as they are called) were fashioned with endless variations and were from the beginning the industry's best seller. They were sold loose by the pound to country peddlers, harness makers, and general stores. From his store, Paul Revere once sold two dozen to Samuel Adams.

Founders of almost all the other Connecticut Valley bell factories learned their trade in the Barton foundry. One of those, one who was to achieve the largest measure of fame from his apprenticeship, was young William Bevin. Free to copy all that he learned under Barton, young William gradually engaged his three brothers—Chauncey, Abner, and Philo—to join him in the East Hampton shop he set up in 1832. Their modest inventory included waffle irons, coffee mills, pots, kettles, and sleigh bells—the last always their most popular item. Today, four generations later, Bevin Brothers Manufacturing Company is operated by descendants who represent (in an unbroken line) one of America's longest standing family ownerships in the industry. The firm has been distinguished for many years as the

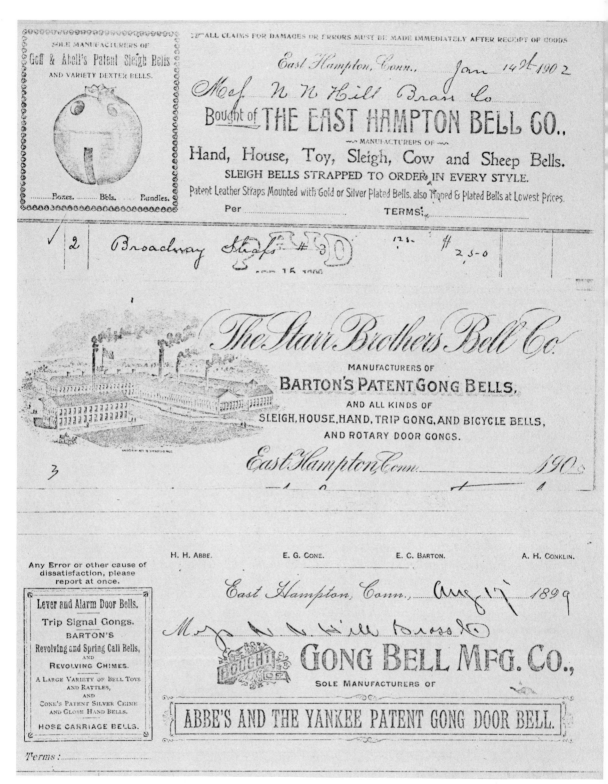

Three turn-of-the-century letterheads from major producers of sleigh bells and other small bells. *Stonecrest Antiques*

Since William Barton established bellmaking in East Hampton in 1808, it is assumed the "Established 1793" refers to his father's firm in Bloomfield, Connecticut, where William learned his craft.

world's leading producer of sleigh bells, and for the past several years as the only remaining member of the industry in East Hampton.

Bevin Brothers' survival may be partly explained by the fact that the company has always maintained a comprehensive production line, everything from tiny turkey bells to large ones weighing two or three hundred pounds, suitable for ship or church. What is more, they have shrewdly adapted to changing demands. No cast sleigh bells have been made since 1951, for very practical reasons. The full, throaty sound of cast crotals is no longer in demand, fortunately, since the cost of hiring foundrymen to make them has become prohibitive. Buyers on today's market require only the pleasant tinkle of stamped steel sleigh bells, bought to decorate doors, mantels, packages, snowsuits, and so on. Even the American Indians, who buy these in quantities, are satisfied with the modern variety of sleigh bell for their dance rhythms.

Most of the original cast types have vanished into private collections, but for those who wish to do so, it is possible still in a few localities to hear the true sound of sleigh bells when the snow flies. Sleigh buffs like the Sawyers of Jaffrey, New Hampshire, take pleasure in sharing their heritage and expertise with paying guests by taking them on sleigh rides over country roads, bells jingling all the way. At their thousand-acre Silver Ranch, the Sawyers maintain rows of sheds housing more than a hundred sleighs, sleds, and carriages. During the winter all sleighs and sleds, as well as the horses that pull them, are decorated with antique bells of various kinds, some of them handed down for many years in this family that has been farming New Hampshire hills for thirteen generations.

Team bells were closely related to sleigh bells in the annals of American transportation, but they were not precisely the same. For the most part they were larger, more penetrating of sound, less polished in appearance. Often they were hand forged, resulting in less uniformity of style. Since vast quantities of these were for use along the frontier, the main requirement was that they combine practical design with durable strength to withstand day-to-day use over a rough and roadless terrain.

Such bells were not necessarily discordant in sound. Quite the contrary, for

117

Left
Because the American frontier was always in motion, its arts were often transient. Nomadic harness makers sometimes took to the road to dispose of their stock. The history of Illinois frontier crafts has on record the name of such an itinerant who roved about selling sleigh bells.

Right
Saddle chimes with colorful horsehair plumes, figural finials, and a full set of pinwheel clappers were the ultimate for special occasions. Circuses featured this type for their parade horses. *Private Collection*

frequently two or more used together were purposely chosen for their chimelike effect. It was the sheer volume of sound, however, that created such a jangling din wherever there were great numbers of wagons. It was a din heard the year around, also, in all parts of the country. There was an unevenness to the tempo of team bells, a certain lilt and tumble not characteristic of sleigh bells—all due of course to the teams' uneven pace over rough dirt roads or bumpy cobblestones.

Even before wagoning reached its zenith, the pack horses used throughout the colonies wore neck bells. They are usually pictured being led out of western Pennsylvania in groups of twelve or fifteen, moving single file, each carrying about two hundred pounds, each wearing a bell (sometimes only the lead horse wore a bell). They were managed by two drovers, who accepted as an unwritten law the custom of belling their pack horses. So invariable was the custom that a drover of pre-Revolutionary days was heard to exclaim, "Only think what a rascally figure I should cut in the streets of Baltimore without a bell on my horse."

The most distinctive of team bells were those used on the six-horse teams pulling the great Conestoga wagons. A full set consisted of two metal harps holding five bells apiece for the lead pair of horses; two harps holding four apiece for the middle pair; and usually only one harp of three bells for the rear right horse (it was customary for the driver to ride at left rear). Sometimes wrapped in fur, leather, or cloth, each metal harp arched high above the horse's collar, its sharp prongs fitting securely into the harness hames. Apparently there is no unanimity of opinion about the origin of Conestoga bells, whether imported or cast in the colonies. Daniel King's is one of the very few brass founders' names connected with them. There is

118

RUSSIAN SADDLE CHIMES.

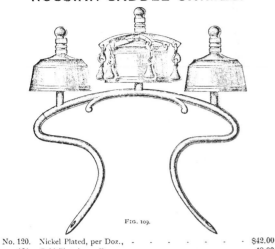

FIG. 109.

No. 120. Nickel Plated, per Doz., - - - - - - - $42.00
121. Gold Plated, per Doz., - - - - - - - - 48.00

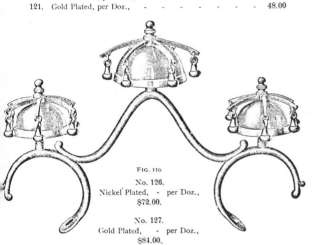

FIG. 110.

No. 126.
Nickel Plated, - per Doz.,
$72.00.

No. 127.
Gold Plated, - per Doz.,
$84.00.

Varying combinations of musical saddle chimes were available from all the East Hampton sleigh-bell firms. The more pinwheel clappers they had, the richer the tone. Gold-plated as well as nickel-plated chimes were listed in this early catalog.

Closed-mouth, or crotal-type, cast sleigh bells were made into a horse collar worn by Potter Palmer's pet saddle horse, which he enjoyed riding through Chicago's Lincoln Park. The crotal referred to as one Mr. Palmer purchased in the Orient is centered on collar. *Private Collection*

Curly is his name. He is a white Bashkir curly breed of horse used for centuries in Russia to pull troikas over the snow. He has a fast, smooth trot for pulling the sleighs that give ranch guests an old-fashioned winter ride. When photographed, he was looking askance at his playful master who was showing him off with all those straps of sleigh bells. *Silver Ranch, Jaffrey, New Hampshire*

Below
Alfred Sawyer, a co-owner and host at the ranch, enjoys a jingling ride behind Click, a dark bay Thoroughbred. *Silver Ranch, Jaffrey, New Hampshire*

Left
The same dark bay wearing his body strap of sleigh bells, with openmouthed shaft bells on the sled, takes guests on a moonlight ride. *Silver Ranch, Jaffrey, New Hampshire*

A snowplow pulled by a single horse was a continuing forty-two-year tradition in Concord, Massachusetts, when this scene was photographed in 1973. To cheer his efforts, a simple horse bell tinkled from Old Dobbin's collar. *The Christian Science Monitor, Robert A. Benson Photograph*

no lack of agreement, though, concerning the clear, resonant quality of their chiming. Many musical combinations were possible in arranging the bells on just one set of harps, yet a practiced ear could usually identify each family's wagon by its bells before it rounded the last bend in the road coming home.

Such chiming headpieces were a traditional part of the whole Conestoga concept, as were the white homespun tops and gaudily painted frames, the big, specially bred, grain-fed horses, and of course the drivers, proudly upholding their unwritten rules of the road. One of those rules revolved around their hame bells, the pride and joy of all drivers. If any wagoner suffered an accident or became stuck in the mud so that he required help from another wagoner, he was duty bound to pay his rescuer with a set of bells. But the fellow who arrived without mishap sang out, "I'm here with bells on!"—thereby introducing a new American colloquialism meaning "I'm here in full regalia."

Originally built by the Pennsylvania Dutch to haul their farm produce, these wagons were named for the valley where they were made, the valley of the Conestoga Indians. The wagons began to appear in appreciable numbers between 1750 and 1755, reaching their zenith about 1830, when fleets by the hundred traveled daily along the Lancaster pike between Philadelphia and Pittsburgh. With their six powerful sleek horses and their chiming bells, they were "the embodiment not only of the American tradition of strength and purpose, but of the joy of life," as one historian expresses it.

Properly applied, the term Conestoga referred only to the huge freighters of eastern Pennsylvania, the same that were pressed into service to haul Revolutionary War supplies for Washington's Continentals. Farther west they had their successors, known in Illinois as Empire Builders and elsewhere as Prairie Schooners. Bells were not a traditional part of those transports, however, perhaps because emigrants were not fond of advertising their route to the Indians. But when freight lines opened from mines to cities in the Far West, Conestoga-type bells were heard again. This time they rang in wild crescendos as drivers braked the headlong speed of their teams down precipitous mountains.

Another use was found for Conestoga-type bells in the Far West, one relatively unknown in the East. They were used on hitches pulling reapers in the wheat

121

This old view of a completely equipped Conestoga wagon shows the driver riding the left wheelhorse, as was customary. *Lancaster (Pennsylvania) Historical Society*

fields, the usual custom being to outfit only the lead pair with bells. When the signal was given the leaders by a jerk on the line, they stamped their feet, causing their bells to ring. Then all the other horses (or mules) in the team would start pulling together. Later, when the harvest was ready for market, the same harvester team would be hitched to a long wagon. Once more, at a signal on the jerk line, the leaders would stamp their feet, ring their bells, and start their companions pulling together for the long haul to market—at the tedious pace of perhaps three miles an hour.

Team bells and wagon freighters—the two appeared and disappeared concurrently as the times dictated. In 1852 the Pennsylvania Railroad opened its first line between Philadelphia and Pittsburgh. This of course foreshadowed the inevitable, the use of trains, not wagons, for hauling heavy freight. As the end of the freighter era loomed closer, the sound of the big freighters' bells grew fainter, until it vanished almost entirely.

Many of the five-harp sets were broken up, for there was still a ready market for one or two harps to use on a single horse, or on a lead pair in the West where freighting and harvester teams were still common. Fortunately some sets were kept intact, out of either sentiment or a realization of their unique association with Revolutionary colonial times. Usually, such full sets as remain are seen in museums, although in rare instances privately owned sets come on the market. At least five private sales within the past quarter-century have been recorded.

Such harvester outfits as this, with its four men and twenty-six mules, could head and thresh forty bushels of wheat a day. The two lead mules wear an especially fine pair of fur-wrapped arches, each with five bells. *Oregon Historical Society, W. A. Raymond Photo*

A jerk-line mule team, 1911, Stockton, California. The leader wears hame bells. *James F. Cooper*

If it is next to impossible to hear Conestoga bells as they once were heard, it is still possible to capture mentally the color and sound of an old wagoning scene by reading a descriptive account based on personal recollection. "Buttin' Blood," a story by Pernet Patterson, provides one such scene that was typical over a wide area of southern tobacco farmlands:

> The drivers sat silent, swaying to the pitch and roll as the wheels lurched from rut to rut. First was Adam's four-mule team—rugged, powerful animals with four thousand pounds of tobacco behind them in the canvas-topped, scow-shaped wagon. Other wagons of all shapes and sizes waited at the crossroads to join the train, stringing out like a fleet of ships along the road to Richmond. Red, brass-mounted cowtail tassels swayed and sparkled from the headstalls of all the big lead animals guiding their ponderous wagons. Brass bells rang comfortingly from their hames, warning on the sharp down grades, awakening shrill echoes from the woodlands. Clattering into Richmond over the ancient cobble-stone streets, their bells bobbing, the mules almost galloped until they reached the wagon yard. With the journey nearly over, the drivers lolled in their saddles, joining together in the time-honored refrain of the tobacco train song:

> > "Car' my 'ba-ac-ca down,
> > Car' my 'ba-ac-ca down,
> > Car'y it down Richmon' town,
> > Car' my 'bacca down."

123

7

LORE OF OUR LAND IN BELLS

Older nations may claim a far greater store of bell lore than can be found in the United States. Nonetheless, for a relatively young nation, the range of historic lore found in our bells is surprisingly wide and varied. Some of the anecdotes, though colorfully told, are based on fact; others are more legendary. Some are known here, there, and everywhere that bell lore is mentioned; others, usually some of the more curious, are known largely to local folk.

A few quotations from American folklore will illustrate the "here, there, and everywhere" tendency of the nation's forefathers to rely on bells as weather prophets:

> Vibrations of tolling bells are fancied as being able to cause rain.
> —*California Folklore Quarterly*
> volume IV, page 27

> Shepherds recognize that it is going to rain by any change in the sound of the bells on their sheep.
> —Wyoming wanagon lore

> If bells are heard more plainly than usual on a windless day, rain will follow.
> —Ozark folklore in *Blum's Almanac*, 1833, page 34

> If loudly sounds the distant bell
> A coming rain it does foretell.
> —Alabama folklore

Farmers over an area of twenty-five miles used the church bell for telling wind direction; by the tone of the bell they could predict the morrow's weather.

—An old New England belief

Tales of belling a buzzard were not uncommon across the southern states a century ago, reflecting a bucolic wit characteristic of a less sophisticated age. Wherever the stories were told, they focused strongly on the superstitious beliefs of those who could never actually place the eerie airborne tinkling but who could hear it from time to time and interpreted it as an ill omen. Superstition, incidentally, accounts for much of the more curious lore of bells, even in the present enlightened age. Otherwise, how can the actions of the city fathers in French Lick, Indiana, be accounted for? In 1939 they revived what can only be considered a law grounded in superstitution, requiring black cats to be belled on each Friday the thirteenth!

One version of "belling a buzzard" was reported in the Sherman, Texas, *Daily Register*, March 28, 1888, thus ending a quarter century of rumor:

For the last twenty-four years people living in different parts of the South have heard strange tinklings of a bell, frequently in the most unaccountable places. At times the ringing seemed to be far off in space and then again it would seem to hover near. Great fear had been excited among the superstitious, who feared the tolling was heralding a great disaster. The real cause of this disturbance was found to be a buzzard of enormous size upon whose neck a bell was fastened and which gave a tinkling sound every time the bird flapped its wings. The buzzard made its appearance in many parts of the South, always returning to Tennessee, where it had probably been raised. Last week while Alex Johnson of Preachers Mills neighborhood was hunting he came upon what he thought was a huge eagle flipping and fluttering upon the ground. He raised his gun and fired, and the monster bird fell, beating the ground fiercely with its wings. Johnson dashed up just as the wings gave the last flutter and saw to his astonishment a bell suspended by a small wire chain of which some links had been worn almost to the thinness of paper. The clapper was missing, accounting for the fact that the buzzard had not been heard for several months. On the bell was written C. W. MOORE, ALABAMA, 1863. The bird measured five feet seven inches from tip to tip. It will be presented to the Historical Society of Nashville, there to be mounted and kept as one of the greatest curiosities of [the] state.

The lad whose name was inscribed on the bell was Charles W. Moore of Sherman, Texas, who as a soldier in the Confederate Army had captured the buzzard and attached the bell. Whatever macabre pleasure Moore derived from his prank, no one knows; but the many rumors resulted in so much publicity over the years that no less a person than the president of the National Audubon Society was moved to write a fictitious tale "The Bell Buzzard"; "[its] dreaded ringing meant death to anyone who heard its chimes."

Horse-in-the-belfry stories, too, are rather common in America's parcel of humorous bell lore. It is humor after the fact, however, that highlights a Georgia ver-

125

sion, where the motive in hoisting a horse into a belfry was wholly serious. As related in several sources, smugglers were to beach contraband on the southernmost coast of Georgia in 1812. The problem was how to evade or, better yet, divert the attention of revenue officers. Gazing ashore, pondering their problem, the smugglers were suddenly inspired to further their plans by using the tallest landmark around, the belfry of the Presbyterian Church in Saint Mary's. Luck was with these feckless fellows when they found that the Presbyterian pastor kept his horse nearby. It was only a matter of waiting for nightfall before the horse was prodded and pushed up into the small belfry, where he was tied in sly fashion so he would not set the bell to ringing.

The next morning the hapless horse, enjoying his lofty view, was the only calm creature in Saint Mary's. The entire population was agog—speculating, grumbling, or laughing, each according to his nature. All were so busy trying to free the horse that they (and this included the revenue officers) did not realize they had been hoodwinked. By the time the truth was known, the smugglers were far out at sea again.

Bells have influenced the names of many places and structures around the country, with usually a dollop of local history underlying such names as Ding Dong, Texas, or Jingle Bells, Florida. Overlooking the village of Truro out on Cape Cod is the Hill of Churches, where in 1826 the Methodists were first to erect a church. Next came the "orthodox," who erected a larger church with an important-sounding bell. Their structure was later known as Bell Meeting House because of a legend claiming the bell could still be heard ringing mysteriously even after the building was deserted. Old Saint David's Church in the little town of Cheraw, South Carolina, was for many years called The Old Bell Church. Completed in 1774, it did not boast a steeple and bell until 1826. Even at that late date, this was the only church bell in the whole countryside around.

When a famous bell vanishes for one reason or another, its tongue sometimes remains to assume a share of the importance formerly attached to the bell itself. The bell that summoned the minutemen to Lexington Green on that fateful morning of April 19, 1775, has long been gone, but its tongue is a proud possession of the Lexington Historical Society—the same tongue that gave voice to the bell just hours before the first gunfire of the American Revolution. When a large Chicago collection of bells went on sale some years ago, many buyers competed for the mighty tongue of the old Chicago Courthouse tocsin that had knelled the Great Chicago Fire. In a far different instance, there might be misgivings about preserving the tongue of a bell that spelled the epitaph of a young man named Amasa Brainard, Jr. As he entered a sanctuary for services on Sunday, "Ye 22nd of Apl, 1798," he received a mortal wound from the church bell's hurtling down onto his head before crashing to the ground. The accident is duly recorded on a lichen-covered tombstone in a Connecticut cemetery.

Unexpected sounds and melodies from bells in a community give rise to humorous stories of purely local interest. Townsfolk in Amherst, Massachusetts, were for years fond of reminiscing about one of their favorite citizens, Squire Dickinson, father of the poet Emily Dickinson. He was treasurer of Amherst College, a state senator, and altogether a pillar of the community. The squire was also a staid gentleman, a stern Calvinist who would never tolerate frivolity in a house of worship. Even so, his behavior was unseemly on the one occasion when, overcome with the beauty of an Aurora Borealis, he rushed to his church and began agitating the bells to call attention to the brilliant display in the sky.

Gates Mill, Ohio, residents were surprised one evening to hear the popular tune "A Hot Time in the Old Town Tonight" issuing from their church chimes. The assistant chimist was said to be a whimsical fellow, and as the hunt club across from the church burst into flames, his whimsical nature overrode his good judgment. The following day he found himself removed from the church payroll. The sixteen-bell chime of Grace Church, Providence, Rhode Island, has been known to cause consternation among listeners—but not because of any unscheduled performance. Traditionally this set of chimes plays Brown University's Alma Mater on the afternoon of each commencement day, and some listeners do not realize the chimes are playing the university's Alma Mater and not "The Old Oaken Bucket." The tunes are the same. Reputedly, one newly installed rector "nearly fell flat on his face" the first time he heard "The Old Oaken Bucket" sounding from the steeple.

All these little pieces of bell lore verge on the ephemeral; but there are other areas of more substantial significance as, for example, the question of whether the silvery tones some bells boast can be attributed to their silver content. Scientifically, silver contributes nothing to the tone of a bell. On the contrary, as has already been explained, it deadens the tone, and there has not been a bellmaker within modern times who would claim otherwise. Nonetheless, legends telling of silver being tossed into molten bell metal are too prevalent to dismiss in a cursory manner, though some metallurgists scoff at the idea as mere scuttlebutt. To cite but three of dozens upon dozens of similar stories: there are people still living in Cincinnati who recall seeing citizens arrive at the Vanduzen Foundry clutching silver dollars to be thrown into the pot from which the monstrous de Sales bell would be cast. In documenting Texas bells, Mrs. Fitzhugh tells of a foundryman who for sentimental reasons reclaimed a little steamboat bell, and together with fifty silver dollars sent it to be recast in New Orleans in 1860.

This silver syndrome reaches Bunyanesque proportions in a bell to be seen at Cairo, Illinois, supposedly cast from one thousand silver dollars. It was originally used on the *James Montgomery*, a Civil War troop transport ship, then later presented to Cairo's Episcopal Church. In 1872, when it was recast, 100 pure silver bars were sent by the governor of the Arizona Territory to add to the original metals. Interestingly enough, the bell has the poorest tone possible, proof that the greater the silver content the poorer the tone. As Chester Meneely once pointed out, however, a minor amount of silver does not affect the tone one way or the other; and on some occasions it has proved next to impossible to deny a request for tossing in a token amount of silver, especially when the request came from a bell donor, who clung to the legendary idea. An instance of such a request came about in 1867, when a director of the Lackawanna Railroad insisted on dropping twenty-eight bright new "cartwheels" into the metal for a bell being cast to put on an engine bearing his name. The bell had a rich, clear tone and took a mighty polish, according to Joseph Bromley, fireman at that time.

Probably the most intriguing of all tales about a bell cast from donated coins concerns one that rang amidst the barbed wire fences of a Civil War camp. Designed as the northern Illinois headquarters for drilling and mobilizing troops, the camp was built on the grounds of Senator Douglas's estate and named in his honor.

127

(This, of course, was Stephen A. Douglas, Abraham Lincoln's famous political opponent.) Later the camp became one of the most noted military prisons of the North, with as many as 5,000 Confederates imprisoned at one time, along with some Union soldiers. It was about 1863 when the prison chaplain established a chapel on the grounds, where services continued to the end of the war. One of the chapel's prized possessions was a bell the chaplain managed to have cast from copper and silver coins contributed by Camp Douglas prisoners of both the Blue and the Gray, as well as by the garrison.

This bell was cast by an ordnance firm that is all but forgotten now, but which ranked as one of the major producers of arms and ammunition for this country and nations around the world. The Ames Company of Chicopee, Massachusetts, began in 1834 with the manufacture of swords and sabres, including presentation swords for Generals Ulysses S. Grant and Zachary Taylor. Arms were not the firm's only concern. It cast bronze statues, fixtures, bells, and even the famous bronze doors for the east-west wings in the nation's Capitol. Many of its bells were for public buildings, notably the city hall in New York City. After the Civil War, the Ames Company encountered problems in finding peacetime business for its huge operations. The two Ames brothers resorted to making skates, mailboxes, and other small specialties, but eventually they had to abandon their impressive chain of buildings along the canal in Chicopee Center.

Despite the excellent documentation the Chicago Historical Society has on the Camp Douglas bell, now in storage at the society, there are those who question the traditional tale of its being cast from so many coins. Be that as it may, Saint Mark's Episcopal Church in Chicago, which was granted custody of the bell by the War Department when peace came, did considerable research on its history. As one rector concluded, even if the money collected from Union and Confederate men was used only to *buy* the bell, this relic is still a historically significant link between North and South.

Being primarily attracted by the sounds of bells, most persons—even students of the subject—have neglected the functionaries who kept them ringing, that is, until the I. T. Verdin Company began electrifying them all. A few, like Robert Newman and Andrew McNair of Revolutionary times, had history-book fame thrust upon them, but the majority are little remembered unless fortunate enough to have merited some special recognition locally.

Newman was the sexton at Christ (Old North) Church in Boston, a position not likely to have immortalized his name had he not been chosen to hang the one-if-by-land-two-if-by-sea lanterns in the church belfry that night of April 18, 1775. Though not overly fond of his work, which he had taken because, as he said, "times are so hard," Newman was a conscientious young chap, making him Paul Revere's logical choice for placing the lanterns. He knew the dusty belfrey so well he could climb up among the bells in the darkness without accidentally knocking one, thereby giving away his mission to the British forces. As sexton, he not only held the keys to the church but also lived conveniently close, directly across the street.

After escaping through his bedroom window, Newman dropped to the street below, where Revere waited to give him his instructions. By prearrangement, Revere was to start crossing the Charles River to alarm citizens in Charlestown, then ride on to spread alarms in Lexington and Concord, where leading patriots Samuel

An annual Lantern Service commemorates this Boston scene from the night of April 18, 1775, when Sexton Robert Newman climbed up into the belfry of Old North Church to place two lanterns in the window. His "two if by sea" signal meant the British were sighted boarding barges to cross the river. *Revere Copper and Brass, Incorporated*

Adams and John Hancock were staying. Newman, meanwhile, was to observe the British approach from the belfry and signal across the river with his lanterns accordingly: one if they came by land, two if they came by sea. Should Paul Revere fail to make his crossing safely, the signal would alert Charlestown. Stealthily Newman mounted the 154 winding steps into the bell loft, crept carefully past the eight bells to show his pair of lanterns in the highest window. It was a dangerous mission, he knew, and despite his cautious movements he was later clapped into jail on suspicion of hanging the lanterns.

Andrew McNair attained his greatest measure of fame on the morning of July 8, 1776, when Philadelphia Sheriff Thomas Dowees instructed him to ascend the State House tower and ring what is now known as the Liberty Bell. McNair was official bell ringer at the State House, as well as doorkeeper.

Traditionally the post of bell ringer is a solitary one, except where change ringing is involved, but in the case of a uniquely patriotic group in Philadelphia there is a certain fraternal association. Appropriately named The Independence Hall Ringers Society, the group was organized in 1950, under the direction of Carroll Frey, to revive an old tradition of ringing the bell in the open clock tower of Independence Hall on certain special days. Only men were permitted membership until the summer of 1974, when the first woman was granted full status in this select group of thirteen, representing the original colonies.

The responsibilities of salaried bell ringers are ordinarily rather routine, but in times of impending danger they are full of risk, and in times of great rejoicing they became noticeably important. During the Great Chicago Fire, the Cook County Courthouse bell ringer continued clanging his alarm across the city until the huge bell fell from the tower. His faithfulness in staying at his post while flames lapped closer by the minute is typical of ringers' traditional devotion to duty. Declarations of peace have always brought the pealing of bells into prominence, sometimes giving the man tugging the rope a niche in history. The *Keosauqua* (Iowa) *Republican* of December 5, 1918 paid front-page tribute to L. C. Fleak, elevating his name to a certain lasting prominence in Iowa history as the most enduring of the state's ringers.

They have a historic old bell at Brighton, Washington County, as well as a historic bell ringer, according to the following news item:

"When news of Germany's capitulation reached Brighton, one of the first bells to give tongue to the glad tidings was the old Fleak house bell, and the ringer was L. C. Fleak who has rung the same bell when victory has crowned the efforts of the Yankee armies in three wars. When victory came to the Union at Appomattox, Mr. Fleak helped spread the news with the Fleak house bell. He again rang it joyfully at the close of the Spanish-American War and again on November 11th. Before him his father rang the same bell when word came of the destruction of the Mormon temple at Nauvoo, Ill."

It was a church centennial in 1946 that spotlighted Conrad Spiegel, who kept the quarters, halves, and hours ringing from the tower in Saint Mary's, the oldest church in Milwaukee, Wisconsin. Named Mary, Anna, and Mary Magdalene, the three bells in the tower were cast a century ago in Cincinnati, then attached to a rare clock from Munich. It was Conrad Spiegel's task, as sexton, to climb the tower morning and evening to wind the clock, also oversee the bells when necessary, thus keeping Milwaukee's timepieces correct. Everyone in the city depended on him for the right time. The *Milwaukee Journal* once reported:

> You can safely bet that there is scarcely a person in Milwaukee who can tell exactly what the bells of St. Mary's do on the hour. Money has been lost and won on the venture. The fact is, the bells ring four for the last quarter and then ring the hour, not once but twice. "That is so that if people miss the hour the first time, they will get it the second time," says Father Grelinger.

In the present age of automation, there are hundreds of people who have heard only the mechanical ringing of bells. They have no realization of the great differences in tonal quality between manual ringing and mechanical ringing. Inevitably, manual ringing is becoming a thing of the past; but by taking the work out of ringing, automatic devices are at least keeping many old bells in service. In fact, according to the I. T. Verdin Company, which electrifies most, if not all, of the nation's bells, electrification has even put back into service many bells long silent for lack of human ringers. Admittedly, the posts of bell ringers would be difficult to fill nowadays.

John F. Allen, now retired, was for years the faithful sexton and bell ringer for First Unitarian Church of Providence, Rhode Island. As such, he had in his care a very special 1816 Revere bell of exactly the same weight as the one in King's Chapel, thereby making it one of the two largest ever cast by Paul Revere. *First Unitarian Church of Providence, Rhode Island*

In the late 1950s, a Verdin robot took over the 2½-ton bell in Harvard College Memorial Church so that it now booms across the yard without a helping hand. But for 311 years, starting in 1643, someone always pulled a rope to sound the bell calling students to chapel or to classes. For fifty of those years the rope was in the hands of Austin Kingsley Jones, or "Old Jones," as he was affectionately called. He was a man of standing on campus, friend of four presidents, confidant of generations of students, but his fondest reminiscences were always about "his" bell. When Old Jones resigned in 1908, he was presented a sheepskin stating that during his fifty years of almost errorless ringing and honorable service he was "an example of fidelity and punctuality to all members of the University."

Arthur Conant was a highly satisfactory successor to Old Jones and became equally skilled as well as knowledgable about his task. He too prided himself on punctuality, once commenting:

> I ring on the hour and the minute, and as far as possible on the second. . . . I've been on the job going on thirteen years, never missed a day, and never had a complaint on the bell being wrong. Two-thirds of the students and professors come to me for the right time, and most of the clocks in the square are set by the bell.

Like his predecessor, Conant was very professional about his techniques in ringing and enjoyed explaining their intricacies. He kept the hourly bell striking for a full minute; the Sunday chapel bell, for three minutes; and on the seven o'clock morning chapel bell he used an old English stroke unique to Harvard from the day the university was founded. "It took me three months of practice with the bell padded with rags to learn that stroke," he said, elaborating still further:

> First I ring it a few times to get it swinging. Then when it reaches the point where it is almost upside down but doesn't quite go over, I hold it there for ten seconds. I let it ring three times, and then hold on the other side for ten seconds, keeping this up for five minutes. I do all this by giving the rope exactly the right pull.

Obviously such pealing can in no way be achieved by the automated ringing of bells in a fixed position, their clappers hitting repeatedly in exactly the same spots.

William and Mary College of Williamsburg, Virginia, has a legacy in Henry Billups, the venerable black bell ringer, mail carrier, and general factotum, who came to the campus in 1888 when there was only one building and remained to "ring in" five college presidents during his more than sixty-five years of service. After the first forty-five of those years, he was never seen without a small gold bell dangling from his vest. It was his fondest possession, the gift of alumni who recalled being summoned to class by the genial bell ringer.

Such college bells and their ringers may have been venerated, but at the same time both were at the mercy of campus pranksters. One joke that always filled students with glee was to prod a horse or a cow into the campus belfry, tie his tail to the tongue of the bell, then await its erratic ringing with every switch of the tail. A less troublesome prank was to steal the tongue of the bell, thus silencing the call to classes and chapel. This widely popular stunt kept administrators busy playing clapper-clapper-who-has-the-clapper. Somehow those at Princeton seemed to play it most frequently, for each year they were forced to order clapper replacements from Meneely's, who had cast the bell. Meneely's did not object to the business, but, thinking it only fair to save a good customer money, devised a method of making the clapper unstealable. Imagine their consternation upon receiving a note from Princeton's dean asking to return the new type tongues in exchange for one dozen of the old stealable type! Princeton's reverence for campus tradition, so said the dean, outweighed any objection to the cost of replacing clappers by the dozen.

Dulcet tones from a carillon sing over the University of Michigan now, in wide contrast to the harsher farm-style tones from a post bell that dominated the scene in the 1840s. This post bell was the university's sole timepiece and also appeared to be the sole target for pranksters, who found their recreational outlets rather limited. The Reverend Theodoric R. Palmer, who entered Michigan in 1843, later recalled the farmlike campus with its turnstile entrance that afterward gave way to posts with room enough between for a man but not a cow. As to the bell:

> Time went according to a bell mounted on a post at the rear, which seemed to have been a prolific source of student humor. It was turned upside down in winter and filled with water, with a corresponding vacation the following morning; the clapper was stolen; and finally in Dr. Tappan's day it was even carried away, post and all. The President, however, was a match for the jokers and simply announced that as the bell was a convenience which the students did not seem to need, classes would be held henceforth without the usual call. As the regulations were very strict as to attendance and four unexcused absences a matter for the higher powers, it was not long before a student arose in Chapel and requested permission to reinstate the Campus timepiece—which was graciously accepted.

Skulduggery of that sort was singularly lacking at Yale University—and unfortunately so, according to one wag, for the chapel bell at Yale was described as "about as good a bell as a fur cap with a sheep's tail for a clapper." But whatever skulduggery Yale lacked, Harvard had in good measure. There an early clock bell in one of the university towers began performing in a most unusual manner. It struck thirteen times at noon, though at midnight it was content to strike the customary twelve times. Clockmakers were called in to examine the mechanisms. They could find nothing wrong, so the perplexing matter went unsolved until one day the culprit responsible was caught in the act. He was a student living on one of the upper floors in a house nearby. Each noontime he sat at the window of his room with a rifle. When the clock struck twelve, with perfect timing the student pulled the trigger to create the thirteenth stroke on the bell.

There was a time on certain campuses when a student could earn a scholarship in return for serving as bell ringer. At Wofford College in Spartanburg, South Carolina, he could earn yearly tuition by making twelve trips daily to the main building, there tugging ten times on the long rope fastened to Wofford's historic bell—a daily total of 120 tugs, averaging out at about two cents each. Of recent years the scholarship has been discontinued; but the bell, cast by Meneely's in 1854, still sounds across the campus from its massive hand-hewn oak timbers that were erected long ago by slave labor.

Until 1959, student ringers kept alive the sound of a fine, storied Caughlan bell in the classic chapel at McKendree College, Lebanon, Illinois. When the clock tower above the chapel was removed in 1959, never to be replaced, a century of pealing was brought to a close with the bell's retirement. Originally found as a Spanish relic in an abandoned Indian mission in New Mexico, it was taken to Saint Louis, where it was recast by David Caughlan, then put on exhibit at the Illinois State Fair in 1858. An account of the fair states that throughout the sessions the bell was kept pealing by visitors testing its superb tone. One of those visitors was the president of McKendree. He too tested the bell, admired it, and promptly bought it for the new college chapel, where it rang for classes and commencements, helped celebrate athletic victories, listened to the clockwinder complain as he worked in the cold, even witnessed a death in the belfry in 1938: a bolt of lightning glanced from the bell and killed one of the first black students on campus. The victim, with another student, was in the tower trying to smoke out a swarm of bees gathered there.

The bell's last important mission before retirement was its fund-raising campaign aboard a truck. It traveled with the blessings of alumni and friends who were hopeful of raising funds sufficient to rebuild the chapel tower. That was not to be, however.

Elsewhere in academic settings there have been other bells well cast, sonorous, closely associated with campus life, each the center of anecdotes long remembered by faculty as well as alumni. More often than not these have been allied with the school's athletic triumphs. The victory song at Weslyan University, Middletown, Connecticut, is "Ring the Bells at Old South College," which has made famous the school's Mears and Stainbank bells given in 1918 by the class of 1863. Less well

McKendree College Chapel (1856-1959) stood as an example of late classical architecture. It was for the stately steeple on this new building that the president of the college purchased a bell cast by David Caughlan in 1858. Chapel, steeple, and bell have all three disappeared from use today. *McKendree College*

One of the very few Caughlan-cast bells thus far located, as it appeared while still in service in the steeple of McKendree College Chapel at Lebanon, Illinois. *McKendree College*

known, but of historical importance because of their limited production, is a Veazy and White bell hanging in Weslyan's chapel. It was cast in East Hampton some-time prior to 1882, when the firm sold out to the Starr Brothers.

Vanderbilt University and Georgia Tech for years had, as an unofficial gridiron trophy, a colorful cowbell that never saw a cow. As intended by the donor and original owner, E. F. Cavaleri, its sound urged many a team to victory whenever the two colleges met on the gridiron. Between meets it served as a traveling trophy kept by the winning team until the next (usually annual) contest—somewhat like

RING THE BELLS OF OLD SOUTH COLLEGE

ANON.   Music by P. P. BLISS

The victory song of Wesleyan University often played on the school's Mears and Stainbank bells. *Wesleyan University, Middletown, Connecticut*

the Big Ten's little brown jug. Students from both colleges twice resorted to theft to possess the trophy. Cavaleri said he thought the bell was gone for good after the 1935 game in Atlanta. "I'd just left the stadium and was taking the bell along to have the scores added. On a side street two fellows jumped me." The bell did not return until it was time for the 1937 game. Apparently conscience-stricken upon hearing a radio plea for its return, two Georgia Tech students confessed to having stolen it.

Cavaleri never attended either college, but, being a football enthusiast, he purchased the big cowbell "just for noise and fun" before the 1924 game. When someone suggested the winner should gain possession, Cavaleri liked the idea and enlarged on it by having the colleges' colors painted on either side—gold and white on one side for Georgia Tech, gold and black on the other for Vanderbilt. Scores and dates were painted over the colors, year by year. Except for gaps in scheduling, they extended from the late 1920s to the early '60s, when all spaces on the bell were filled.

With their archives to preserve such anecdotes, universities have an advantage over secondary and elementary schools. Yet the news media, school administrators, patriotic groups—all are becoming more conscious of the heritage enveloping many early school bells. As belfried schoolhouses of yesterday are demolished to make way for sleekly designed new ones, a fair number of bells are being rescued to be placed as mementos somewhere on the grounds of the new structures.

The *Cedar Falls* (Iowa) *Record* of April 2, 1940, found that an eighty-seven-year-old elementary-school bell in that town had been the first schoolhouse bell west of the Mississippi. Research revealed it had been bought by women of the community in 1853, with funds raised at a festival. When it was to be cast aside about 1900, the president of the school board convinced the other members they should buy it as a matter of historic preservation. Mr. Humbert was more convincing than he knew, the *Cedar Falls Record* reported, for the board not only purchased the bell, but with an appropriate bronze marker placed it at a new school eventually to be named after their foresighted president. If Cedar Falls residents could no longer hear it, they could at least view it as a tangible "first" in their city's history.

Probably the earliest type of primary school bell known in America. Mrs. A. S. C. Forbes made copies like this from one used at an Indian school in a Spanish mission. *Drawing by Dorothy Cole*

The bell in a little schoolhouse at California, Ohio, had been silent since that first Armistice Day following the First World War. When the building was to be converted to other purposes in the 1950s, Indian Hills chapter of the Daughters of the American Revolution had the bell cleaned and tested. Its tone was still mellow. As a result, it hangs now in beautiful Indian Hills Church as a memorial to Senator Robert A. Taft, who is buried in the church cemetery. When it was cast by the Vanduzen Foundry in 1871, it cost approximately $75; the same size today would cost more than $1,000. Along with the politically elite attending the rededication of the bell in its new role were the family who had donated the schoolhouse property prior to the Civil War (as well as the bell itself), a gentleman who at age six had begun his education in the little school the day it opened, and the wife of a Vanduzen employee who had helped cast the piece in 1871.

Bells in Hand

Among myriads of types cast, the simple handbell with its well-worn wooden handle was the most ubiquitous of all, for obvious reasons: it was far-reaching in tone, convenient to ring, easily totable. A recital of its varied uses would seem endless. It became so much a fixture on the rural schoolma'am's desk as to be almost symbolic of her position. A town crier could not function without one; its lusty jingle-jangle was invaluable to the street hawker wanting to advertise his presence in a neighborhood.

Many a great or near-great personality has owned a handbell that even years later seems almost synonymous with his role in life. The sound of one vigorously rung became Alexander Woollcott's signature on his "Town Crier" radio program in the 1930s. Brigham Young's household prayer bell was a large one of this type with a natural wood handle. It is exhibited with other memorabilia at the Mormon Temple Square Museum in Salt Lake City. A widely known Virginia auctioneer used a sturdy brass handbell formerly rung by Mrs. Mary Washington, mother of the first President. Lacking a post bell at Ferry Farm, where George spent his boyhood, his mother used this to call field workers. Later acquiring it for himself, N. B. Kensey used it for over forty years to summon bidders to his famous sales, never conducting one without it. Rather than have it pass into other hands, Mr. Kensey asked to have it placed in his casket, a wish that his family granted.

The colonial town crier admitted to a fondness for ringing his bell—its strident voice carried even farther than his own familiar "Oyez! Oyez! Oyez!" (Hear Ye! Hear Ye! Hear Ye!). Thus he assured himself of a large audience. Always it was an attentive one, too, for he was the colonists' only source of news and his pronouncements carried importance. Wistfully Nathaniel Hawthorne once exclaimed, "Who of all that address the public eye, whether in church or court house, or hall or state, has such an attentive audience." It is safe to assume that large audiences everywhere awaited colonial town criers on the morning of April 19, 1775. In the once fabulous collection of bells assembled for display at Mission Inn, Riverside, California, there was an uncommonly large handbell that had been used that morning to assemble the citizenry of New Bedford, Massachusetts.

Another authentically significant town crier's bell is preserved at Williams-

The handbell was a fixture on the desk of every rural schoolteacher.

YE COLONIAL CRYAR

Colonial town criers apparently felt their importance: they were the colonists' sole source of news.

In March 1666, the "town of Boston" voted that two town criers were necessary "to crie lost or found Goods." Each was to be paid six pennies for "cryinge three publique days."

burg, Virginia. When plans were being formulated for the first Williamsburg Award, the trustees sought an appropriate symbol to accompany the monetary gift to be presented. They chose a hand-forged replica of this colonial original, so emblematic of a peoples' vigilance in defense of their liberties, as the trustees expressed it. The replica passed to appreciative hands, for the recipient was none other than Winston Churchill, then the most vigorously eloquent living champion of liberty and justice.

At times, gathering a wide audience became a practical matter of good busi-

Winthrop Rockefeller, then chairman of Colonial Williamsburg boards, presenting the first Williamsburg Award Town Crier's bell to Sir Winston Churchill. The ceremonies were held in Drapers' Hall, London, December 7, 1955. *Colonial Williamsburg Press Bureau*

ness for the town crier. In Spanish Texas a handbell was customarily used in auctioning property. The sale was announced publicly by the crier, who clanged his bell for nine days while "crying the wares." Then, as prescribed by law, followed a "crying of the sale" for three days. Finally, on the third day, the goods were auctioned.

The post of night watchman, like that of town crier, was a paid, highly respected one, though the pay was small. One shilling per night was the common rate. In some New England colonies the post carried the more elegant title of "bellman," but the rate of pay remained about the same; and, regardless of his cognomen, whoever filled the post was expected to watch for thieves, fires, or other disorders. Not finding anything amiss, he would ring his all-is-well each hour. Any who wakened to the sound might hear him sing out the hour in rhyming couplets of his own composition perhaps. For example:

"Hear, Brethren, Hear! The hour of nine has come.
Keep pure each heart and chasten every home."

or

"The clock is six and from the watch I'm free;
And every one may his own watchman be."

When any news of great importance needed reporting, the watchman turned town crier, temporarily abandoning his habitual dingdong, singsong rhythms. One October night in 1781, when the colonists were desperate because victory over the British seemed hopeless, sleeping Philadelphians were awakened by an old German watchman trudging along banging his bell and yelling at the top of his leathery lungs, "Basht dree o'glock, basht dree o'glock and Gornvallis ish dakendt!"

Ringing the curfew was often the responsibility of either the town crier or the night watchman, using their handbells, especially in communities having no town bell. Otherwise curfew was customarily sounded by the official town ringer. Its sound, like the crier's and the watchman's bells, was a familiar one from the Old World, the laws governing it varying but slightly from place to place. Basically, curfews warned citizens to be off the streets, inside their houses for the night. Sometimes there were several bylaws, as in eighteenth-century Dorchester, Massachusetts. Here one bylaw read, "Constables are to take up loose people who do not heed the ringing of the nine o'clock bell." Another required that the town bell ringer, besides sounding the nine o'clock curfew each evening, should also toll the day of the month—an extra duty to which the ringer roundly objected.

Pre-Civil War Charleston, South Carolina, had a rather involved system of curfew. Two bells were rung each evening at eight and ten o'clock in the summer but at seven and nine o'clock in winter. The first signaled all children to get to bed; the second signaled the night watch to assemble, and after that no servant might step outside his master's house without a special permit.

A brief, unsuccessful revival of curfew principles came about in present-day America during the confused '50s and '60s. Many communities saw in the idea a deterrent to rising crime. Whatever potential the idea may have held was never fully realized. Communities found that the commanding effect the curfew once had could never be widely duplicated in this permissive age. It is a sound that is, except in times of strife, forever a part of the past.

The whole galaxy of perambulating merchants so dear to yesterday's child also maintained a close affinity with their bells. One and all, they held to the notion of adding the call of a bell to their own cry of "Hot roasted p-e-a-nuts!" or "Fresh v-e-g-e-tables!" Most of those circulating merchants vanished from American neighborhoods years and years ago, though there have been a few comebacks. The Eskimo Pie man with his jolly jingles has proved a worthy successor to the old Hokey Pokey Ice Cream vendor. In some areas the popcorn man is seen again, sometimes with a bell tinkling from the handle of his cart as he pushes along.

So numerous were doorstep vendors in days past that everywhere there are people sure to have fond memories of a favorite among them. One essayist, in writing of his boyhood, recalls the waffle man with his horse-drawn wagon as the aristocrat among street vendors. He roamed the streets in midmorning, just when a

A scene showing a New Orleans milkmaid using a handbell to announce her presence. Circa 1900.

boy began feeling before-lunch hunger pangs. It was pure bliss to run along beside the wagon with its glass windows, peeking at pitchers dripping with sweet syrup or at black waffle irons steaming with tantalizing aromas. Even those who had no pennies to buy eagerly awaited the waffle man because he had a special feature on his cart that fascinated them. That was the bell up on top, not the usual tinkly sort heard on an ice-cream cart but a miniature edition of a locomotive bell connected by a long cord to the horse's bridle. As the horse bobbed its head up and down, the bell sound penetrated the neighborhood. Excited children hurried to run alongside the horse and watch him "play" the bell.

People who grew up in a rural setting like to recall the country peddler, who in one way or another often announced his approach with the sound of bells. In her memoirs, Mary Wilkins Freeman recalls the peddler's cart that visited her girlhood home. Around the top were little handbells, tin cups, cookie cutters, and other small wares suspended like fringe, tinkling with every step Old Dobbin took. No need for that peddler to carry a special bell.

All these different hawkers like the muffin-and-cracker seller, the milkman, the puffed rice popper, the butcher—too many to enumerate—had an option when it came to ringing their way along the streets. They could fasten one or more bells to their wagon or cart, to ring at each turn of the wheels, or they could carry a handbell to dingdong whenever or wherever they pleased. The majority opted for the totable handbell, so it is not surprising that these were made in many sizes, resulting of course in many tones. The effect of such a medley may have created quite a cacophony along crowded city streets, but the hawkers themselves were a friendly, respectful lot with seldom an identity crisis. Each knew his place in the scheme of street-selling.

Among the vendors who opted to fasten bells to their cart, the most commonly remembered sound came from the scissors grinder's bells playing a plaintive three-note cadence. In the lore of doorstep vendors, history will quite likely credit the scissors grinder with being the most enduring of all those who sold services. One of the last to be heard in the Midwest was photographed as recently as 1955. Others, like the umbrella mender, the chimney sweep, or the dustman had already more or less disappeared from America.

Apparently this scissors grinder chose to travel bell-in-hand, carrying his sharpening machine piggyback.

At large houses staffed with servants, these street merchants usually stopped at the servants' quarters to dispense their services or wares. There they must have been vaguely familiar with an entirely different kind of hand-operated bell belonging to a complex wired servant call system. Such sets were installed along the kitchen wall, each bell attached to a fancy pull in some particular room. When a member of the family tugged on a pull, connecting wires activated one particular bell so that servants knew to which room they were being called. Call systems of this description played an important part in the architectural styles and social customs beloved by the elite. Their manufacture and installation provided employment for countless people; and judging from advertisements appearing in eighteenth- as well as nineteenth-century newspapers, the business of installing the apparatus became quite a competitive one.

Among the earliest to advertise was John Elliott, who, like many craftsmen of the period, was skilled in a diversity of trades. Today he is best recalled for his looking glasses and cabinets, yet his advertisements indicate that he took special pride in his trouble-free installations of house bells:

> Imported from London and to be sold by John Elliott, cabinet-maker in Chestnut Street, the corner of Fourth Street, a Neat Assortment of Looking Glasses, viz. Piers, Sconces and Dressing Glasses, Joiners and Sadlers Furniture, Ec. Fine Waisted patterns for Jackets . . . and completely fixes up House bells and Cabbin bells in the neatest and most convenient manner as done at London, with cranks and wires, which are not liable to be put out of order, as those done with pullies. N. B. Said Elliott has on hand a few books, entitled Second Thoughts Concerning War.
>
> —*Pennsylvania Gazette*, December 30, 1756

At a later date, Alexander Smith was likewise advertising in Philadelphia, but in a manner not very flattering to his competition:

> He also hangs bells after a new, best, and least expensive plan, never before made use of. As he has worked in some of the first shops in London, he flatters himself to give satisfaction to those who may be pleased to employ him . . . N. B. As the making of jacks, and hanging Bells has yet been imperfectly performed in this place, he hopes that a little experience of his performance will entitle him to the friendship of his employers . . .
>
> —*Royal Gazette*, September 19, 1778

As the nineteenth century advanced, professional bell hangers became more professional, engaging perhaps in two trades but not twelve. In Baltimore business directories between 1845 and 1850, for example, most of these men identified themselves in only one other trade—as locksmiths. Apparently their work as locksmiths gave them a special technical know-how for installing a central operating system that would ring bells from every room in a house. Many inventive ideas were being patented for improving the operation of all these wires that at first had been left exposed along the walls or ceilings. Eventually patents provided for wires encased in metal tubes that could be hidden in the walls, thus affording much more dependable, louder ringing because there was less risk in tugging hard on a pull.

The results of an even more innovative patent are visible in the kitchen of the Adams family home in Quincy, Massachusetts, where the house bells were preserved as a part of the restoration. A servant of course was attracted by the ringing of any bell, but unless each had its own distinctive tone he must see the bell move in order to know in which room he was needed. At the Adams house a rubber ball was suspended from each spring. The ball continued to swing even when the bell stopped ringing, making it easier for a servant to catch his call if he had been too busy to notice it at first.

Unless they have visited a historic showplace that still has a set of house bells in working order, few people today are aware that such elaborate systems of hand-operated bells even existed. Most of them were ripped out long ago, the bells salvaged to sell individually to collectors, some of whom had no knowledge that their bell on its sturdy spring was once part of a system of servant call bells. Once observed, however, such an operating technique intrigues viewers, much as it did mischievous little boys who lived in houses equipped with similar systems.

Tad Lincoln is the "hero" of the classic story about a mischief-maker creating his own fun with these bells. During his early days in the White House, Tad and some young friends explored from basement to roof, mentally cataloging items of interest. In the attic they found the controls for the manual system of bells scattered through the White House. Before long Tad had sorted over the maze of pulleys and cranks to find the master yoke. By tugging on this with his full might, he rang all the bells at once. They jingle-jangled everywhere, creating utter pandemonium. Doors slammed, clerks scurried about, servants ran back and forth "like ants gone mad." Being an indulgent father, President Lincoln thought it all very amusing and simply said, "I think you had better find Tad."

Gay, beautiful Dolly Madison had her own reason for remembering the bell-pull system in her home, for it may well have saved her life. One evening as she stood before her bedroom mirror, she saw—reflected in it—an Indian gazing at her from behind a screen in the room. Appearing unconcerned, with as little movement as possible she reached beside her mirror to pull the cord of her bedroom bell. Far off in the kitchen the bell rang to summon servants, who managed to persuade the Indian to leave.

From the Quincy homestead in which four generations of the Adams family lived, including two presidents of the United States. Along the kitchen wall hangs a set of house bells, three of which are shown here. If servants failed to hear a bell ring, they could see it as it continued to swing and thereby know which room needed service. *United States Department of the Interior, National Park Service, Adams National Historic Site, Quincy, Massachusetts*

The mistress of a great house was not so concerned over the mechanics of these bells as over decorative pulls to attach to the ceiling wires that stretched to the bells. Had she, for instance, been mistress of Nottoway, a famous New Orleans sugar plantation, she would have needed fifteen pulls. Out of fifty rooms at Nottoway, fifteen connected with the bell system. Made of rich velvet or satin, of damask, linen, or wool, the pulls varied in width from three to five inches, in length from three to five feet (to fall within easy reach of the user). The pull served as a handle, so to speak, but usually its end was ornamented with some easy-to-grasp object like a metal clasp, a tassel, or a glass ornament.

It was the needlework on the pulls that made them decorative, whether it was cross-stitch, crewelwork, petit point, brocading, beading, or some self-created stitchery. In a day when needle art was one of the social graces, younger daughters in a family were often given the task of designing and creating the pulls, so there was considerable personal attachment to them on the part of the family. House bells therefore became unique in that their "handles" were considered far more valuable than the bells themselves. When bells were no longer in use, or in Civil War days when plantation families were forced to flee, at least one bell pull was kept to treasure with other family mementos whenever possible. On the present antiques market a handsome old bell pull brings a far greater price than does the type of bell used with it.

Left
Advertisement from the Baltimore Business Director of 1850. Like his competitors, of whom there were several, Stewart listed some of his other services besides bell hanging.

Right
Decorative bellpulls, showing the various types of "handles" attached to them. *Drawing by Dorothy Cole*

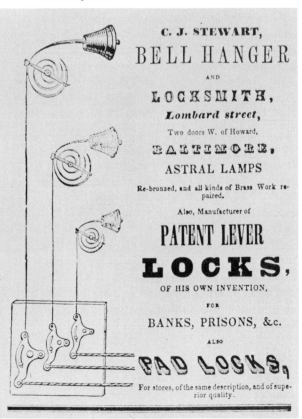

8

THE COLLECTOR'S ROLE

Seeking and sometimes restoring bells from an earlier day, cataloging and, whenever possible, documenting them—all this spells out the obvious role of the collector, one that is being avidly pursued by more than 2,000 individuals from coast to coast. Their interests are far ranging and inclusive, but even the collector with specimens representing many cultures is inclined to favor bells of one certain cultural era or perhaps of one certain type cutting across several cultural eras. For many, this inclination leads to an interest in bells relevant to American social patterns. Some take special pride in finding large tocsins from towers, locomotives, ships; others like to display bells of smaller proportions, representative of any of a multitude of uses: belled objects once a part of religious services; examples of advertising premiums from American business firms; or small bells in the figural likeness of persons prominent on the American scene.

Among all the possibilities is one category that is proving popular now in a day and time when the nation tends to reflect on the way of life of an earlier America. It encompasses bells associated with home and family, especially during the long Victorian era spanning the years from 1830 to 1880. All bells are societal objects, and therein lies a great part of their appeal, but the ones in this category—like the mechanical house bells just described—are always closely identified with a family's domestic social customs. Consider the ornate plated silver table pieces, each with a bell somewhere in its ingenious design. These were indicative of a more leisurely time when, as a matter of course, everyone gathered around a well-set table for an unhurried meal morning, noon, and evening. There were casters, spoon holders, toast 'n' jam racks, and sugar bowls, along with a host of other comparably elegant pieces produced by American silversmiths.

Left

Handsomely cast bell from The Jones and Company Troy Bell Foundry, Troy, New York. Dated 1878, the 1,800-pounder is one of several large examples Mr. Davis keeps on display at his Bell Manor, each completely authenticated. The Jones bell not only called parishioners to the Presbyterian church at Meridian, New York, but for a time also served in a civic capacity as a town bell. *Guy O. Davis Collection*

Right

Rare example of a candle lantern bell, found near the Canadian border in Maine. The other three sides of the lantern are of colorless glass, one pane of which is original. Many church services, such as burials and processions, once required the use of bells as well as candles out of doors, especially in rural areas. Catholic hospitals used such lanterns for the Sisters as they went about the corridors while communion was administered to patients. *Stephen Foster Memorial*

Prices of silver, even plated, have quadrupled two or three times since advertisements such as this appeared in the late 1940s:

> Very unusual Rogers A-1-1878 table bell stand 21" high, lovely base, top toothpick holder one side, vase spoon holder other side, odd push button bell. $7.50.

Nonetheless, regardless of price, silver pieces of this general type are being sought. Usually well marked and dated, they permit the collector to assemble a rewarding fund of information on nineteenth-century American silversmiths.

Production reached an all-time high among dozens of manufacturers centering in Connecticut and Massachusetts. Eventually this nucleus was dominated by the two great houses of Meriden Britannia Company (now International Silver Company) and Reed & Barton, the two vying with each other in producing an unbelievable variety of "combination" pieces incorporating a bell with some utilitarian

Books on life in colonial days tell of church deacons collecting contributions during the middle of the sermon by passing *sacjes*. These were small velvet bags hung on the end of a pole six or eight feet long. Usually there was at least one little bell on the *sacje* that rang when a coin was dropped in. *Private Collection*

Left

Rare desk registry and call bell set from Vanderbilt House, Syracuse, New York, rated the "finest hostelry in Upstate New York, with accommodations for 300. . . ." While Vanderbilt House operated (1870-1913), this registry advertising area merchants reposed on the counter. Front receptacles were for ink and matches. Those at the back held registry slips and advertising fliers. *Guy O. Davis Collection*

Right

An unusually heavy commemorative depicting Samuel Champlain, who in 1609 discovered New York State's scenic Lake Champlain. The bell does not commemorate that event, however, but the tercentenary of Champlain's founding of Quebec one year earlier. The bell bears the dates 1608-1902 along with the name Champlain. *The Mickey Collection*

object. The silver industry might have been highly competitive but it was also supportive: it was common practice for firms to trade parts belonging to pieces in their output. Thus, objects of the same design were shown in different manufacturers' catalogs with only slight modifications. For example, otherwise identical table casters may have a fixed tap bell under the base or on the stem or, perhaps, a free-swing bell hanging from the finial.

The vast majority of combination "bell wares" are found trademarked by the largest manufacturers. One of the pleasures of collecting, however, lies in finding a piece from a less recognized name in the industry. A small, beautifully crafted table caster with its bell midway up the stem seemed for a time to defy identification because its trademark had been partly obliterated when the piece was replated. The caster proved to be the work of R. Gleason and Sons of Dorchester, Massachusetts. Their business was begun by R. Gleason in 1822, listed as a pewterer. After 1850 the firm made mostly plated silver until it closed in 1871. Noted for quality craftsmanship, the Gleasons used as a trademark a convex medallion depicting an American Indian in feathered headdress, holding bow and arrows. The patent date 1859 does not appear with the trademark but is expertly engraved on a silver furl on the stem.

146

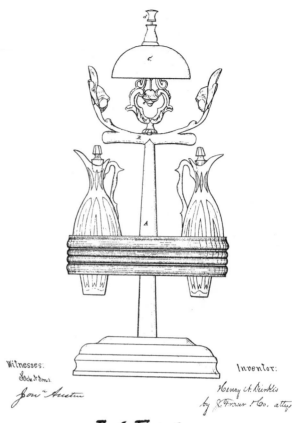

This unusually small early caster with a bell, four bottles, and a salt dip shows the curious trademark used by R. Gleason and Sons of Dorchester, Massachusetts, plus a patent reissue date of 1859. The firm began as a pewter shop in 1822, later becoming noted for fine-quality plated silver between 1850 and 1871, when it closed. *Private Collection*

Above right
According to letters of patent issued for this design in 1860, "the paramount object of my improvement is the protection of the operating mechanism of the bell . . . by arranging the handle directly beneath . . . protecting the bell from . . . having its interior parts hit by the tops of the bottles. . . ." *United States Patent Office*

During the second half of the nineteenth century, the patent office was besieged with innovative ideas for using bells—more than a quarter of all the patents issued were for dual-purpose bells. The unique feature of this "Call-bell and Caster Stand" was a concealed bell that revolved in one direction as the touch rod was depressed, in the other when the rod was released, producing a chime effect. *United States Patent Office*

The practicality of the early Victorians was exceeded only by their love of the ornamental, which explains their admiration for large silver articles on their tables or sideboards. Silver table casters with a complement of five or six bottles for vinegar, oil, mustard, and other condiments were the special delight of every housewife. In vogue from the late 1850s through the 1870s, they were seen in a variety of sizes and designs.

Later other trends developed when the Victorians reversed their priorities. Their practicality began exceeding their fondness for the ornamental, and designs gradually became more classic. Still eminently functional, the articles were less ornate, less ostentatious. Sculptured scrolls, foliage, ribbons, and the like were executed in lower relief, in keeping with the more classical overall lines. The Victorian penchant for silver began taking new directions toward more personal accessories for men and women to use on chiffoniers or dressing tables, many of them with a bell as part of the total design. An elegant three-tier silver holder for the Victorian gentleman's collar and cuffs exemplifies all these later trends. A monogrammed bell swings from the handle, to summon his valet. At intervals around the cylindrical tiers different breeds of hunting dogs peer out from the berried foliage. Just as this place typifies an age that was still unhurried, it typifies also the technical excellence still paramount with manufacturers. The sliding hinged sections are fitted together with precision to move effortlessly.

As the larger ornate pieces of a plated silver service became less fashionable, small sterling tea bells grew in popularity around the turn of the century. Illustrat-

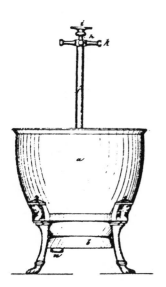
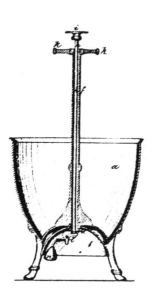

Design for a "slop-bowl or sugar-bowl with bell," to quote from the letters of patent. The slop bowl was used on the table for emptying the dregs from teacups. *United States Patent Office*

Gentleman's three-tier collar-and-cuffs holder in silver, with monogrammed bell for summoning the valet. The knob on the middle tier swings it open. The sheaf-of-wheat feet add grace to the classical lines and delicate detail of this 1880 piece. *Stephen Foster Memorial*

Page from a 1940 catalog illustrating the few traditional-type silver tea bells then being produced. *Samuel Kirk and Sons*

ed catalogs from American silversmiths reflect the demand for these; later they reflect the declining interest. Reed & Barton's catalog of 1900 showed ten different tea bells among their assortment of sterling hollow ware. They were embellished with classical acanthus leaves or with naturalistic floral designs that characterized the Art Nouveau movement then flourishing. These small but elegant sterling table appointments enjoyed a long run of popularity. Samuel Kirk and Son, in their 1940 catalog, still advertised sterling tea bells in four styles, but in their current catalog only two of the four are being shown.

The present mania for rolling back the current view of American culture a century or two is mirrored even in antique buffs' search for babies' gold or silver eating implements and rattles. From colonial days on, many of these were decorated with tiny bells. The most diligent searching nowadays rarely turns up any such charming baubles from the colonial period (most extant examples are family heirlooms or in the keeping of museums), but even an academic interest in them brings to light a fascinating, prestigious group, the colonial gold- and silversmiths. The earliest worked almost exclusively in either New York or Boston, although at a later date cities like Philadelphia or Baltimore, as well as smaller towns, supported scores of silver artisans. All together, 500 are known to have been at work in the colonies at one time or another before the American Revolution—a surprising fact inasmuch as British America produced virtually no silver or gold. Craftsmen were obliged to melt down coins or odd pieces to an acceptable standard of purity. There was no assay office on this side of the Atlantic until 1814, and so each silversmith was duty bound to maintain the customary London standard of 92½ percent; yet not one piece of colonial silver has ever tested below that standard.

149

Stub-type sterling baby rattle of punched silver with mother-of-pearl handle; tentatively attributed to Unger Brothers, Newark, New Jersey. *Private Collection*

Jacobus van der Speigel (1668-1708) fashioned this solid-gold pap spoon for a wealthy New York infant named Jacques de Peyster. Two bells are fastened to the end of the "dog-nosed" spoon. *The Mabel Brady Garvan Collection, Yale University Art Gallery*

Colonial silver rattle with coral handle; unmarked. *Museum of the City of New York*

These were men of probity, eminently gifted. At a time when other decorative arts were scarcely developed, silversmiths were turning out babies' whistle-bells, coral-and-bells, bell-handled spoons, and so on, along with other objects. Such bells served several useful purposes for the colonial infant—amusing him and, as some believed, frightening off evil spirits by their sound. The coral-and-bells carried double indemnity, for to the colonial mind coral itself was imbued with magic. Incidentally, supposedly it was the parents or nursemaids who jingled and whistled such baubles. Experts on the subject question whether infants could have been entrusted with these fairly sharp-edged objects or tiny bells small enough to be swallowed.

Such playthings, of course, were not so important as other items on the silversmith's inventory. Consequently they were produced in limited numbers, primarily for the well-to-do. Famous gold- and silversmiths known to have offered them include one John Hull (1624-1683), who is regarded as the first to learn his art in this country, and also Jacobus Van der Spiegal of the same period. In 1763, Philip Syng, Jr., of Philadelphia offered "a silver gilt whistle and corel with eight bells," and about that time another famous Philadelphia silversmithing family, the Joseph Richardsons, were listing similar objects in their daybooks. In Boston, Paul Revere was one of several making silver rattles and "wisles," for frequently there appeared advertisements of "a very handsome Gold Whistle with Bells and Coral" made by silver craftsmen in the city. In New York, Daniel Christain Fueter made exquisite specimens for many socially prominent families.

A little name-dropping quickly links the whistle-and-bells to colonial history. In 1775, while he was governor of Massachusetts, John Hancock married the daughter of Judge Edmund Quincy. After the birth of their first child, the couple were forced to spend the winter in Philadelphia for reasons of safety during the Revolution. The family already had an extensive collection of silver, but they searched Philadelphia in vain for gold or silver bells with coral for their baby. Fortunately a handsome "wissel and bells" was located in time for the infant's christening. This little episode would make it appear that these much-sought-after playthings were not available in any great abundance.

The John Quincy Adams family and Martha Washington also purchased coral-and-bells for the infants in their families, as did the parents of John Jay, first chief justice of the United States Supreme Court. A portrait of Jacques De Peyster shows him with a gold and rock-crystal whistle-bell. In fact, infants of wealthy parents were rather frequently painted with a whistle-bell in one hand; it was more or less a status symbol.

Silver rattles remained a status symbol until the mid-nineteenth century, when they became more readily available. By then, such familiar-sounding firms as The Gorham Company and Samuel Kirk and Son were manufacturing them in wide assortments. In their 1888 catalog, Gorham showed eight types of the stub rattle alone. Unger Brothers advertised baby rattles having mother-of-pearl handles mounted with sterling likenesses of cupids, jesters, Billikins, and other favorite childhood figures—each bobbling with bells.

Bells from another segment of American craftsmen were popular as colorful, decorative appointments in parlors and bedchambers of the nineteenth and twentieth centuries. These were the output of glasshouses producing blown, molded, and—later—pressed glass artwares. Color was the dominant characteristic; whether pale or vivid or shaded, it was always used with great skill by talented glass designers like Nicholas Lutz or Louis Comfort Tiffany, who individually or in conjunction with noted glasshouses created varieties with exotic-sounding names like Peachblow, Burmese, Rubina Verde, Spanish Lace, Wavecrest, Favrile, or Vasa Murrhina. Decorative bells were to be had in these as well as other types of glass, in a fantastic diversity of patterns, shapes, and textures that have been imitated within modern times but never equalled.

The epitome of loveliness was seen by some in iridescent Tiffany glass, which included bells of a rich peacock blue. These came from the studios of Louis Comfort Tiffany, who in 1893 began to experiment with satinizing glass through the use of gases and oxides to make it iridescent. He termed his specialty Favrile, a trade name meaning "handmade." His output of bells was minimal, and there is a scramble for possession whenever one comes on the market—not only for the bell's intrinsic worth, its reflection of new art trends in its day, but because of its creator's significant place in American creative arts. His name was practically a household word after 1892, when no home seemed complete without a Tiffany stained-glass light fixture. In the world of art he was looked upon as something of an avant-garde figure actively promoting the Art Nouveau movement with its free-flowing forms, a feature seen in some of his bells.

Bells of colorless glass became relatively commonplace around the home after the Philadelphia Centennial Exhibition of 1876 popularized pressed glass, stimulating the making of tableware glass at the same time. By 1879 there were seventy-five glass factories in Pittsburgh alone, nearly a third of them specializing in table-wares. There were also lovely cut glass bells, always expensive, quite in a class by themselves. Painstaking imitations have never achieved the brilliant refractory qualities brought out by skilled cutters in the glasshouses of the Brilliant Period of cut glass, from 1880 to 1915. The cutting shops of that day are long gone, T. G. Hawkes & Company in 1963 being one of the last to close its doors. The *Buffalo Evening News* of May 25, 1963 reported from Corning, New York: "An era that began in the 1870s has ended with the closing of T. G. Hawkes & Company, glass engraving and cutting. It was the last of the fine cutters . . . at one time had more than a score of glass cutting shops, and employed more than 1000 glass cutters." So ended the making of heavy, brilliant cut glass bells with their sparkling ring.

It is a small triumph today to own a signed Hawkes bell from the Brilliant Period or an exquisite example cut by Christian Dorflinger even earlier (1830-80), when fine line cutting and color flashing characterized much of the work. Just a single bell suggests something of the sparkle that formerly marked fashionable dinner tables, especially that in the state dining room at the White House. The first buying Mrs. Lincoln did after she became First Lady was to order a set of cut glass dinner ware.

Colorless pressed-glass bell-covered butter dish in Daisy and Button pattern with double lacing around the edge of the dish. Such dual-purpose bells in glass or china were inspired by the silver-plated varieties. *Ringland Collection.*

Below

Cut glass bells from the Brilliant Period, as shown in *American Cut Glass for the Discriminating Collector* by J. Michael Pearson: *left,* with X-cut vesica, hobstar, and fan; *middle,* a large bell 7½ inches in height; *right,* with flashed star in a diamond field. *J. Michael Pearson*

Small crystal bells for table use were also made by Steuben Glass works when Frederick Carder was in charge from 1903 to 1932. Steuben has long been a recognized name in crystal, one considered worthy for diplomatic gift giving, where guidelines decree the gift be representative of the finest in American artistic productions. As a wedding present, President Truman sent Queen Elizabeth a Steuben Merry-Go-Round bowl. President Eisenhower was also partial to Steuben, and, on his trip to Communist China, President Nixon chose a Steuben crystal prism as his gift to Premier Chou En-lai.

Victorian whatnots displayed all manner of little curiosities and sentimental objects. Since small bells were popular as souvenirs, they were likely to be included in the display, which reflected a family's varied interests: a visit to some great exposition then attracting throngs of Americans, or a summer at a favorite resort—all these places had little bells for sale as mementos.

Writing desks also displayed bells made to follow the vagaries of Victorian decorative fashion: weighted brass bells depicting personalities admired by American society, twirlers with an eagle finial, or tap varieties showing a patriotic motif like a simulated thirteen-star flag. Even more distinctive were the call-bell inkstands, designed while artisans were still intrigued with the idea of creating dual-purpose, sometimes multiple-purpose, objects.

During the second half of the nineteenth century, the United States Patent Office was besieged with innovative ideas for using bells. Of 200 or so patents issued on the subject, at least 60 pertained to ingenious ideas for combining bells with

Left
Novelty souvenir bell from the New Orleans Mardi Gras of 1884. Dog's head nods as the clapper moves; the perpetual calendar in one paw is stationary. The "dog tag" around the neck on a chain is a commemorative token from the Mardi Gras. *Stephen Foster Memorial*

Right
This handsome eight-inch desk twirler is dominated by the figure of an eagle poised for flight from a globe of the world. The base decorated with satyr heads is heavily ornate in the Victorian manner. *Barbara Lewis Collection*

A neatly designed inkstand with every fitting for the convenience of the user —even a brass loop on the candle-holder, for cleaning pen points. The brass fittings and fluted-glass wells contrast pleasingly with the black frame notched to hold pens. A turn of the white porcelain knob rings the servant call bell. *Barbara Lewis Collection*

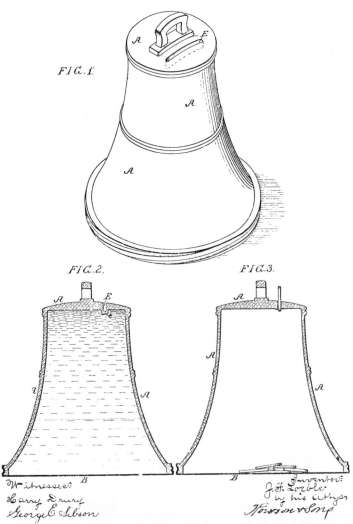

(No Model.)

J. F. LOEBLE.

COMBINED JELLY GLASS AND MONEY BOX.

No. 326,757.   Patented Sept. 22, 1885.

FIG.1.

FIG.2.   FIG.3.

Loeble's combination jelly glass and money box molded in the likeness of the Liberty Bell was made not only in milk glass but in glass of various colors. When the receptacle had been emptied of jelly, it could be converted to a toy money box by punching out the bottom of slit E. Examples in mint condition have a tin screw-on base stamped with the name and address of the Philadelphia manufacturer. *United States Patent Office*

household pieces like inkstands, table casters, waste bowls, or money banks. Inkstands naturally held a rather limited appeal, largely for the wealthy class. Among the relatively few firms manufacturing such stands were Barton Bell Company, of Connecticut, and Woodside Sterling and Gould-Mersereau Company of New York. Gould-Mersereau made them as late as 1899, the Barton firm as early as 1783.

The point must be obvious that bells—both functional and decorative—were *very* common accessories in the Victorian household. This brief excursion into the subject by no means exhausts all aspects of their use. Older infants were protected at play with either web or leather reins studded with sleigh-bell-like crotals. Kirby Manufacturing Company's (Middletown, Connecticut) 1903 catalog of bell toys illustrated no fewer than twenty-six styles of belled reins. For the slightly older child there were the endlessly varied, fascinating mechanical bell toys that came on the market around 1870. Designed to be drawn or pushed along the floor, they rang at intervals either by internal motion or by the action of animated figures riding on top. Adults wanting to buy one as a gift must have had a field day choosing among bell ringers representing such assorted subjects and actions as The Kicking Mule, Teddy Roosevelt and the Rough Riders, The Acrobats, Jonah and the Whale, or Goose with Rider. These toys were of iron or other metals, with quality bells from the bellmakers themselves. They were deftly designed with an appealing artistry and a sound altogether lacking in the plastic bell toys of today.

Many that displayed the cleverest action were produced by the makers of mechanical banks—J. and E. Stevens Company, for instance—but the two most

Left
A decorative Victorian floorpiece of uncertain provenance, a very musical dinner chime. Brass plates marked for notes of the scale are fitted across the frame, above the graduated gongs.

Right
Catalog illustration (from the Kirby Manufacturing Company, 1903) of a child's rein studded with sleigh bells.

KIRBY MFG. CO., MIDDLETOWN, CONN.

REINS.

All Leather Rein.

Per Gross.
No. 320. Four 1¼ inch and twenty-four ⅞ inch Nickel Bells, $144 00

A monkey rides a tricycle on this automated bell-ringer toy.

Most popular of all bell toys were the pull types with either a horse or mule pulling a bell suspended between a pair of large wheels. The bell rang when the wheels revolved. *Stephen Foster Memorial*

prolific producers were the Gong Bell Manufacturing Company and the N. N. Hill Brass Company, both of East Hampton, Connecticut. Surprisingly enough, they remained in business until relatively recent years. Each had an annual output of bell toys reaching into thousands upon thousands. What has become of them all, collectors wonder, now that it takes a small miracle to acquire even a single bell toy at any price. Being expendable to start with, these toys saw hard usage, so there never was a time when great numbers of them survived.

If adults took pleasure in selecting bell ringers, many of them also took pleasure in selecting bells for their bicycles, as did their school-age children. Bicycle bells are heard today in limited, rather cursory fashion, but never the heavy cast brass ones with their musical, resonant sound; and it is doubtful whether great thought is given to choosing them. They are merely a required accessory. For the Gay Nineties cyclist, however, there were literally dozens of models to choose from, the Bristol Liberty Bell Company alone making thirty-two different styles under

In 1897 the Bristol Liberty Bell Company was making 32 styles of bicycle bells under the trademark *Corbin Bells*. On the handle of this example, the company name and the style number are engraved. *Barbara Lewis Collection*

the trademark of "Corbin Bells." In 1897 there were dozens of firms equipping 10,000,000 bicycles with bells, another million cycles being sold annually. Then came the automobile to challenge the bicycle's popularity; yet in 1926 there was still enough demand for cycle accessories to warrant Bevin Brothers' issuing a forty-two page catalog devoted exclusively to bells and a few other items. Their catalog groups the bells according to the emblems displayed on them—good luck symbols, fraternal insignia, patriotic motifs, and so on. One of the most unusual cycle bells illustrated is the "Royal Tire Bell" that presumably operated by contact with the sides of either tire.

It sometimes seems that collectors are dedicated to looking only toward the past, but that need not always be the case. There is ample proof that a collection does not have to be limited by mere earliness. In the wake of changing concepts among museums, which are much more admissive of the contemporary than formerly, most private collectors have likewise liberalized their thinking. Just how much attention should be given to the contemporary is a matter of personal choice. Even reactionaries are coming to realize that some of America's foremost art mediums today are but a continuation of famous long-established names. A contemporary Steuben bell, for example, has a long tradition of fine glassmaking behind it.

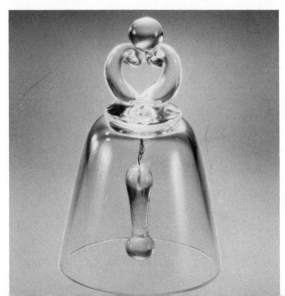

A modern Steuben crystal bell with heart-shaped handle. Manufacture of this bell was discontinued in 1949. *Steuben Glass*

To acquire a Steuben piece of recent make is to help perpetuate a great tradition in American crystal wares. Authorities on art glass are similarly inclined to add a contemporary example, perhaps a Peachblow from the Pairpoint Glass Company, now producing a limited number of bells.

Contemporary Pairpoint glass has been made again since 1968, under the aegis of the former manager at the old Pairpoint Glass Company, using methods little changed from those used at the firm's earlier factory in New Bedford, Massachusetts. But, claims that gentleman, "This may be the last generation for offhand glassmaking, at least the highly skilled offhand glass work that we have become accustomed to the last 300 years. . . . Experts believe there may be as many as 10 master gaffers in the world at present, but that is all. One day there will be none."

With the tempo of life accelerating and the number of people wanting finely crafted pieces increasing, the limited work of America's top craftsmen has become quickly collectible—almost overnight in some instances. Edward Marshall Boehm's small porcelain bell in the likeness of an inverted tulip enjoyed that kind of escalation. It represents the eminent naturalist-sculptor's only attempt to design a bell, before his death in 1968.

In the realm of American metal arts there has been an extremely limited production of really fine table bells by the traditional silversmiths presently in business; in bronze, on the other hand, there as been no tradition of crafting ornamental table bells, as in Europe. Some very creditable experimenting is in progress, however, casting by the age-old lost-wax process. Beginning in 1972, Ballantyne Specialties began issuing annual bronze bells in limited edition, each year's design including a full-length figural handle representing a renowned person, either fictional or real.

Examples of contemporary glass bells being made by Pairpoint Glass Company. Those shown here are in opaque French blue with delicately enameled floral decoration and air twist handles. *Pairpoint Glass Company*

Wallace is one of the few great silversmithing firms to hold to the tradition of producing some type of bell. Since 1971 the firm has been issuing a limited edition sleigh bell that will never herald the approach of a sleigh but is a versatile ornament. This is the 1971 edition, encircled with sprays of holly. *Wallace Silversmiths*

Right
Hans Brinker's figure forms the handle on the 1974 annual Ballantyne bell made of bronze by the lost-wax method. *Ballantyne Specialties*

Collecting by Viewing

Collecting by viewing is an activity open to interpretation from several angles. For those who by choice or by circumstance are not travel oriented, there are rewarding areas for research, armchair style. Viewing old prints or paging through county archives often turns up pertinent information of a sort not found in books, the little human interest stories behind noted bells. With any luck at all, concentrating on one certain event, place, or time can result in a brief study of lasting significance. For instance, under the influence of the Bicentennial, journalists pounced on the idea of looking at several great American expositions marking other anniversaries. Bell buffs can adapt this idea to rounding up information and views of bells featured at certain of those expositions. The Philadelphia Centennial Exposition of 1876 has stories to offer in that connection, as does the Chicago World's Columbian Exposition of 1893.

Stretching for about six hundred acres along the lake, that Chicago fair was planned to commemorate the four-hundredth anniversary of the discovery of America. More than 27,000,000 visitors attended, more than at any previous fair on American soil. All of them must have carried away special memories of new taste treats, such as concoctions like Cracker Jack, which was introduced to the world at the fair; new thrills in entertainment furnished by scandalous Little Egypt's dancing; or new experiences in sound, hearing the magnificent bells that highlighted exhibits.

No one could miss hearing the nine-bell tower chime ringing out from the Liberal Arts Building or the golden notes floating down from Belgium's carillon. Only a privileged few, however, heard the bell used at the Columbian Dinner given for distinguished guests attending the dedication ceremonies. According to official accounts, dinner was announced by the ringing of a huge dinner bell in the hands of the chef, who was clothed in crisp white jacket, apron, and cap. After ringing it, he bowed and hung the bell from a mammoth wishbone of burnished gold, the hosts' official emblem, in the center of the banquet table. The chief justice of the United States Supreme Court, who was among the guests, afterward termed the affair "the most remarkable dinner ever given on this continent."

Memories were all that anyone had of the Columbian Liberty Bell especially ordered for the occasion by the Daughters of the American Revolution. It was the finest likeness of the Liberty Bell yet cast, stood over six feet tall, weighed six tons, and would scarcely seem to be on anyone's list of losable bells. Nonetheless, when the fair closed, the bell was nowhere to be found and its disappearance remains shrouded in mystery until this day. *Collier's Magazine* featured the complete story of the Columbian Liberty Bell, calling its disappearance the greatest mystery surrounding any such object in history.

According to the magazine's story-behind-the-bell, people all over the country had been invited to send contributions of metal from which it would be cast—more or less a patriotic gesture on the part of the Daughters of the American Revolution, who had planned after the exposition to use the bell in promoting world peace. More than 250,000 pennies were contributed by schoolchildren from every state. Silver spoons by the hundreds and thimbles by the peck went into the pot. Many contributions were historic pieces. There was a copper kettle once belonging to Thomas Jefferson; a surveyor's chain that had been George Washington's; the keys to Jefferson Davis's home; and two Civil War bullets that had met in midair to form a perfect U, to stand for the Union. Altogether, over 200,000 men, women, and children contributed gifts of gold, silver, copper, tin, iron, and bronze. Said Chester Meneely, whose foundry cast the bell, "It came out all right, although we were plenty skeptical when all those old patriotic relics started melting and became just so much leaden mix to deaden the vibrations and dull the tone."

Aside from bells purposely designed for each exposition, there were always some special ones brought in on loan. Manufacturers liked to advertise their workmanship in this way. At the Columbian Exposition, the Clinton Meneely Bell Company won many favorable comments. Of all the bells on special loan along The Midway, two were of the greatest interest. One was the Liberty Bell itself, which had been given a continuous ovation during its journey along the lake front, wreathed in flowers and resting on a triumphal float drawn by thirteen jet-black horses.

The other bell that drew more than passing interest was the first church bell to ring in the New World, brought over by Christopher Columbus on his second voyage. It was a gift from King Ferdinand, its graceful appearance considered a tribute to that monarch's excellent taste. An image of Saint Michael, a raised Gothic letter F in honor of the donor, and two sets of concentric circles made up the ornamentation. For a bell so modest in size—only eight inches tall, in the manner of early Spanish Renaissance bells—its history was as colorful as it was unique. After nearly a century, an earthquake destroyed the Santo Domingo town where it hung, and the bell lay buried for three hundred years or more. It came to notice when a hardy fig tree pushed up through the ruins carrying the bell along on one of its branches. A shepherd who saw the relic gave it to Manuel Galvan, who in turn presented it to a church in Santo Domingo as a talisman sacred to the memory of Christopher Columbus. When plans were being formulated for the great Columbian Exposition, Señor Galvan was instrumental in arranging the loan of the bell.

For a little memento of the World's Fair, various souvenir bells were sold by exhibitors. Even those who did not attend the fair could find on the market all kinds of objects inspired by the four-hundredth anniversary of Columbus's discovery of America. Charles A. Bailey, a great mechanical toy designer, created a large animated bell toy showing Columbus at the prow of his ship with some of his crew. The toy was patented by Bailey in Cromwell, Connecticut, and manufactured there by the J. and E. Stevens Company.

Among other souvenir bells from the fair of 1893 was one of crystal, beautifully etched in three different commemorative designs. The one most commonly seen in collections has a swirled, ribbed handle of frosted glass. Etched on the side are the words WORLD'S FAIR 1893; in embossed letters circling the base of the handle, WORLD'S COLUMBIAN EXPOSITION, 1893. The two modifications are a bell with etched scenes of Columbus and his ships landing in the New World and one bearing merely an escutcheon for Columbus.

By tradition, these glass souvenirs have been ascribed to Libbey Glass Company, on the assumption they were actually made at that firm's Industrial Palace on The Midway Plaisance, purposely erected to publicize the company's wares. However, in recent years, authoritative advice from the Antique Historic Glass Foundation made it seem probable that this trio was not produced at Libbey's pavilion; in fact, was not even of Libbey make, inasmuch as their glassware was customarily trademarked or signed, and no specimen of the bells was known to be so marked. Then, a short time after that opinion was advanced, a dealer offered for

Commemorative etched glass bell tentatively attributed to the Libbey Glass Company and presumably made at their Industrial Palace erected on the grounds of the Chicago World's Fair in 1893. *Mrs. B. Ellsworth Young*

Edward Drummond Libbey's huge Industrial Palace at the 1893 World's Fair, where a series of commemorative glass bells may or may not have been made.

sale one of these glass bells marked LIBBEY GLASS COMPANY, WORLD'S FAIR, 1893. Perhaps the bells were produced on the fairgrounds after all!

A further look at the company's showplace there helps us to visualize the circumstances under which these attractive commemoratives might have been made at the exposition. Edward Drummond Libbey demonstrated his business acumen along with his showmanship by obtaining exclusive rights to the manufacture of glass on the fair grounds. He invested $200,000 in his huge Industrial Palace, where he employed 150 glass blowers and cutters to demonstrate their craft. The pieces the craftsmen made were sold by the thousands, profiting Libbey so handsomely that he was able to finance Michael J. Owens's invention of a bottle-blowing machine. Thus was born Owens-Illinois glass.

Even if subsequent evidence finally proves these etched glass bells were not made at the Columbian Exposition, or that they were not even made by Libbey, that would not negate their historic import. They are souvenirs with commemorative status—that is certain, even though considerably more research is needed before a final exact identification can be made. As the Antique Historic Glass Foundation points out, at best there are many unanswered questions about markings on Libbey glass. (Here is another of those areas in identification waiting to challenge the collector.)

Anyone with an investigative turn of mind can contribute substantially to state and local history by making a survey of significant bells that have played a part in the settlement or development of his particular locality. In a dozen or more states, including such widely separated ones as Rhode Island, Illinois, and Colorado, individuals or small groups have done just that, and enjoyed seeing their findings in print. There are likely to be fringe benefits to such surveys, in the form of unexpected, heretofore unknown, facts. A magazine columnist compiling a survey of bells throughout Illinois was routinely checking old catalogs when suddenly he noted a picture of a shedlike structure with an unmistakable sign on the roof reading R. T. CRANE BRASS & BELL FOUNDRY. Eventually a link was established between this early business and the present-day Crane Company noted for fine plumbing fixtures. There the story stopped. Company officials knew nothing of any such enterprise in their past history. To their credit, however, they were as curious as the columnist who found the old picture. Within a few weeks a special delivery letter confirmed the existence of such a manufacturing phase in the early development of the Crane company in Chicago. From the founder's grandson the company acquired a photograph of a documented brass animal bell cast by R. T. Crane, and learned that the old factory bell that once summoned their workers was supposedly cast by him, too. It was then (1953) still in evidence at the Chicago branch, but without documentation.

The more travel-minded enthusiast, preferably with camera in hand, will find equally varied opportunities to contribute to the overall history of bells. An awareness of their roles in American society can easily be gained by viewing specimens in museums or, better still, wherever they can be found in their original locations. Some museums have quite extensive, well-documented displays of a particular type, like the ship bells to be seen in maritime museums all along the eastern seaboard. Others beckon the viewer with only a few historic bells of special note (or even a single specimen), but almost always ones that merit a special trip. The Oglebay Institute Mansion Museum at Wheeling, West Virginia, has on exhibit three superbly colorful art-glass bells produced by Hobbs-Brockunier, Wheeling's leading name in the American art-glass era.

It is not uncommon to find historic homes or other restorations featuring one or more bells, usually of a functional type, dating back to days when the structures were occupied. Hanging in the entrance hall of Abraham Lincoln's home in Springfield, Illinois, is one of those curious doorbells on a spiral wire, with another wire attaching it to the front door. It is sometimes identified as a "Lincoln" doorbell, although it is a type commonly used in ante-bellum homes along the mid-sector of the country and southward, and probably elsewhere as well. The charming ante-bellum house now used as the Washington-Wilkes Historical Museum in

Re-creation of the little old foundry that stood on Crane Company's Chicago property until destroyed many years ago. A replica replaced it in 1925, but was destroyed by fire in 1940. *Crane Company*

Re-creation of the interior of the R. T. Crane Brass and Bell Foundry, made in connection with the company's centennial. R. T. Crane poured his first mold here on July 4, 1855. *Crane Company*

On permanent exhibit at Oglebay Institute Mansion Museum in Wheeling, West Virginia, are three large art glass bells made at the famed Hobbs-Brockunier glasshouse there. *Left*, cranberry-colored bell with raised swirl design and milk white handle; *right*, opal-color bell edged in cobalt blue with an applied clear glass handle; *middle*, cranberry-color bell with iridescent hobnails and a hollow amber handle. *Oglebay Institute Mansion Museum*

Washington, Georgia, has a bell of this type as an original part of its mid-nineteenth-century furnishings.

Surprisingly, even certain resort complexes offer an opportunity to see and hear bells either on exhibit or in actual use. Midway along Florida's east coast a unique collection draws attention around Driftwood Inn at Vero Beach. It represents the worldwide hobby of Driftwood's founder. The collection contains a number of significant American bells, including one from a New York elevated train, another once used by Harriet Beecher Stowe, as well as the bell from Casey Jones's locomotive. Unlike those in many exhibits, Driftwood's bells may be and are sounded—for meals, arrivals, departures, or simply for the unalloyed pleasure of hearing their voices.

Merely recording the locations where bells can be viewed (or heard) is a contribution in itself, not to mention any data that may be found in the process, but there is a still more purposeful role for the roving bell buff. That consists of making

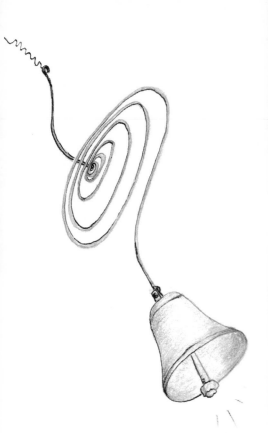

Left
A pre-Civil War doorbell of the type seen in Abraham Lincoln's Springfield, Illinois, home, where it hangs in the entrance hall. A wire stretches to the door, and the coiled spring vibrates to ring the bell with each opening and closing of the door. *Drawing by Dorothy Cole*

Right
At Driftwood Inn, Vero Beach, Florida, some one hundred bells hang here and there, to be rung at will. Some weigh a ton, some much less. They have been garnered from various sources—farms, churches, ships, and so on. *Driftwood Inn*

a pictorial record of endangered bells and the now equally endangered towers that house them, or perhaps photographing some of America's more curious belfries, often in out-of-the-way locations.

Belfries, church belfries especially, are sometimes as historic and fabled as the bronze-throated bells they enclose. Architecturally, they are related not only to the church proper, but frequently to the local topography as well, and always they bear some relation to the bell(s) inside—or lack of them, in some instances. Take as an example the beautiful Monte Cassino Chapel that until recent years stood picturesquely on the Benedictines' hillside of vineyards near Fort Mitchell, Kentucky. It has a belfry so small the Benedictines could never find a bell for it—at least, one of sufficient tone. Some seventy years ago two monks quarried the stone to build this shrine, which accommodates only three worshipers and has become known as the world's tiniest church. Of late years it narrowly escaped the ignominious end that comes to historic structures surrounded by housing projects. Fortunately the chapel was saved by moving it to the grounds of Thomas More College in Fort Mitchell.

In the heart of the Ozarks at Eureka Springs, Arkansas, another curiosity rises from a hillside, probably the only belfry known to serve as the entrance to a church. At Saint Elizabeth's, to reach the chapel visitors must descend from the belfry down a deep stairway. Viewed from any angle, Saint Elizabeth's was obviously planned to suit the topography, in a town where many homes are also of unusual design for the same reason.

In Vermont a movement is currently underway to save an oddly belfried structure known as the Old Round Church, situated between Burlington and Montpelier. In reality, it is a sixteen-sided church crowned with a bell-shaped roof surmounted with an open octagonal belfry in which hangs a fine old Henry Hooper bell. Legends, now largely disproved, have developed around the building's unusual shape. One declares seventeen men erected the church about 1813, sixteen of them building one side apiece and the seventeenth adding the belfry. However, at least eighteen men participated in erecting the structure, which was the joint undertaking of four or five denominations. Henry Ford dearly wanted the Old Round Church for his Greenfield Village, but was unsuccessful in having it relocated. It stands where it was built, a prime example of American carpenter folk art—and a highly photogenic one, with its Hooper bell clearly visible. In September, 1974, The *Magazine Antiques* used a superb color photograph of this landmark as its frontispiece. The graceful octagonal belfry, with its bell silhouetted against a deep blue autumn sky, is a noticeable feature.

As spinoff ideas to pursuing the matter of curious belfries, oddly positioned bells and significant inscriptions present a further challenge to both the camera buff and the bell buff who want only to view certain bells at close range. Such challenges are well met in a state like Texas, with its countless vintage bells. The Little Church of La Villita in San Antonio is extremely difficult to photograph; its 1844 bell is even more so, receding as it does into thick vines trailing across a right-angle juncture of walls where the bell hangs. The distinctive architecture and history involved here, coupled with the oddly positioned bell, make it a worthy camera subject, nevertheless. In fact, a close-up of the bell is doubly useful because it

In Richmond, Vermont, the famous Old Round Church has a Henry Hooper bell in its octagonal belfry. *Vermont Historical Society*

Left
The historic bell at San Antonio's Little Church of La Villita may be seen high up in the vines, where two walls join at the right of the entrance. *Thomas J. Collins Photograph*

Right
Close-up of the bell at La Villita, known historically as the De Vilbis bell since its early history was associated with John Wesley De Vilbis, who spreached the first Protestant sermon in San Antonio. *Thomas J. Collins Photograph*

seems to help substantiate one of two opposing stories on its origin.

The structure, built in 1876, began as a German Methodist Church on a site selected by John Wesley De Vilbis, who preached the first Protestant sermon in San Antonio in April, 1844. In the hope of building a church, De Vilbis returned to the North in search of funds, at the same time purchasing a bell in Cincinnati. Upon his return, he erected a wooden frame on his property along Villita Street, where he hung the bell to summon his parishioners. His custom was to "swing it lustily, then cross the river and meet his congregation in the Courthouse a quarter of a mile away." As it appears in a camera study by Thomas J. Collins, the bell does have the overall proportioned appearance of bells cast in American foundries like those in Cincinnati, where *Ramsdell's Historical and Pictorial Guide* claims it was purchased. However, La Villita's own church history says the origin of the present bell is unknown "other than it came from old Mexico."

Time, the elements, fire, and other assorted hazards have a way of eroding inscriptions on bells, especially on those with the wording cast in low relief. Here again, though, working at close range to decipher or to photograph an old inscription may yield unexpected rewards in making possible the correction of a heretofore inaccurately quoted inscription. Such was the experience of Mr. Collins when making a photographic study of another San Antonio bell, the one to be seen in the small bell cote over the vestry door of Saint Mark's Episcopal Church. In a quite literal sense, the origins of this bell were embedded in Texas history, for it was cast from a cannon found buried near the outer wall of the Alamo. In 1874 Meneelys of West Troy transformed the almost pure copper cannon into a 526-pound bell, placing on one side of the waist a large Texas star with the word ALAMO in the center and on three points the dates 1813, 1836, 1874. The middle date refers to the year heroes of the Alamo made that name the focal point of Texas history. Below the star are these words: CAST FROM A CANNON FOUND BURIED IN THE ALAMO.

Left
Saint Mark's Episcopal Church in San Antonio has a bell valued not only for its unique inscription but for its origin deep in Texas history. *Thomas J. Collins Photograph*

Right
Close-up of the Texas star and the word *Alamo* on one side of the Saint Mark's bell. *Thomas J. Collins Photograph*

Covering the waist on the opposite side is this unusual but highly appropriate inscription for an instrument of destruction and hate that was reborn in an instrument of hope and goodwill. Exactly as cast on the bell, the words read:

> "YE MUST BE BORN AGAIN."
> THE MASTER SPAKE OF MAN'S NEW BIRTH
> BY WATER AND THE SPIRIT;
> BUT I INTO MY MOTHER'S WOMB
> RETURNED AND HAVE BEEN BORN AGAIN
> FROM WORK OF DEATH TO WORDS OF LIFE
> THROUGH CHRIST'S ETERNAL MERIT.

Inscriptions range over the whole spectrum of human emotions and provide interesting accretive insight into the spirit of the times in which they were cast on a bell—as, for example, eighteenth-century inscriptions in freedom's cause or as testimonials to an unwavering religious faith. Often the latter are brief, direct quotations from the Bible; otherwise, they are usually simple, standard phrases used by bell founders for generations. Paul Revere's favorite was that old familiar admonition, "I to the church the living call—and to the grave summon all."

Sleuthing around in search of old inscriptions is not all solemnity, however. Now and then they reflect human foibles, especially those of their donors:

> AT PRAYER TIMES MY VOICE I'LL RAISE
> AND SOUND TO MY SUBSCRIBER'S PRAISE

or they are unwittingly humorous in their quaint wording:

> AMOS LEVITICUS GAVE THIS RING
> IN THE VILLAGE STEEPLE FOR TO DING!

168

9

REVIVAL IN RINGING

All evidence points to a dwindling of the sound of bells across the land. To admit to a current revival in ringing, then, seems on the surface of things to be a contradiction. But, understood in correct perspective, the sounds being created today in no way resemble the scrambled tintinnabulations of bells formerly used in everyday life under varying and haphazard situations. Rather, they are an outgrowth of the bronze-throated cadences heard from the country's finest peals and chimes. The accent is on music, played usually in a concert atmosphere. In other words, it is programmed ringing, and whether it issues from chimes, carillons, or handbell choirs, it has a certain homogeneous quality because it is being played on tuned bronze instruments.

All three of these ringing forms were introduced to America at relatively early dates, but they were slow to attain their present status. With developing aesthetic tastes in modern America, however, and a wider acceptance of all performing artists, chimists, carillonneurs, and handbell ringers have now become recognized performers.

The few early chimes brought over from England to be installed in colonial churches were greatly cherished, yet it was not until the year of the nation's centennial that *Harper's Monthly* could report, "Full and partial chimes are now to be found in all parts of the country." Among those listed were the two earliest sets to arrive. The very first, cast in 1744 expressly for Christ (Old North) Church in Boston, were to become the bells of Paul Revere fame, and his story has already been told. The next arrivals, ten years later, were those cast in London, at the request of Queen Anne, for Christ Church in Philadelphia. Another ten years saw the installation of Charleston's mellow chimes, but Trinity Church in New York City did not receive its famous "ring of bells," otherwise known as a partial chime, until 1797, on the good ship *Favorite* direct from London.

169

Ringing the chimes at Trinity Church in New York City about 1870, after five more bells had been added to the original "ring" of four.

More than a few of the chimes listed by *Harper's Monthly* had been made in America, proof that domestic foundries were perfecting their skills sufficiently to produce sets of acceptable standard; that is, a number of bells—as few as eight or as many as eighteen, but preferably ten or twelve—attuned to one another in diatonic succession. After the Blake Bell Company cast the first chimes ever made in America, in 1825, other foundries such as those in Troy and Cincinnati took up the challenge. Installations multiplied rapidly until well after the turn of the century, when a combination of circumstances brought about a lull in developments. There seemed to be a dearth of individuals interested in ringing.

When chimist Arthur C. Sharon of Holy Name of Jesus Church in New Orleans was interviewed in 1944, he estimated there were "not more than ten chimists and carillonneurs combined in North America. . . ." He himself was proclaimed the only person in his city who could get anything approaching music from the city's church bells. As for women in this field of music, Mr. Sharon admitted they were capable of playing a carillon, but he declared, "I don't know of any hefty enough for chimes." Although neither of his statements gives a wholly accurate picture of chiming at that time, combined they point up the relative rarity of such music during a long period of years and the almost total absence of women performing it. The pendulum was about to swing in the opposite direction, however.

For the first time in its history, the University of Chicago had just appointed a woman student as official custodian and ringer of the Mitchell Tower bells on its campus. The announcement made newspaper headlines, one of which read, "Woman Tolls Mitchell Tower Bells to Break Long-standing Tradition." Somehow it seemed fitting that a woman be appointed to play these particular bells, given and inscribed in honor of Alice Freeman Palmer, the university's first dean of women. Philosophy student Cicely Woods was described as a very agile performer, playing without benefit of a clavier, plucking the strings in harp fashion, but with considerably more animation. Her repertoire of tunes included everything from a hymn by Haydn, to *Yankee Doodle*, to the Alma Mater. This last was the tune beloved by the university's enduring gridiron coach, Alonzo Stagg, who presented officials with a gift of $1,000 to ensure the continued playing of the Alma Mater each evening.

About this same time, unknown to Mr. Sharon, two other women hundreds of miles apart were chiming their way to fame. At Grace Church in downtown Providence, Mrs. Wilfred Pickles was the principal performer; at the University of California in Berkeley, Margaret Murdock already held an enviable record of ringing the chimes in Sather Campanile, a campus landmark. On June 15, 1972, surrounded by television cameramen, news reporters, and photographers, Miss Murdock formally entered her fiftieth year of playing noontime concerts, with a group of special selections ranging from *Sturdy Golden Bear* to *The British Grenadier*.

A slight person weighing only a hundred pounds, and already past her seventy-eighth birthday, Miss Murdock attributed her energy and spryness to her many years of playing the twelve-lever clavier in Sather Campanile. Wrote one reporter, "Watch her doing it and you will understand why." He was quite right! It does require an enormous fund of energy to maintain a constant, melodious flow of sound from bells weighing hundreds, even thousands, of pounds. Most chimes in American towers, though originally hung in a different manner, were eventually fixed in a stationary position, with their clappers connected to a keyboard of claviers resembling pump handles. In other words, the clappers move to sound the bells when the player exerts tremendous influence on the claviers. Powerful springs control these levers; after a vigorous downward push, each lever must be released before it can snap the player's wrist. Mr. Sharon recalled wearing wrist bandages for weeks while learning to play the chimes at Holy Name of Jesus Church. It is all this manual dexterity, however, that brings out the full potential of which chimes are capable—the long, short, loud, soft, and otherwise expressive notes—and which permits the chimist to give each tune his own interpretation.

Time was when chimes were used largely for hymn playing. It is said that for more than one hundred years nothing but sacred music was heard from the steeple

Margaret Murdock in 1972 as she was about to ring in her fiftieth year of playing the chimes on the twelve-lever console in Sather Tower at the University of California campus, Berkeley. *Oakland Tribune*

of Old North Church, until a fire broke out in it. After that was extinguished, the alarmed people were so overjoyed they refused to leave until the bells played "Oh, Dear, What Can the Matter Be?" America's chimists of modern times have contributed greatly to the resurgence of interest in this form of music, through their willingness to experiment with some popular tunes that are likely to give more listeners more enjoyment. Their selections are naturally limited, to a degree, by the size of the chime and colored by their own preferences or perhaps by regional customs. Even so, modern repertoires run the gamut of musical composition from favorite hymns to jigs and capers. In New Orleans, Arthur Sharon set a good example years ago. He knew many listeners would always prefer hymns, but he felt it was also appropriate to play spirituals, old plantation songs, and, for parishioners in the immediate neighborhood, some Irish melodies.

The bells in McGraw Tower at Cornell University, Ithaca, New York, exemplify the pleasure both "town and gown" can derive from hearing varied programs. Cornell's chimes can be heard all around Ithaca and have become very much a part of the community. The programs are played by ten different chimemasters in turn, the competition for the posts being extremely keen. This in itself is indicative of young peoples' interest in chimes as a musical instrument. Because Cornell's bells number eighteen, a considerable range of selections is possible. There are three fifteen-minute concerts daily, marked by one traditional campus air at each performance. One of these, the "Jennie McGraw Rag," is heard each morning in tribute to Miss McGraw, the donor for whom the tower is named. A quixotic tradition is observed each Halloween when the tower clockfaces are disguised as jack-o'-lanterns while the Alma Mater is played in a minor key at midnight.

The Cornell University chimes are an especially fine tribute to the Meneely family of bell founders who cast them. The original set of nine was first heard in 1868 when the university opened. In 1891 nine more were added, perfectly tuned to the original set, thus doubling the tonal range.

Another notable set of Meneely chimes can be heard on special holidays from the City Hall tower in Minneapolis, Minnesota. For forty-seven years Joseph Henry Auld played at least thirty recitals yearly on the Minneapolis instrument, with selections appropriate to the holidays. Since Mr. Auld's death in 1969, his son Edward has continued the tradition. The transition has been a natural one, for music —especially that of bells—has been almost a way of life for the Auld family. Father and son occasionally performed duets on the city chimes; at other times, Mr. Auld's wife took time from her piano teaching to perform as guest chimist, and for years this widely known pair envisioned themselves chiming a duet on their golden wedding anniversary—some such melody as "Drink to Me Only with Thine Eyes." Perhaps it was Joseph Auld's personal affinity for bells that gave his playing that extra "something," that certain touch, that made the chimes so responsive. He was a collector of sorts, partial to handbells. In his own words, he hankered for bells at the age of twelve, and by age twenty when he moved to Minneapolis to begin tuning clocks and pianos, he was given his first opportunity to ring tower bells.

Since the Minneapolis City Hall chimes constitute a civic instrument, Joseph Auld's position made him an official representative of the city. As such, he cherished certain memorable moments, his two most exciting coming on November 11, 1918, and on August 29, 1929. On the first date, awakened by a *Minneapolis Journal* staff member at 1:45 A.M., he raced to the City Hall by bicycle in eleven

Joseph Henry Auld as he prepared for his 1952 Flag Day recital from atop the Minneapolis City Hall. Independence Day that same year marked his fortieth anniversary as city chimemaster. *Minneapolis Star*

minutes, then climbed the 252 stairs to the bells (there is an elevator now), and played intermittently for several hours, to celebrate the end of the First World War. On the August date, a man in his seventies walked up the steep stairs with Auld to inspect the city's chimes; he pronounced them "very fine bells." The man was John Philip Sousa of the United States Marine Band.

The use of campaniles and bell towers as civic instrumental landmarks has much to recommend it, for usually the structures offer visitors an unsurpassed view of the countryside or at least of the city. Too, the music of their bells can be experienced by countless persons who might otherwise never hear this type of playing. In one of the oldest Puritan cities in New England—Springfield, Massachusetts—a campanile of architectural beauty is offering citizens and visitors just such pleasurable experiences. Its slim shaft lances skyward between two other buildings of classic design, the municipal auditorium and the city hall. The whole scene is reminiscent of an Italian court square, with the campanile dominating. From the observation deck around the 300-foot tower, the Connecticut Valley can be viewed for thirty miles on a clear day.

The present use of Springfield's campanile demonstrates so well what is happening in the world of chiming—the favorable and, in the estimation of some, the less favorable. In 1962 *The Springfield Republican* decried the small number of visitors to the tower, but by 1975 attendance was zooming when, for the second successive summer, the tower was open to the public—on an extended seven-days-a-week basis that year "because of last year's tremendous success," claimed the city's mayoral aide. More than 5,000 had visited it during the summer of 1974.

Springfield's chime tower has not always found favor with local citizens, as evidenced over the years by more than just the small number of visitors throughout the 1960s. For a time, it stood completely silent for want of someone to play its bells. Few seemed to care. More than that, it suffered open hostility and would-be annihilation early in its history. At the time of its dedication in 1913, the campanile was hailed as the nation's finest. No less a person than President William Howard Taft gave the dedicatory address for the whole municipal complex. Regardless of all that, there were thrifty Yankee citizens who openly opposed the campanile.

There were also disgruntled workmen who hated the sight of the structure after they had struggled to extend its height by twenty-five feet during construction. The architects, despite their careful planning, found it was not high enough to house the twelve Meneely bells with their aggregate weight of 12,000 pounds. Present-day city fathers can be thankful neither group succeeded in their threats to blow up the campanile in 1911.

The original chimemaster, Ernest Newton Bagg, is credited with making Springfield aware of the full potential of its chimes as a civic symbol. He initiated the custom of concerts to honor famous visitors, among them John McCormack, Enrico Caruso, and General John J. Pershing. In 1921, Bagg played what is said to have been the first chime concert broadcast by radio. It was heard as far away as Alaska. In his opinion, however, the campanile belonged, above all, to the people of Springfield, and he knew how to make them aware of this. During the First World War he played memorial hymns requested by the families and friends of men killed in battle. He also played favorite melodies for residents of the almshouse, the old people's homes, and the city jail.

Before his death, Mr. Bagg had a repertoire of 5,000 selections. After he was gone, however, all chime concerts ceased because no successor could be found. Fortunately, one Springfield business executive finally determined to reestablish them. With permission from the mayor, he began to experiment until he was skilled enough to offer three of four afternoon concerts each week from a repertoire of seventy-five operatic and classical selections.

Today, visitors and townsfolk hear the same bells that Mr. Bagg and his successor played, but the quality of their sound has changed because they are now played electrically. This, to the purist, is the less fortunate aspect of America's renewed interest in bells as musical instruments. To him, electrified bells are to

The slim shaft of a beautiful civic campanile lances skyward in Springfield, Massachusetts. A Meneely chime was installed in the campanile at the time of its dedication in 1913. *Springfield Chamber of Commerce*

manually operated bells what the player piano is to the concert grand. To express it another way, according to one purist, chimes today have taken on a computerized voice. Played from an electric keyboard, their sound lacks whatever interpretation the chimist could give with his touch on those awkward-looking handles at the clavier—plow handles, someone has called them. Moreover, if the chimes are completely automated, the range of selections used is necessarily limited. Nevertheless, though this is difficult for purists to acknowledge, it is this latest development—the electrifying of tower bells—that has returned hundreds of long-silent ones to use.

It is a fact of the times that with burgeoning budgets and shrinking dollars, with sometimes a lack of qualified chimists outside metropolitan areas or college campuses, communities must keep their bells ringing (if at all) with the least expenditure of time, money, and trouble. So, like most innovations, the modern manner of ringing has both its attractions and its drawbacks.

Chimes, melodies, tunes—all are terms so closely associated that one fact is often overlooked. Neither melodies nor tunes were heard on the first sets of bells imported from England. Instead, the colonists heard the changes being rung in a manner peculiar to the British Isles. Never a popular art in America after the close of the colonial period, change ringing is drawing an ever-growing number of performers now. For those not engaged in the art, however, it remains a complex endeavor almost beyond comprehension—ringers use such cryptic terms as "dodging," "Grandsire Triples," "plain hunt," or "Kent Treble Bob Major." They ring according to intricate rules that are unintelligible to the layman. Basically, these involve a scheme for numbering the bells, then ringing all of them in rotation, with the provision that no sequence be repeated without a change and no bell ever be shifted more than one place in each change.

If a ring of seven bells is numbered and rung in order the first time, the next five changes might be represented thus:

1-2-3-4-5-6-7
2-1-3-4-5-7-6
2-3-1-4-5-6-7
3-2-4-1-6-5-7
3-4-2-6-1-7-5
4-3-6-2-7-1-5

The number of changes possible on any given set of bells is astronomical, increasing tremendously with a larger number of bells. Using six, for example, over 700 permutations can be rung; using eight, the number jumps to at least 40,000. When a mathematical sequence of at least 5,000 strokes has been completed without error or interruption, a peal is said to have been rung. A peal, therefore, does not necessarily constitute all possible variations on a set of bells. In the records that are always kept for each peal completed, the accomplishment is classified according to the number of bells used. A peal on a set of eight bells, for example, is a "Major." Increasing the number of bells to twelve makes it a "Maximus."

Ringing the changes, then, is a method of varying the order in which bells are rung, to bring forth ever-changing harmonious sounds. No melodies or tunes are attempted, though the bells are tuned to harmonize. They are rung in such rapid succession that the effect is one of a great mingling of sound surging through the air, wave after wave. To achieve that effect, each change ringer uses a hand rope attached to a wheel that revolves to swing his bell up and over, full circle, to bring out all its tonal value. It is a performance that demands strength, endurance, perfect timing, teamwork, and mental application. The performers have no time to read sheet music. They are far too busy pulling, releasing, counting.

Since this unique manner of ringing was the accepted one in the colonies, it was practiced not only at Boston's Old North, Philadelphia's Christ Church, and New York's Trinity, but at almost all others boasting a set of chimes. As Joseph Warren Revere pointed out, "Bells made here and in England are intended to be rung by a wheel, by which method the Bell strikes the tongue and frees itself almost at once." Then, whether due to independent developments in the colonies or whether a reflection of a temporarily ebbing enthusiasm for change ringing in England, the popularity of such ringing in the United States dwindled after 1800. The public began to prefer tunes to changes. It became increasingly difficult to find qualified ringers—so difficult, in fact, that when Dr. Arthur H. Nichols of Boston wished to revive change ringing in the city sometime after 1900, he had instead to reintroduce it: It had become virtually unknown, and he found it necessary to import a group of English change ringers to perform and instruct.

To Dr. Nichols, the study of bells had been almost a lifelong avocation when it climaxed with his reintroducing change ringing to Boston. The *Evening Transcript* for January 17, 1914, devoted the better part of a page to reviewing the arrival of Dr. Nichols's skilled English ringers, plus his own introduction to that form of ringing while on a visit to London some years before. It was early in the 1890s that he was walking in the city on a summer morning and heard for the first time a peal of bells ringing changes. He did not know the name of the process, but he did know it resulted in music of high complexity, of a kind unknown to Americans—whose notions of bell music were limited to "a chime of 'dead' bells tapped by a tongue whack! thwack! clank! in 'The Last Rose of Summer' (slightly off key) or a hymn tune."

After long months of practice, Dr. Nichols himself became proficient at ringing, was invited to join an English guild, and with their help eventually arranged for a group to settle in Massachusetts, where they could demonstrate their skill while instructing others. There were four peals in the Boston area where the Englishmen could perform: in Christ (Old North) Church, the Hingham Memorial Tower, Perkins Institute for the Blind, and Groton, with the peal at Boston's Church of the Advent then undergoing repairs to make it a fifth. Of all the performances put on by the little guild of Englishmen, one more than any other brought their art to the notice of the American public. As reported by the *Evening Transcript:*

> When last autumn our local ringers performed a wedding peal on the bells of Christ Church in honor of the marriage of the President's daughter, the fact was telegraphed from coast to coast. Directly, letters began to pour into Dr. Nichol's mail requiring to know what a wedding peal might be, how it was rung, and what ailed their bells that the peal could not be executed by them. It had occurred to numerous persons for the first time that the poets, novelists and historians when they spoke of wedding peals meant a specific kind of bell ringing and that the custom

176

would be both dignified and joyous. Thus at one leap, we are plunged into the differences which it may as well be acknowledged at the start, are for the most part to the disfavor of ourselves.

Though the United States, especially the Boston area, developed a certain fondness for this novel, joyous sort of bellmanship, it gradually reverted to its even greater fondness for bells that played tunes; so Dr. Nichols's "artistic epoch," as *New England Magazine* called it, faded away. Yet enough interest had been generated to keep change ringing alive in at least a few locations. Groton has been fortunate in having a succession of enthusiastic ringing masters, starting with S. Warren Sturgis, whose teaching career at this elite school spanned forty years. During his long tenure he persuaded many boys to take up English change ringing. Some of the most distinguished men in the United States, while students at Groton, heard the changes. Franklin D. Roosevelt was among them.

Perkins Institute became heir to its peal through chance, and perhaps for that reason experienced a certain excitement in continuing its ringing. A woman had offered to present a ring of English bells to the Boston Customs Tower, where its voice would sing out over city and waterfront. How wonderful, she thought, to hear bells rung from that high tower on public occasions by paid expert ringers. But Washington frowned on the proposal. Any gift to a federal building had to have official approval, which in any event was not forthcoming for English bells! Perkins Institute was the gainer.

True to its tendency to cycle upward in popularity, downward, then again upward, every century or so, change ringing is cycling upward now after leveling off for a time on a rather low-interest plateau. Several happenings have given impetus to the latest upward cycle. In the early 1960s newsmen were heralding the installation of a large ring of bells in the nation's capital. One news service explained:

> The English technique of change ringing, in which bells are pulled by hand rope, is almost unknown in the United States. But the situation will soon be remedied when the new 10-bell ring of the Washington National Cathedral of St. Peter and St. Paul begins sounding in 1964.

Just prior to that pronouncement, attention had also been drawn to change ringing when, at Eastertime, 1960, six students at Kent School in Connecticut completed the ringing of a quarter peal. No ringers on this side of the Atlantic had accomplished such a feat for twenty-five years. What was more, it was attempted against the advice of experts who assured the school that young boys could never swing such heavy bells "up and over."

In 1974, nationwide news coverage focused on the hallowing of another new peal—in the contemporary chapel tower of Melrose School, a private country day school near Brewster, New York, operated by the mother general and sisters of an Episcopal order. The blending of contemporary architecture (the work of Burton Rockwell, F.A.I.A., of San Francisco) with the mechanics for an ancient form of ringing is in itself unique, as is the fact that the Melrose bells and ringers may be seen simultaneously through windows—the only arrangement of this kind known. Ordinarily the eight-bell peal is rung by pupils of the school, some of the parents, and interested friends, under the direction of Frank Roberts, Esquire, the English-trained Master of the Melrose Ring. For the hallowing of the bells on January 31,

Left
Eight ringers perform the changes in the ringing chamber of Washington Cathedral. At far left is Richard S. Dirksen, bellmaster of the cathedral. *Washington National Cathedral*

Right
Above the ringing chamber are the ten bells manufactured for Washington Cathedral by the Whitechapel Foundry in England. *Washington National Cathedral*

1974, however, a band of expert guest players assembled from Canada and the United States to execute the changes. After the brief service, The Most Reverend Michael Ramsey climbed to the belfry to bless the bells, calling out the names chosen for them by church dignitaries and school patrons. Given in memory of a noted community benefactor, Cornelius V. Starr, the bells peal over the beautiful hills and valleys Mr. Starr called home, just as he had one day hoped to hear them.

Other developments that augur well for the future of change ringing are its revival at the Advent Church in Boston, after years of neglect, and the restoration of the ringing mechanism in Hingham Memorial Tower, which stands about fifty yards from Old Ship Meetinghouse. The tower belongs to the town, since it was built by popular subscription as a memorial to immigrants from England who settled around the cove where Hingham is located. It holds eleven bells on which melodies can be chimed, with ten of them now operative as of old to ring in the English manner. Citizens enthusiastic about the project employed the expert help of English ringers, who trained a local group to initiate the program of pealing heard there now.

Chicagoans, too, have been privileged of late to learn more about this almost sportive old type of ringing that was in its heyday while the American Revolution was being fought. Just last year the *Chicago Tribune Magazine* featured an exceptionally lucid description of change ringing, paying tribute to the University of

The contemporary blends with the traditional in this new chapel for Melrose School, Brewster, New York, designed to accommodate bells for practicing the old art of change ringing. *Melrose School*

Chicago's small guild of performers. Twice weekly, members scramble up the stairs to the ringing chamber in Mitchell Tower, where they practice under their energetic young director, Robert Gruen, a college English instructor. At the time of their installation, the ten bells in Mitchell Tower were fitted for both chiming and change ringing, but no records have been found of ringing the changes on them for any date beyond 1908, the year of their initial use, when a band rang the 720 changes of Plain Bob Minor.

Bicentennial preparations offered great incentive to this musical form because its advocates see it as a living link with the nation's colonial past—a joyous, vital sound befitting the country's two-hundredth birthday. Historians, as well as campanologists, agreed that the peals of Old North Church in Boston and Christ Church in Philadelphia, above all others, should swing and ring free once again as they did in 1776. Ironically, though, grave problems—financial and otherwise—beset the restoration committees at both these historic shrines. Long months of consultation among experts were needed to ascertain whether the tower at Old North could withstand the pull and stress of freewheeling bells. On Patriots' Day, April 19, 1975, Boston had its answer. On that anniversary of the hanging of the

Close view of the bells at Melrose School. They can easily be viewed in action through the glass wall. *Melrose School*

lanterns in the belfry, the very same bells that had witnessed the hanging originally sent forth such volumes of sound from the tower as had not been heard there for forty-five years.

Beautiful old Christ Church in Philadelphia set up a restoration fund for reactivating its original peal, on which change ringing had been discontinued some years before when a large pipe organ was presented to the church. At that time the room where the ringers performed was needed for enlarging the organ chamber. Unlike the eight bells in Old North, the eight in Christ Church are not *all* in their original state. Two have been recast—one in 1835 after a tumble that presumably broke it; the other for tuning adjustments when three additional bells were being added in modern times "to make a noble chime." Even so, considered as a whole, this peal has a lineage richly associated with events hinging on America's struggle for freedom. Incidentally, it was on Christ Church bells in Philadelphia that P. T. Barnum's band of English ringers asked to execute a peal before returning home. This they did, June 9, 1850, it being the first successful peal ever heard in America.

The original eight were cast in London by Thomas Lester, the same Whitechapel founder who made the original casting of the Liberty Bell. The peal was brought to Philadelphia by Captain Richard Budden in his brig *Myrtill*. Captain Budden refused to charge for transportation, so in gratitude the bells were rung every time the *Myrtill* docked. They tolled at the captain's death in 1766, and for generations afterward upon the death of a descendant. In the affections of early Philadelphians, the Christ Church peal was second only to the Liberty Bell, for both had shared many great moments in the American Revolution. When the loss of the city seemed imminent, the eight bells were removed from their steeple to be

Steeple view of historic old Christ Church in Philadelphia, a Georgian masterpiece begun in 1727, when Benjamin Franklin organized three lotteries to help finance its construction.

sent, with the Liberty Bell, for safekeeping in Allentown—they jounced and joggled side by side in the same wagon on that fearsome journey. When returned to their steeple, they joined with the Liberty Bell in sounds of celebration. The sounds, of course, were the changes ringing out—as campanologists want to hear them ring out again.

The Carillon in America

Those who have familiarized themselves with carillons exhaust their superlatives attempting to describe them and the music of which they are capable under the hand of a master carillonneur. The nobility of the bell world . . . the grand pianos of the sky . . . the apex of bell casting—such expressions show up repeatedly in the vast literature that has grown up around the subject. Yet there are still many who do not differentiate between a carillon and a chime, who use the two terms interchangeably in describing one and the same instrument.

A well-defined difference exists between the two. Strictly defined, a carillon is comprised of at least twenty-three bells of traditional shape, perfectly tuned to the chromatic scale—that is, it embraces notes that correspond to both white and black keys on a piano, so that varied effects of harmony may be realized. A chime consists of fewer bells, usually tuned to the diatonic scale, encompassing only the white keys and therefore precluding the harmonics possible on a carillon. Commonly known as claviers, the keyboards for the two instruments and the manner of playing them also differ. The standard carillon clavier consists of two rows of levers, the upper row usually for the black notes, the lower for the white. These are not only grasped and pushed downward, as for a chime, but must sometimes be punched or thumped with a closed fist, with some fancy footwork on the pedal board at the same time.

In America, carillons swept into popularity during the decades following the two world wars. Though not entirely unknown before that time, they were few in number. When, in 1914, William Gorham Rice (a former ambassador to Belgium) published *Carillons of Belgium and Holland,* he listed all those he knew. Only two of these were in the United States, though there were actually three others of which he apparently had not heard. In contrast, another list compiled in 1956 showed more than seventy in the United States and Canada, thirty of them having been installed between 1951 and 1955. In the decades since, their number has more than doubled. It is estimated that in time there will be as many carillons in this country alone as there were in the entire world in 1924. The total world count then was believed to be 184.

Whereas change ringing was England's contribution to the world of campanology, carillons were the special pride of the Low Countries, where the story of their entry into America begins. Even before the *Mayflower* landed, Flanders and Holland were leading Europe in musical culture. To Flemish and Dutch ears, bells chiming one by one were not enough. They wanted harmony, but harmony on just any bells was impossible owing to their complex structure of overtones. The purest of tones were required; so it was that carillon bells came to be perfected and a new instrument was born. Carillons reached their highest development during the seventeenth century, but—ironically—the long-sought art of tuning bells perfectly was a secret too well kept. It died out before being passed on to the next generation and was lost for more than a century. When bell founding was resumed on the Continent, France was casting more carillons than the Low Countries, Bollée at Le Mans and Paccard at Annecy-le-Vieux taking the lead.

The first few installed in America came from these founders in France. The very first one was ordered at the request of missionaries of a monastic order who came from the Mother House in Le Mans to found Notre Dame University. Naturally they were acquainted with the bells Bollée was casting, and eventually they realized their dream of installing a carillon from Le Mans at their university. At that time, 1856, their twenty-three-bell instrument was considered fine indeed, but by present-day standards it no longer qualifies as a perfectly tuned carillon, and it is no longer used as such. The only ones of its bells still heard are those connected with the clock, which ring every fifteen minutes. Though no longer played, Notre Dame's carillon is nevertheless cherished because of the pioneering effort it represents in a movement that would one day make America the most carillon-minded of all nations.

The year 1922 marked the start of the modern carillon in America, when Taylor Bell Foundry of Loughborough, England, installed a twenty-three-bell instrument donated to the Portuguese Church of Our Lady of Good Voyage in Gloucester, Massachusetts, to ring the fishermen out to sea and signal their return. Two years later Saint Stephen's Episcopal Church of Cohasset, Massachusetts, acquired a carillon from Gillett and Johnston of Croydon, England. These were the first in a series of installations in this country, a series to be interrupted only by the Second World War. The two British firms in Loughborough and Croydon were taking the lead in producing perfectly tuned carillon bells. Not until they closed their doors on bellmaking would Holland and France again take the ascendancy.

To demonstrate the Flemish style of carillon playing so much admired on the Continent, as well as encourage its study, two Belgian campanologists were brought to America. One was Kamiel LeFevere, who was later to preside over the great Riv-

The twenty-three-bell carillon installed on the Notre Dame campus in 1856 is no longer used, but it is prized for its historic importance. Its tonal quality can still be appreciated, though, as the clock in the steeple of Sacred Heart Church is connected to a few of the bells, and they sound every fifteen minutes. *University of Notre Dame*

erside Church carillon in New York City, but who came originally to play at Saint Stephen's Episcopal Church in Cohasset. Mr. LeFevere was amazed at the interest aroused by his summer concerts. People by the thousands flocked to this small coastal town after Boston newspapers covered the concerts as important events. A reporter for the *Evening Transcript* aptly explained at least one facet of the carillon's appeal when he wrote: "Here is an essential form of music—public, because you can hear it without paying for the opportunity; public because it can't be shut within four walls, but must travel across space to the ears of many who are passing by or sitting at home doing their work."

To LeFevere goes considerable credit for bringing carillons to the attention of the American public and establishing their use in the New World as regularly scheduled concert instruments. He was in great demand as a guest artist, particularly at the dedication of new installations. When he gave the 1932 dedicatory concert on the Laura Spelman Rockefeller Carillon at the University of Chicago, 50,000 people sat in their cars or on the lawn to listen. His admiration for the instrument and his mastery of it were apparent. But there was something else, perhaps less apparent to anyone except another carillonneur: his talent for arranging a balanced, appealing program of selections.

LeFevere attributed his versatility in arranging to his study with Jef Denyn in Mechlin, Belgium. It was Denyn who had been working to elevate the status of carillons, to restore their prestige, by introducing their use for recitals as opposed to their traditional use for playing hourly tunes or for observing special occasions. Denyn's formal evening concerts at Mechlin began drawing international acclaim. He was also a masterful teacher, one who was somehow able to convey to his students the delights of making the carillon a folk instrument of sorts, its music to be enjoyed by the entire populace within hearing range. On this point, his star pupil's training was put to a test one Christmas during the Second World War. LeFevere was then presiding over the carillon at Riverside Church. The voices of all the "singing towers" in Europe had been stilled, and so the Office of War Infor-

Kamiel LeFevere, the first carillonneur to preside over what was then the world's largest carillon, in Riverside Church, New York City.

mation asked LeFevere to record Christmas carols of foreign lands for shortwave broadcast to occupied countries. Little music for carillons had been written except such arrangements as individual players were making. Consequently, LeFevere found himself scurrying around to French pastry shops and restaurants that catered to different nationalities, where he persuaded the proprietors to sing favorite carols of their native lands while he jotted down the melodies he would later transcribe for the carillon. The proprietors needed little persuasion; they were overjoyed to be helping their countrymen.

The standards and patterns LeFevere so enthusiastically established have been endorsed just as enthusiastically by today's growing number of carillon performers. Some have studied and graduated with highest honors from the world-famous school for carillonneurs in Mechlin. At least two have written authoritative texts in their field; several have been moving spirits in arranging for carillon instruction to be given at fifteen or more schools, colleges, and churches. The University of Michigan offers a major in the subject.

Membership in the Guild of Carillonneurs in North America provides a convenient yardstick for measuring the constantly increasing interest in playing these "grand pianos of the sky." The guild organized in 1936 with fewer than twenty qualified members. This number doubled during the next quarter century and shows no signs of lessening at the present time. A count of women members in the guild is especially interesting, in the light of the search for new areas of performance for today's women. At mid-century, only four held professional rank in the guild. Now there are not only many more, but there are new "firsts" for women year by year. "This year marks another victory for women's liberation in the carillon field," announced the University of Chicago in a program brochure for its 1975 summer concert series on the Laura Spelman Rockefeller Carillon. For the first time, three women recitalists were performing. At the conclusion of the third feminine recitalist's concert, a quite different "first" was established—for a carillon tower, that is. To celebrate the forty-second summer of recitals, a select group of guests climbed the 280 steps to the clavier room—usually not the scene of revelry and dining, but on this occasion the setting for a catered fondue dinner!

The Wellesley College Carillon at Wellesley, Massachusetts, played a key role in elevating women's interest in becoming carillonneurs. It was the first such instrument to appear on a women's college campus, but for thirteen years after its installation in 1931 it contributed little to daily life there. Its music was heard only on special occasions until, by 1944, through the happy collaboration of a few campanologists among alumnae and faculty, this situation was reversed. A period of instruction and practice was offered all interested students, about fifty of whom were chosen to organize their own guild. Once it was organized, the girls began playing in relays three times a day. Mrs. Charlotte Nichols Geene, donor of the bells, had visited Belgium's Royal Carillon School and been allowed to copy many of the songs and exercises later used by the Wellesley girls.

As a footnote to women's early role in carillon playing, the name of Miss Mary Griffith of the Griffith Music School in Atlanta should not be overlooked. At the Chicago World's Fair of 1893, this stouthearted lady watched an Old World carillonneur at the heavy wooden clavier of the carillon from Belgium. Unable to forget the beautiful music, she was determined to have that instrument in Atlanta for the Cotton States and International Exposition in 1895. She persuaded the Cot-

Left
In Wellesley's imposing Gothic bell tower one of the first campus carillons on this continent was dedicated in 1931. It has played an increasingly important part in campus life. *Wellesley College*

Right
One of the early members of Wellesley's own Guild of Carillonneurs takes her turn at the clavier. *Wellesley College*

ton States' official committee, but with the proviso that the carillon would have the right notes to play "Dixie." She herself would act as recitalist, though she was totally without experience. Miss Griffith's arduous preparation for her debut consisted of practicing all the preceding summer on a number of baseball bats heavily weighted on one end.

The story of carillons in this country is not complete without mention of John D. Rockefeller, Jr.'s determination to build in New York a greater one than the largest in Europe. Through his scouts (spies, as some jestingly called them) he learned that the largest on the Continent had fifty-one bells, so he ordered one with fifty-three bells for the Park Avenue Baptist Church, in memory of his mother, Laura Spelman Rockefeller. The year was 1924, but before too long the congregation moved to Riverside Church on Morningside Heights, where eventually the size of the carillon was increased to seventy-four bells, making it for many years the largest in the world. The bourdon, always the largest bell in a carillon and the lowest in pitch, weighs twenty tons and is more than ten feet high. Three huge clappers activate the bell for different purposes, two outside and one two-ton clapper inside. This Riverside bourdon remains the largest tuned bell in the world, although the carillon's aggregate size has been exceeded by the seventy-seven bells in the Kirk-in-the-Hills at Bloomfield Hills, Michigan. Nevertheless, John D. Rockefeller, Jr., set new records in belldom when he donated the Riverside instrument, and this fact is noted for posterity in the inscription encircling the base of its bourdon:

FOR THE FIRST TIME IN HISTORY, A CARILLON
COMPASS OF 5 OCTAVES IS HERE ACHIEVED
AND EXCEEDED

The largest tuned bell in the world is the bourdon, or lowest base note, in the carillon of Riverside Church, New York City. It stands ten feet high and weighs twenty tons.

Riverside's sister carillon in the Rockefeller Memorial Chapel at the University of Chicago was also the gift of John D. Rockefeller, Jr. It contains seventy-two bells, with a bourdon weighing only two tons less than its New York counterpart. Considered the masterpiece of its founder, Gillette and Johnston, the Chicago carillon is noted for the qualiy of its bass bells, a quality unmatched in any other instrument. For nearly thirty years after their dedication in 1932, those sonorous bells charmed the university neighborhood with Wagner's "Parsifal Tune" to mark the hours and quarter hours. Then a crisis developed. Sensing a threat to the quality of tone emerging from the great Gothic tower, the carillonneur climbed up to inspect the four bells used for the Parsifal notes. Just as he feared! All those years the clappers had hit the same spots continually—582,175 quarter-hour performances—and the bell walls were worn. The usual practice is to have the bells given a quarter turn every quarter century. With the Chicago bells being uncommonly heavy, however, the cost appeared prohibitive; the alternative was to change the tune.

Mr. Blackwood, a composer on the faculty, was called upon for new music to mark the time. He carefully avoided a tune using the worn bells, featuring instead the $30,000 low E bell of rare "gorgeous sound," a favorite with every carillonneur who has ever presided over the Laura Spelman Rockefeller Carillon. When the new tune was first heard, consternation and disbelief enveloped the neighboring community. After all, Wagner's "Parsifal Tune" had become almost a landmark melody. Caught at the crunch point between tradition and need, the university had no choice but to cope as best it could with unhappy listeners. Mr. Blackwood's new tune remained.

186

Midway between the Gulf of Mexico and the Atlantic Ocean, in Florida's heartland, what is reputedly the world's most beautiful carillon rises from Mountain Lake Sanctuary. It is rightly called Florida's Singing Tower and America's Taj Mahal. To build this sanctuary was an early and persistent ambition of author-editor Edward W. Bok, but it was not until the 1920s that he discovered a suitable place for what was to become a remarkable garden, a meditative tower ringing with music, a natural resting place for birds, and a sanctuary for millions of Americans seeking renewal of spirit. President Coolidge dedicated Mountain Lake, with impressive ceremonies, February 1, 1929.

Bok's fondness for nature and for music stemmed from his boyhood in the Netherlands. There his grandparents, to whom Mountain Lake Sanctuary is dedicated, had transformed a sandbar off the Netherlands coast from a barren pirate-infested reef into a garden haven for birds crossing the North Sea. There, too, he had lived within sound of that unforgettable music from fine old singing towers, as they are called in the Low Countries. In presenting his singing tower to the American public, Bok implanted something of the Old World in the adopted land that had given him stature and wealth, so it was eminently fitting that he call upon a carillonneur of the Old World to make the bells truly sing. His choice was Anton Brees, who shared rank with Kamiel LeFevere as the foremost carillonneurs in the world at that time. Brees had trained under his father, Gustaf Brees, who for fifty-six years was bellmaster at Antwerp's fourteenth-century cathedral. At seventeen young Brees gave his first recital in the same cathedral, going on to become a recitalist at great carillons around the world. On becoming bellmaster at Florida's Singing Tower, he brought with him the Old World concept of the bells as a folk instrument. Long-hair music he would not play. He used to say:

> Ninety-five per cent of my listeners probably don't understand what makes good music. Even fewer are experts on bell music. The minstrel, true to himself and his mission, sings the ballads and the hymns of

Left
Bok Tower, often referred to as the Singing Tower, is mirrored in the quiet waters at Mountain Lake Sanctuary in Florida. *State Photographic Archives, Strozier Library, Florida State University*

Right
Anton Brees playing the Singing Tower bells for a 1946 Governors' Conference. *State Photographic Archives, Strozier Library, Florida State University*

Bringing the Bok Tower bells from the port at Jacksonville. Like all carillon bells, they were hung stationary, on five levels, with the largest (a 23,000-pound tenor) at the bottom and the smallest (an 11-pounder) at the top. *State Photographic Archives, Strozier Library, Florida State University*

the people. His approach to the people is simple—mindful that it is better to use five notes with understanding than ten thousand notes in a strange tongue.

Bree's most requested songs were "The Bells of St. Mary's" and, among hymns, "The Old Rugged Cross."

The shaft of the Singing Tower, which rises from a base of native coquina rock, is constructed of golden Florida stone and salmon pink Georgia marble. Floridian birds like flamingos and cranes crown the pinnacles around the octagonal summit. The seventy-one bells were made in Loughborough, England, and tuned on the Taylor "True Harmonic System," giving them a remarkable sweetness and purity of tone. Their music, always best heard at a distance, carries through faience grilles to blend with the songs of the sanctuary birds—over 100 species thus far noted.

Though a large number of bells obviously permits a greater tonal range, size need not be the sole criterion for a pleasing carillon. The Hoover Tower on Leland Stanford's campus in California is proof. There, thirty-five bells are housed in the tower of Hoover Institute and Library on War, Revolution, and Peace. They were cast in Belgium for the Belgian Pavilion at the 1939 World's Fair in New York, then later given to Stanford in appreciation of the former President's humanitarian work in Belgium during the First World War to relieve its starving, war-stricken people. Dedicated to peace, the tower is looked upon as a working symbol of its purpose, as is the library filled with documents and mementos of the man who believed peace could best be achieved by alleviating human suffering.

Carillons in the New World never have assumed important civic status, like those in Europe. Their role on school and college campuses is the closest they have come to that status. Fully one-third are located where their music not only adds pomp and dignity to traditional academic ceremonies, but relates as well to daily campus life. To try to name the most outstanding, even the top ten, would be to risk grave omissions, for there are many superb campus installations. The three already named offer some insight into ways a carillon can be adapted to varying architectural situations on each campus: at Wellesley, it is within the administrative complex; at the University of Chicago, in the Rockefeller Memorial Chapel; at Leland Stanford, in conjunction with a special library.

At least a scattering of singing towers belies the belief that all such instruments were made abroad. Though this country at various times produced chimes as fine as any from England, very little concentration was ever directed toward manufacturing carillons. One exception must be made, however, in favor of the Meneely firms, which cast perhaps a dozen in all. The original bells in the unique Deeds Carillon of Dayton, Ohio, were the work of Meneely Bell Company; the original ones for Washington Memorial National Carillon at Valley Forge, Pennsylvania, the work of Meneely and Company.

On Easter Sunday, 1942, a uniquely beautiful shaft of thirty-two bells rang out for the first time from Carillon Park in Dayton, this being the Deeds Carillon, gift of Mrs. Edward A. Deeds to her community. Before embarking on the enterprise, Mrs. Deeds—an accomplished musician herself—viewed many carillons at home and abroad while making a careful study of bells. That she entrusted the Meneely firm with casting bells of the quality she wanted is a tribute to their skill. The designers of Rockefeller Center in New York City were chosen to carry out the donor's vision of a tower that would mount the bells entirely in the open, thus ensuring a better carrying power. The result is a veritable chandelier of bells suspended from four perpendicular shafts forming an open tower. The bells are all easily visible, with the largest, weighing 7,000 pounds, at the top, the cluster then tapering down to the smallest. Since this is in direct contrast to the usual arrangement of

On his way to work on his political papers at Hoover Institute, the former President was frequently seen passing the carillon tower on the Leland Stanford campus, given in his honor. *Hoover Institute Archives*

The unique Deeds Carillon in Carillon Park, Dayton, Ohio, has been likened to a veritable chandelier of bells. *Carillon Park*

keeping the largest bells at the bottom, it involved additional engineering problems, but Mrs. Deeds's noted architects met every requirement (and more, for the shaft was so well constructed that it is now easily supporting ten more bells added within recent years). The bells are played not from a traditional-type clavier but from a keyboardlike console controlling a ringing mechanism. The total aesthetic effect is one of openness and spaciousness, the music of the bells cascading down over land that few realize was once only a bushy swamp.

Meneely and Company's special pride centered in the lowest twenty-eight of the bells that make up Washington Memorial National Carillon at Valley Forge. All the bells here—now fifty-eight in number—represent the apex of achievement on the part of their founders, inasmuch as the instrument has evolved gradually over a long period of years. This has required that bells added at different times be tuned to those already in the tower, a very difficult feat. The inspiration for the Washington Memorial bells came from the founder of the chapel in whose tower they are housed. Thirteen Peace Chimes representing the original colonies were dedicated July 4, 1926, commemorating 150 years of American independence. To the Peace Chimes was added a large National Birthday Bell bearing a star for each state and, bordering the base, the name of each.

Those chimes marked only the initial steps toward a noble national carillon encompassing one bell for each state, aside from those already dedicated to the colonies, plus the National Birthday Bell. The additional ones were to be assigned states in order of their population in the 1920s, the largest being for Illinois and weighing 8,000 pounds. Even that plan for forty-nine bells was enlarged by adding still others to allow for greater musical expression, these to be assigned the nation's territories, with the smallest—for Wake Island—weighing just over thirteen pounds.

A carillon consisting of one bell from each state, plus a national birthday bell, sounds from the noble Washington Memorial National Carillon at Valley Forge. *Washington Memorial National Carillon*

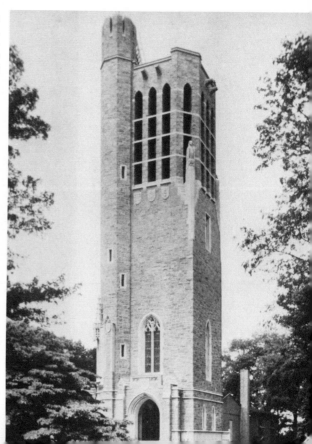

The majestic bell tower seen at Valley Forge today was finally completed in 1953. The entire undertaking had been the responsibility of the Daughters of the American Revolution, whose members made a special pilgrimage to dedicate the carillon in 1956. Appropriately, considering the unusual significance of the instrument, there exists an exceptional and continuing rapport between the carillonneur and his bells at Valley Forge. Carillonneur Frank Pechin Law was on hand with professional assistance while the tower was under construction, played the dedicatory recital, and has remained in charge of programming and playing the bells since that time. His early training was under Kamiel LeFevere, and also Percival Price, former Dominion Carillonneur of Canada and presently professor of campanology at the University of Michigan. Mr. Law himself is now one of the few teachers of carillon music in the country.

With America enjoying lasting supremacy in the world of carillons, it is worth taking another, closer, look at the harmonics involved in their music. Thousands who enjoy such bell music remain mystified by its appeal, which has no equal in the musical world—and for good reason. The term "harmonic" is described in *Webster's Dictionary* as an overtone, especially one produced by vibration. Each bell, it will be recalled, sounds five such overtones, and these five must be in perfect tune to produce a perfect chord. This is the simple principle of bell tuning. Consider, then, the carillon, where several bells are sounded at one time. Each rings a perfect chord in tune with whatever other perfect chords are ringing. Add to this the varying degrees of touch each carillonneur lends to his playing, and the unusual quality of the sound becomes more understandable.

During recent months, the American public has been brought face to face with a limited suggestion of the inner workings of a true carillon, plus the beauty of the bells per se, through open-air concerts on the traveling Pepsi Carillon assembled by the I. T. Verdin Company. It is the only portable unit of its kind in the United States, one of four worldwide (one in Belgium, two in Holland). The bells, covering three musical octaves, were cast and tuned by Petit and Fritsen, Ltd., of Aark-Rixtel, Holland, a foundry dating to the seventeenth century, now partly owned by the Verdin firm. The youthful carillonneur for the portable unit is Larry Weinstein, the youngest person ever to receive the coveted diploma from the Netherlands Carillon School and the first American to be awarded first place in the Dutch Carillon Society's national competition.

Of the various forms of ringing now experiencing a renaissance in America, the art of handbell ringing has won the greatest following. No one of the other forms cuts across generations to the same extent. Performers can be found among preteens and grandparents alike, not only in bell choirs as a medium of worship, but in ringing bands organized purely for musical enjoyment at schools, retirement centers, museums, homes for the handicapped, clubs of every description, or just privately among neighborhood friends. The popularity of this type of performing art is not difficult to explain. It requires the usual discipline needed for rhythmic coordination; but, other than that, it is a flexible activity for groups either large or small, with anywhere from one to five chromatic octaves of bells, with or without a director. Concerts can be given in the open as well as indoors, and under a variety of situations, whether in Grand Central Station to cheer Christmas travelers or at a garden wedding reception.

Usually the players number about ten or twelve, each controlling two or more

The traveling Pepsi Carillon assembled by the I. T. Verdin Company never fails to attract interested listeners and observers. *I. T. Verdin Company and Pepsi-Cola Company*

bells of different pitch. A common technique is to have them stand before a table on which the bells are placed in chromatic order, upright or lying down with their handles toward the players. Using this technique, each person can control from three to five bells; however, if the table is omitted and performers hold one bell in each hand all through the concert, those are ordinarily the only ones he can very well manage unless he carries a third on a cord around his neck. Some handbell artists prefer solo ringing, in which case they can work creditably well with an octave of bells—even more, if they are skilled performers—arranged on a table. Each bell is fitted with a flexible leather loop for a handle, making it easy to manipulate with a flip of the wrist. Each also has a felt or a leather clapper "trapped" in a device that permits it to strike only when the bell is deliberately rung with a forward movement of the wrist.

Handbells were first made almost by accident, when men ringing changes in English towers sought some way to practice without standing in drafty bell chambers and letting the whole countryside hear their mistakes. Whitechapel Foundry experimented with a small graduated set of tuned bells that could be carried into the village pub for practice sessions. The idea was immediately popular

Children are drawn to the beauty and the mechanics of the big bells at close range. *I. T. Verdin Company*

with pub patrons, who began clamoring to hear familiar tunes on similar bells. Ringing bands suddenly flourished, to vie with one another in exciting contests that drew huge crowds. It was a prize band named the Lancashire Ringers that impressed America's circus showman, P. T. Barnum, in 1844. He wasted no time in booking the group for an American tour, promising great fame and fortune, but they must appear not as Lancashiremen but as the more colorful Swiss bell ringers. Despite their objections, Barnum insisted they grow long mustaches and wear Alpine costumes. When the troupe protested that, in any event, they could not speak the Swiss language, he told them to use their natural dialect, since nobody in America would know the difference. No one did!

Barnum is sometimes credited with introducing handbell music to America. In truth, however, the Peak family had already been entertaining with bells for several years when Barnum arrived in 1847 with his campanologians, as he called them in his autobiography. The Peaks, in turn, had competition from the Raniers, who entertained with bells, yodeling, and Alpine songs; and from another group billing themselves simply as Swiss Bell Ringers or Campanologians. Both were native Swiss troupes, so it is quite possible that Barnum took his inspiration from seeing costumed Swiss ringers like these. At any rate, so popular were the real Swiss performers and Barnum's close imitation of them that before long almost all such entertainers were assuming the title Swiss Bell Ringers. Thus the long persistent misconception that all handbell music is indigenous to Switzerland.

New York heard its first such concert in 1844. "Musical jugglery," the *New York Daily Tribune* called it, that "astonished and delighted" capacity crowds at Niblo's Gardens. At the end of a dozen or so concerts, one reviewer wrote, "We have listened to all kinds of music, but never to any which so completely thrilled us as the magic tones of those bells as they flung upon the quivering air magnificent pieces. . . ." The repertoire as listed in advertisements included: Haydn's Surprise Symphony, "Polonaise" by Bellini, "Philomenia Waltz" by Strauss, and "Blue Bells of Scotland."

Many later itinerant ringing troupes capitalized on the prosperity that eventually followed the close of the Civil War. The Spauldings were perhaps the best known, organized in Boston in 1856 with bells considered to be of superior tone. Not to be outdone by their closest competition, the Peaks, they advertised their program as "the most complete, most artistic, and most pleasing entertainment in this country." Boston found that the Spauldings lived up to their advance billing when in 1867 they gave a July Fourth concert for an audience of more than 9,000. The press declared the program the best entertainment of its kind ever given in Boston.

Like so many of the handbell teams, the English Handbell Ringers Concert Company, under auspices of Redpath Lyceum Bureau of Boston, was a family enterprise—in this case, of the four Shipp brothers, who originally emigrated to Massachusetts from Cambridgeshire, England, where William Shipp had been a change ringer. The brothers reached their peak of popularity when they were awarded a contract to play at the World's Columbian Exposition in Chicago in 1893. Theirs was typical of the smaller ringing teams that sprang up in the late 1800s. Even entertainers who were not primarily musicians sought handbells to increase the appeal of their vaudeville acts. Years later, a popular couple of radio fame, Fibber McGee and Molly (Jim and Marion Jordan), owned and operated the

Metropolitan Entertainers early in their career, before the days of radio. Along with
other stage attractions, they gave concerts on a handsome set of handbells.

A series of economic depressions beginning with the Cleveland administration
discouraged some of the handbell groups, until gradually many disbanded or returned to their native lands. Then, too, in another decade or so, the vaudeville era
would come to a close. All in all, bell ringing as a performing art seemed destined
to end. As it happened, though, that relatively quiet span of years early in the present century was only prologue to a most astounding and unforseen renaissance that
would place handbell ringing almost entirely in the hands of amateurs rather than
professionals.

The principal promoter of this musical form in its modern version was Mrs. Arthur A. Shurcliff, daughter of Dr. Arthur H. Nichols, the noted Boston scholar and
author who had reintroduced change ringing to this country. From a trip to England as a young girl, to try her own hand at change ringing, Mrs. Shurcliff returned
with a set of English handbells such as change ringers were using for practice. Playing them became a lifelong interest with her, and as her children learned the art
together, they started the custom of trooping through the snow on Christmas Eve,
ringing carols on Beacon Hill. When Mrs. Shurcliff organized a group known as the
Beacon Hill Bell Ringers in 1923, it was one of the first handbell bands of the modern period, one that would influence the formation of other groups, especially in
New England.

From there on, successive steps in the development of handbell ringing were
paved with various milestones. In 1937 the New England Guild was founded under

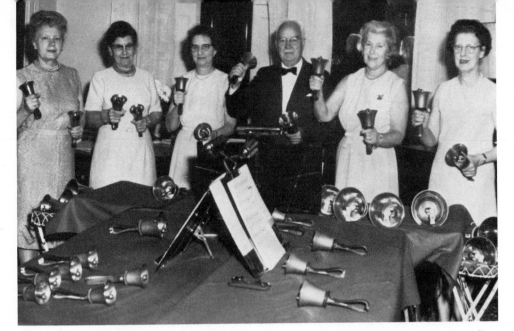

The Beacon Hill Bell Ringers as they appeared in the mid-1960s, performing "Saint Paul's Steeple," their theme tune. The ringers (*left to right*) were: Mrs. Harriet Glick, Miss Vivian Schumann, Miss Amy Stone, Mr. Raymond Myrer, Mrs. Raymond Myrer (leader and arranger), and Miss Florence Berlin. *Mrs. Robenia Myrer Smith*

Mrs. Shurcliff's direction; then in 1954 appeared the American Guild of English Handbell Ringers (AGEHR), also under her direction. Within a quarter century the New England Guild counted practically one hundred member groups, which held a highly successful annual festival at Ipswich, Massachusetts. In less time than that, in a mere four years, the AGEHR numbered at least one hundred ringing bands and choirs on its membership roster, scattered over twenty-five states. With such a geographical spread of interest, it was at about that time that handbell ringing was "discovered" by the American public. As a result, AGEHR accelerated at an even faster rate during the '60s. Now, at the national festival for members, over 1,000 individuals come from forty-odd states, to ring and to listen to others perform. That is quite a bit of ringing!

Any number of unique groups represent milestones during AGEHR's formative years. One of the charter member groups, a quintet named the Blue Bells of Saint Louis, was believed to be the only bell-ringing grandmothers' organization devoted to entertaining. The group not only averaged four concerts each week, but, out of 650 groups being auditioned, was chosen to appear on the Ted Mack television program.

Much of this suddenly expanded interest is explained by the interest churches have shown in forming so-called bell choirs. The introduction of handbells into the music program of the famous Brick Presbyterian Church of New York City in 1947 was a milestone. For a number of years, certain of the choirs drew wide attention while cheering holiday travelers in Grand Central Station; the choir members accompanied their carol singing with handbells. Their impressive bell-ringing processionals down the avenue to the church, for such special services as Easter, were also widely covered by the press. The combination of mellow-toned bells with choir voices and with other traditional instruments of worship has proved an invigorating asset in church music. Who could find less than devotional inspiration in hearing an antiphonal descant rung while the congregation sings "God of Our Fathers"? Or

195

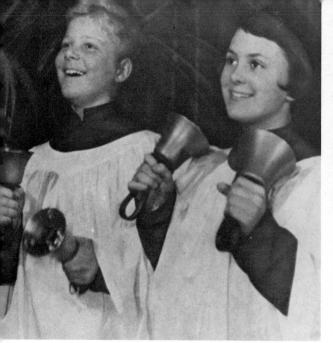

Left
Two enthusiastic youth choir members from the (then) recently introduced form of worship with handbells at New York's Brick Presbyterian Church. *Brick Presbyterian Church, New York City*

Right
The Wesleyan Bell Choir of First Methodist Church, Lake Charles, Louisiana, is a very concert-minded group. In recent years, they have averaged fifty public appearances annually. The director, Donald E. Allured, is not only director of music at the church but also national president of the American Guild of English Handbell Ringers. *First Methodist Church, Lake Charles, Louisiana*

the Dutch carol "Let the Heavens Be Joyful," arranged for handbells and trumpet? An arrangement for handbells and oboe of the "Pontifical March"? Or a stunning performance of the "Allelujah!" with combined bell choirs and organ?

If youth groups now outnumber all others in performing on handbells—and they do—it is because young people find in this form of music a flexible, versatile, rhythmic group activity that discourages boredom and challenges creativity. In the present music-conscious era, the superbly cast handbells available to groups (the top favorites are from Whitechapel) are capable of producing tonal music equal to that from any other fine instruments. These modern bells and the modern manner of playing them bear scant resemblance to the vaudevilian ones, often of a more tinkly type played with the greatest possible rapidity. With the more measured ringing of modern sonorous bells, even young children find it musically pleasing to hear themselves play just simple tunes in unison. They can graduate to rounds or basic harmonies, then work up to fairly elaborate sacred and secular selections, with perhaps something like "Baubles, Bangles, Beads, Bells, and Bongos" for occasional variation.

Adapting so readily to almost limitless possibilities, handbell music as it is known and played in America today is quite likely here to stay. The evaluations of this ongoing art made by Scott Parry in his *Story of Handbells* are as true now as when he made them in 1957. He claimed the number of ringing bands was growing annually, and televised concerts and press articles growing more numerous, so that handbells are as familiar to the average person today as they were to stage audiences of a century ago.

196

10

BELLS IN STORY AND SONG

Because of their emotional impact—to a lesser extent because of their rhythmic ring-ing—the sound of bells has for centuries appealed to writers and composers. Their varied individual reactions are reflected in the records they have left. Poets of im-portance, as well as those who aspire only to verse writing, have been especially sensitive to bells as a poetic theme. Some, like Henry Wadsworth Longfellow, used them as their inspiration more than once. The best known of such poems by Long-fellow, "I Heard the Bells on Christmas Day," is familiar principally because it has been beautifully set to music that is still widely sung as a Christmas hymn. Frequently one or more of the last stanzas is omitted in the singing, so it sometimes comes as a surprise to learn that Longfellow was not writing about just any bells, but about those ringing out hope during the darkest days of the Civil War. The whole emotional reaction the poet was experiencing when he heard those particular Christmas bells is wrapped in the last stanzas.

Among that cluster of New England writers every schoolchild associates with Longfellow were others, such as John Greenleaf Whittier, Henry David Thoreau, and Emily Dickinson, who found their own personal inspiration in bells according to their interests. Being a passionate abolitionist, Whittier wrote his "Laus Deo!" upon hearing of the constitutional amendment passed to abolish slavery. It is an ex-ultant poem, opening with these lines:

It is done!
Clang of bell and roar of gun
Send the tidings up and down
How the belfries rock and reel!
How the great guns, peal on peal,
Fling the joy from town to town!

> Ring, O Bells!
> Every stroke exulting tells
> Of the burial hour of crime,
>   Loud and long, that all may hear,
>   Ring for every listening ear
> Of Eternity and time!

A host of poems from other American writers appeal in a variety of ways, from the lighthearted lines of Eugene Field's "Why Do Bells of Christmas Ring?" or Rachel Field's "Doorbells" to more reflective work such as Thomas Walsh's attempt to express the almost inexpressible in "The Carillon" or Walt Whitman's moralizing in *Sea-Drift*.

From Book XIX, Sea-Drift:

ABOARD AT A SHIP'S HELM

Aboard at a ship's helm,
A young steersman steering with care.

Through fog on a sea-coast dolefully ringing,
An ocean-bell—O a warning bell, rock'd by the waves.

O you give good notice indeed, you bell by the sea-reefs ringing,
Ringing, ringing, to warn the ship from its wreck-place.

For as on the alert O steersman, you mind the loud admonition,
The bows turn, the freighted ship tacking speeds away under her
*   gray sails,*
The beautiful and noble ship with all her precious wealth speeds away
*   gayly and safe.*

But O the ship, the immortal ship! O ship aboard the ship!
Ship of the body, ship of the soul, voyaging, voyaging, voyaging.

Rural tintinnabulations mark a trio of poems from Robert Nathan, Lew Sarett, and Pulitzer Poetry Award winner Robert P. Tristram Coffin. For Robert Nathan, no particular tintinnabulations beckoned him, just "Bells in the country/They sing the heart to rest." For Lew Sarett, the jang-jangle of the lowly cowbell echoed through his mind as it does through lines in his "Cattle Bells," telling "What patient strength of earth their tones disclose/The peace of stars like quiet falling snows. . . ." And for Mr. Coffin, it was the unexpected sound of a distant, misplaced cowbell when "Suddenly, two thousand miles from home and boyhood . . . this sound/Of a bell he would have known/Over half the world around/A cool, cool bell from balsam hills/Here in the palm-trees' flat hot home . . . ."

Both Edgar Allan Poe's and Bret Harte's impressions live through their rhythmic meters imitating bells "Keeping time, time, time/In a sort of Runic rhyme," as Poe expressed it in his immortal poem "The Bells." Bret Harte fell under the spell of the Spanish missions, being quite carried away with the sound of their bells. Of his several titles using this poetic theme, "The Mission Bells of Monterey" was chosen by the great French composer Charles Gounod to set to music. He could sense the dip and swell of sound with every line of Harte's "O bells that rang/O bells that sang/Above the martyr's wilderness." An Edgar Guest verse falls into this same category of poetic impressions popular for their rhythmic imagery of bells as well as their sentiment about them. "I'm not the kind that loves the past and all that's modern scorns/I merely say that sleigh bells were more musical than horns."

Bells as a theme in American literature have received their best treatment in the realm of poetry. Though they appear less often in the fictional field, there are exceptions. An assortment of tales has been told by short-story writers of stature like Nathaniel Hawthorne, Irvin S. Cobb, Martha Ostenso, Edgar Allan Poe, and Elizabeth Yates. Here, again, the stories are as varied as the moods their creators conjured up for the reader. "The Devil in the Belfry" almost anyone would immediately associate with Edgar Allan Poe. But "The Bell That Rang for Love" is in the gentler mood that characterizes Martha Ostenso's style.

Novelists, however, have done little in developing any similar themes against an American setting. One exception is the *Miracle of the Bells*, an inspriational novel about four days when the church bells rang day and night in a small Pennsylvania town. The ringing was a publicity stunt, but this fact was overshadowed as the plot unraveled, until the story became one of transforming a mining community from poverty to concerned brotherhood. Russell Janney, author of that original, dramatically told novel, was well qualified to write it by his experience as a theatrical producer and a creator of lyrics for stage revues.

Writers of juveniles and stories for the very young have given freer rein to the possibilities in creating stories around a bell. The result is a wonderfully fine collection of children's and young people's books in this area. Many, like Leo Politi's *The Mission Bell*, are based on facts interesting in themselves. Politi's picture story relates the travels of Father Junipero Serra in the California wilderness and the building of the missions. Katherine Milhous's *With Bells On* is an equally authentic tale, actually a picture story, capturing the spirit of Pennsylvania farm life in the days when Conestoga bells rang out.

For young people, some of the mysteries centering around a bell combine historical fact with fanciful lore. John Scott Douglas's mystery, *The Secret of the Undersea Bell*, was winner of the *Boys' Life* Dodd Mead Prize Competition. It deals with California divers who constantly hear a bell tolling beneath the surface of the sea. Lillian Budd combined realism with a hint of mystery in *The Bell of Kamela*, set up in lumberjack country. The story centers around a bell that sounds a name every time it moves in the wind. Flashbacks explain its needful origin for a pioneer family trekking to Oregon.

Writers of juveniles have done an equally excellent job in the nonfiction field. There is Elizabeth Coatsworth's *Boston Bells*, her account of a few days in the young life of John Singleton Copley during the Knowles Riots, thirty years before the Boston Tea Party. British soldiers were roughing up resistant Boston folk, including John's family. In desperation, citizens found a voice for their fury in Boston's church bells, which they put to ringing so loud that their menacing din frightened off the British.

Considered all together, stories and historical retellings such as those just mentioned give young readers quite a few points of reference from which to view the usefulness of bells from colonial times on. There is still another area, however, in which some of the very best writing of all is found, designed to relate fully the events surrounding the Liberty Bell on the eve of the American Revolution, to correct the image too many schoolchildren have been given of that climactic moment in history. *The Bell That Rang for Freedom*, a masterful account by Olga Hall-Quest, is almost telegenic in its vivid, moving scenes.

Writing such as this, picturing Revolutionary times, is a far cry from the sometimes legendary, even distorted, versions once given every schoolchild. Undoubtedly the most widely read story in American history for many years was George Lippard's fictional tale about the Liberty Bell that he wrote and published in 1846, telling of an aged man standing tensely in the tower of the Old State House, waiting to ring the bell when Congress had finished signing the Declaration of Independence, July 4, 1776. Downstairs was "a flaxen-haired boy with eyes of summer blue," ready to signal him when Congress's quill pen had squeaked its last signature. In fairness to Lippard, when he published his account in the Philadelphia *Saturday Courier*, he plainly labeled it one of a collection of *Legends of the Revolution*. But it had such great dramatic impact that other writers immediately appropriated it, even enlarged on it by picturing the flaxen-haired lad climbing a ladder to the bell tower, crying, "Ring, Grandpa, ring!" The legend was reprinted in the Franklin Fifth Reader and other school readers, so that generations of Americans grew up believing that whole fanciful July Fourth scene as it never really happened. It even became the subject of a supposedly historic American painting.

The thematic use of bells in music may not have reached any great heights with American composers, though it has been continuously popular, more or less on a folksy level. For either voice or instrumental use there is a never-ending list of selections composed as reveries with chime effects; but for increased listening interest, there are a few somewhat more imaginative musical scores creating special sound effects, as in "Signal Bells at Sea" or in "Silver Sleigh Bells." Among Abraham Lincoln's favorite songs was "The Silver Bell Waltz," with dance rhythms imitating the sound of little tinkling bells. It was Lincoln's close friend Lamon Crosby who, on learning of Lincoln's fondness for music, presented him with a copy of this waltz in 1864. The President was touched by such thoughtfulness in troubled times, for Crosby was not only a warm personal friend but one of the Union's most trusted spies in the War Between the States. War Department files credit him with supplying much of the information that enabled General Grant to force the Confederate surrender at Appomattox.

John Philip Sousa's spirited martial airs like "The Liberty Bell March," though not ranked by critics among higher musical efforts, have nevertheless proved enduring with the masses—and it was the masses, not the elite, to whom Sousa catered. As the "Pied Piper of Patriotism," Sousa found in the Liberty Bell a fitting symbol for his newest march "to make people stand erect, proud to be called Americans." Its publication marked a happy upturn in Sousa's fortunes, for he had been treated less than honorably by his publishers, who were collecting all royalties on his music. For this newest march, he contracted with another firm, John Church Company of Cincinnati. As a result, "The Liberty Bell March" netted him $40,000 within seven years, whereas such other famous marches as "Semper Fidelis" had brought him only $35 from his previous publishers! The new march became a regular feature of each tour after it was introduced in 1893. Cornets, trumpets, and trombones would come to the front of the stage and face the audience for a striking

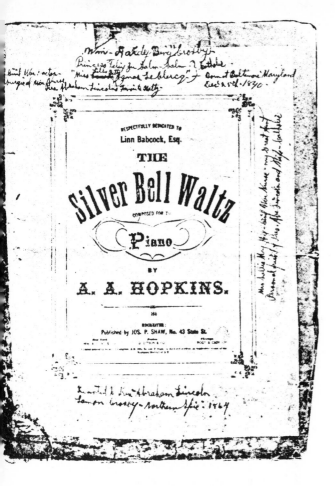

The copy of "The Silver Bell Waltz" owned by President Lincoln. After his death, Mrs. Lincoln returned it to the donor, in whose family it has been handed down.
Abraham Lincoln Book Shop

finale using "The Liberty Bell March." Strangely, Sousa's original band score for this number was lost for thirty-five years. After it was found, it was donated to the United States Marine Band on November 6, 1967, the anniversary date of the "March King's" birth.

Folk songs and composed songs dwelling on love's tribulations and tragedies and growing out of the American environment—neither of these groups should be overlooked in searching for musical areas responsive to the sound of bells. A perennial favorite among composed songs is "Serenade of the Bells," harmonized to accompany the poignant love story of a Spanish couple who could not marry until the mission bells (then broken) were heard again. For a random trio in the folk area there is "Sleighing Song," with its trotting rhythm that sets the sleigh bells a-jingle, and the richly chorded spiritual, "Hear Them Bells!"—both traditional—along with a balladlike South Carolina Christmas folk song called "Heav'n Bell Ring."

Time was when hymn writers were noticeably alert to popularizing their work with the sound or the image of bells. Most of their efforts are missing from twentieth-century hymnals, but in their day they were favorites and the stories behind their composition were well known in many instances. The occasion of Ira D. Sankey's writing "The Harbor Bell" was one such instance. As often repeated, Captain Selden of the revenue cutter *Wyanda* donated a clear-toned ship's bell to the newly erected Episcopal Church of Port Townsend, Washington, in 1865. One condition of the gift was that the pastor should ring it on foggy days. Sometime later Ira D. Sankey, famous co-worker of Evangelist Dwight L. Moody, was a steamboat passenger near Seattle. Bewildered in a thick fog, the pilot was about to run aground when he heard the welcome sound of this bell floating down from the bluffs above. Mr. Sankey was so impressed with the incident that before reaching Seattle he wrote "The Harbor Bell," which proved a very popular hymn at revivals.

"Ring the Bells of Heaven" is another tune missing from modern hymnals, but for post-Civil War congregations it was a favorite. It was written by William O. Cushman, whose gospel hymns were sung up and down America with leading evangelists at the turn of the century. One day Cushing received from George Frederick Root, composer of "The Battle Cry of Freedom," a fascinating tune that kept singing in his mind for days while he kept trying to give it a religious setting. Those who have sung "Ring the Bells of Heaven" can understand why Cushing was attracted by the melody. As a writer of soul-winning hymns, he was interested one night to watch a particular man seek the altar at the close of an evangelistic meeting. Suddenly he thought how the bells of heaven must be ringing in gladness for a sinner's return. "Then," as he later reported, "the words . . . flowed at once into the waiting melody and the new hymn was written."

A few devotional songs have come to be associated with the music of certain bells that inspired their composition. Carrie Jacobs Bond was one of that elite group of writers privileged to live in the cloistered quarters of California's Mission Inn during its noteworthy days, with its unrivaled collection of bells, melodic chimes, and a multitude of other attractions. It was there that she was inspired by the chimes to compose "At the End of a Perfect Day."

The bell in the open turret of the quaint village church at Wayne, Illinois, is said to have a certain association with the famous song "When They Ring the Golden Bells." It was the gift of the village shoemaker to The Little Home Church by the Wayside when it was dedicated in 1871. At that time the schoolhouse where the congregation had been meeting was converted to a dwelling, and it was here, while listening to the shoemaker's bell, that Dion de Marbelle wrote the song that made the little church so famous it drew visitors from all over the world.

An Artist Looks at Bells

Considering the medium of self-expression artists use, it would be natural to assume that they are less drawn to the sound of a bell than are composers and writers, that they are more attentive to projecting images of them in some natural perspective. Such an assumption would be misleading to a certain extent. When the American artist Edwin H. Blashfield conceived his famous painting *Christmas Bells* in the late nineteenth century, his great desire was to relay to the world the joyous message of Christ's birth as no hymn or verse had ever done. He found his chief inspiration in the sounds of the famous bells gracing the belfries of Europe's great cathedrals. Who or what could tell the glad tidings more eloquently than those silver-tongued bells? To help project his idea, Blashfield showed bells in motion, ringing, just as he had heard and studied them in Giotto's tower in Florence or in the Church of Saint Laumer in Blois, France (now the Church of Saint Nicholas).

Blashfield's celebrative angels add to the reality of motion, to the suggestion of a joyous message sounding forth. His inspiration for including them came from a book, by John Addington Symonds, telling of angels gathering in swift squadrons "to ride upon the clanging bells" among the arches of Europe's Gothic cathedrals. So, again, sound was involved in the artist's choice of ideas for his painting. When the canvas was put on exhibit in the late nineteenth century, it won immediate acclaim.

The original canvas of *Christmas Bells* is sixteen by twelve feet. It was completed during the Golden Age of mural painting, executed in the grandly turgid style of the period, with Renaissance borrowings. Although a recognized easel painter and a member of the National Academy, Blashfield had an inborn affinity for mural painting of the type so much in vogue in his day. After returning to America in 1881 from his years of European study, he executed a number of large murals, including one for the World's Columbian Exposition, another for the great central dome in the Library of Congress, as well as several panels for the Bank of Pittsburgh. His style was eminently admired, bringing him prestige as one of America's foremost mural painters. Of course his work in the grand style that murals required had its influence on certain other of his canvases, such as *Christmas Bells*.

Attention focuses on the sounding of a bell, actually a gong, in a water color by Ohio artist Walter DuBois Richards. Called *Thirty Minutes for Supper*, the scene portrays in great detail the arrival of an early steam locomotive at a railroad station on a snowy day. A white-jacketed waiter stands outside the station's Fred Harvey Restaurant, hammering on a large brass gong to summon passengers to a hot meal. Little seems to be known of Mr. Richards professionally, even by museums owning examples of his work, though he has to his credit an impressive list of awards and honors, according to *Who's Who in American Art*. He is listed as a Cleveland area artist, with water colors in the Cleveland Museum of Art and the Cleveland Public Library. In 1940 he was known to be affiliated with a New York studio.

Left
Christmas Bells, a canvas by Edwin Howland Blashfield (1848-1936).

Right
Thirty Minutes for Supper, a watercolor by Walter DuBois Richards (b. 1907). *Fred Harvey, Incorporated*

The careful techniques and fidelity to fact so apparent in *Thirty Minutes for Supper* are reminiscent of historical painters like J. L. G. Ferris. Richards was obviously trained to paint with fidelity to the facts he assembled for his subject. The rearing of the frightened carriage horse as the locomotive snorts to a standstill, the polished brass bell with eagle finial on the engine, the high beaver hats, the muffs, and other details of Victorian dress—all are faithfully reproduced in the colorful Fred Harvey scene.

Several names predominate among historical American painters who took a special interest in reproducing scenes with the Liberty Bell as the chief focal point. Henry Mosler (1841-1920) stressed the fictional in his *Ring, Ring for Liberty!* Apparently he was influenced by George Lippard's fictional tale telling of an aged man in the Old State House tower, ringing for liberty. It is altogether probable that, as a schoolboy, Mosler read Lippard's version of that first ringing, for it was reprinted in many schoolbooks and widely accepted, as noted here earlier. Mosler is not only represented in the Corcoran Art Gallery and the Metropolitan Museum of Art, but is a recognized name on the Continent as well. His most notable achievement there came with the sale of a canvas to the French government for a museum, the first painting by an American to be so honored.

Jean Leon Gerome Ferris (1863-1930) is the most widely known of the historical painters who shared a common interest in portraying the Liberty Bell. His canvas *The Liberty Bell's First Note* has undoubtedly been reproduced more often than any other artist's depiction of the same subject, but it is only one of many that he painted to show episodes from American history. Though he was Philadelphia born and completely devoted to working with American historical subjects, Ferris's manner of painting derived to a great extent from study under French masters,

Left
Ring, Ring for Liberty!, a painting by Henry Mosler (1841-1921), based on a fictitious story about the ringing of the Liberty Bell.

Right
Testing the Liberty Bell in the shop of Pass and Stow, who recast it, a scene originally painted by Ferris that was imitated by several artists. Traditionally, Benjamin Franklin, Isaac Norris, and Isaac's niece are among those shown attending the ceremony. The artist who painted this version of the scene is unknown.

who taught him to apply a certain deft extravagance to his figures of fashionable ladies and gentlemen of the Revolution. At least four of the individuals assembled to test the bell are identifiable in Ferris's scene. One is John Pass, in whose foundry the group is standing, while a young lady relative of Isaac Norris lifts a hammer to make the test. Next to Isaac Norris, Benjamin Franklin engages that gentleman in conversation.

There was little in the famous Winslow Homer's (1836-1910) early career to foreshadow his later achievements, especially in depicting the sea and those who earn their livelihood from it. Out of his interest in the sea came one of his best-known paintings, *The Lookout—"All's Well,"* a painting as much described, discussed, praised, and criticized as any in American art.

With a theme in mind, Homer's method was to spend a long period in thoughtful preparation. Two of his prime concerns for *The Lookout—"All's Well"* were a satisfactory bell as a model and mastering the right technique to give his scene the moonlight atmosphere that was to unify it. A contemporary in whom Homer reputedly confided reported that he ransacked waterfront shops in Boston to find exactly the bell he had in mind. Not being able to find it, he modeled one in clay in the antique style then rarely seen any more. On another trip to Boston, he went aboard a ship at night to study the effect of moonlight on masts, rigging, and particularly on the ship's bronze bell. Back at Prout's Neck, he set up his bell out of doors, put a sou'wester on his favorite model, John Gatchell, and posed him as if he had just struck the bell before turning to give the traditional call. The moonlight was bright that evening, and Homer proceeded to paint the entire picture by the light of the moon. When he sent his finished canvas to Doll and Richards Gallery in Boston in 1896, he priced it at $850 but said he would willingly take $600. Later he confided, "I have made $100 cash—that is my season's profit."

Not all Winslow Homer's biographers accept the story of his modeling a bell from clay and working by moonlight. Regardless of that, the painting is universally recognized as one of those "Japanese fragment" compositions Homer came to handle so adeptly (he had become acquainted with Japanese prints while studying in France). So unconventional a manner of handling a composition comes as a surprise in this most American of painters—but there it is in *The Lookout—"All's Well,"* as in an *ukiyoe* print, the frame cutting the mariner's figure and the bell serving as a symbol of the entire ship, while just over the railing the foamy crest of a wave suggests a whole expanse of ocean (*see* frontispiece).

The ship bell Homer used was essential to his purpose of giving artistic recognition to a seaman's everyday life and work. Similarly, in his woodcut *The Morning Bell,* that ringing object on the roof of the mill was the essential catalyst that set the scene in motion—rural New England mill employees (mostly girls) trudging across a footbridge to enter the world of factory life, a life regulated by the ringing of that bell. Homer first painted this scene as an oil, just after the Civil War. Later he converted it to a wood engraving for publication in *Harper's Weekly,* December 13, 1873.

A lighthouse fog bell along the New England coast made an admirable subject for a print by lithographer Stow Wengenroth (b. 1906). His *Fog Bell* is far more than an accurate rendition of a metal object, however. Mr. Wengenroth kindles the imagination. In the background, a creeping fog suggests the approach of foul weather, but the sea is not evident in the scene although its nearness is suggested

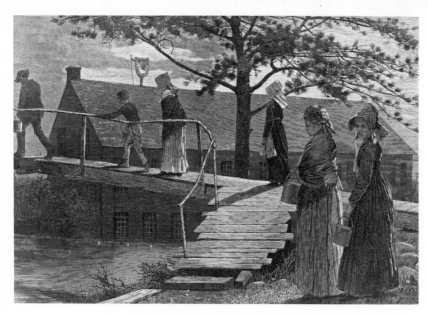

The Morning Bell, a wood engraving after a drawing by Winslow Homer. *Smith College Museum of Art*

by the high footbridge needed to reach the beacon light, apparently just offshore from the bell on its shingled support.

For the observant individual, there are any number of paintings or prints using bells in a tangential way. The average viewer will perhaps scarcely glance a second time at the place bells play in the overall design, yet they reveal various period customs, and the artist always had valid reasons for including them. For example, a little primitive oil on cardboard portraying Potpye Palmer with his garbage wagon and bell typifies the use of such attention-getting devices by the lowly street criers. The nineteenth-century artist William P. Chappel shows Potpye energetically ringing the bell as he trundles his garbage wagon around New York, along "East Side of Elizabeth corner of Pump St Wm & Groddy Post Paint Mill." The bell is but one small detail among many, but it is there. Without it, the same scene would be less than authentic.

The dustman (otherwise known as the rag picker) is immortalized in an unidentified print dated January 1, 1806, as well as in a lengthy rollicking verse. The verse, last printed in its entirety in 1912 by Mary J. Taber in her quixotic anthology, lends credence to the dustman's custom of using a bell on his rounds. These two stanzas especially illustrate the mood of the print:

Fog Bell, a lithograph by Stow Wengenroth (b. 1906). *Courtesy of the Print Department, Boston Public Library*

A detail from *The Garbage Cart*, an oil on cardboard by William P. Chappel (19th century). *The Metropolitan Museum of Art; bequest of Edward W. C. Arnold, 1954; the Edward W. C. Arnold Collection of New York Prints, Maps, and Pictures*

The New York Dustman's Bells

Of all comical sounds in heaven or earth,
A combination of sadness and mirth,
There's nothing to my imagining tells
More wonderful tales than the dustman's bells.
   As wrangling, jangling, to and fro,
   There notes are heard wherever you go.

. . . .

From among these old rags and fragments so
    packed,
From many a garret and cellar ransacked,
Are bits of old garments a century old,
That marvelous bits of history unfold;
   As wrangling, jangling, to and fro,
   These bells are heard wherever you go.

—DANIEL RICKETSON

Unsigned print dated January 1, 1806, portraying the dustman, or ragpicker, with his handbell.

Portraits of children toying with their coral-and-bells are another tangential use of bells by the artist. But a far more prolific use of this sort is seen in the Currier and Ives prints of boats, fire wagons, sleighs, and railroad trains. Currier and his partner Ives lived through the period when all those forms of transportation developed, so they were firsthand observers. Out of some fifty railroad prints they made, for example, several give a glimpse of changing styles in engine bells. A bell with an ornately scrolled hanger is seen in *The Route to California*, which shows the Sierra Nevada run along the Tuckee River. An ornate pillared type shows up in *Prairie Fires of the Great West*.

The use of a bell in any form by metal sculptors is a rarity. Among the few known examples, some of the most interesting pieces came from European sculptors using American subjects—or at least subjects close to the heart of the American people. French sculptors found the American Indian a fascinating model. A pair of bells as handsome as any ever cast in bronze are signed French depictions of American Indians "beating" their bells in tom-tom fashion.

An imposing statuesque bronze figure bell of Jenny Lind in concert attire is signed by F. (Friedrich) Gornik, an important name among Austrian sculptors and industrial artists. The Nationalmuseum in Stockholm comments, ". . . we do not see any connection between Friedrich Gornik and Jenny Lind." There may seem to be very little connection, but an artist's reasons are his own when it comes to choosing a subject, and his horizons are infinite. The gifted Swedish soprano, whom he could have known only by reputation, must somehow have won Gornik's personal admiration.

America has always felt some claim on the Swedish singer's affection, for it was here that she met her husband, whom she married in Boston in 1852; and for years she kept up correspondence with many people she came to know while living in America. Probably no other personality in the nation's musical world is remembered in larger collections of memorabilia. It is especially fitting that this rare bronze bell in Jenny Lind's likeness is on permanent display at the Stephen Foster Memorial in White Springs, Florida, along with one of the beautiful square grand pianos used in her concerts.

Large bronze bell sculptured in the likeness of Jenny Lind as she appeared on the American concert stage, 1850 to 1851. It is signed F. (Friedrich) Gornik. *Stephen Foster Memorial*

INDEX